Computer Resources for People with Disabilities

"An Outstanding Academic Book of 1995." — *Choice* magazine

"This book on assistive technology speaks directly to people with disabilities and their families. Technology is vital for attaining independence. This book can assist you in finding out how to get it into your life." — **Ed Roberts,** late President of the World Institute on Disability

"This book gets beyond the jargon, beyond the commercialism and beyond the theory to address the real needs of people with disabilities who want to use technology in their lives." — **Vicki Casella, Ph.D.,** Professor, Department of Special Education, San Francisco State University

"The Alliance for Technology Access has produced an indispensable guide for anyone interested in using computers or assistive technology to expand their horizons in employment, education or any other area of their lives . . . . If you're ready to take the plunge into the world of computers, but lack the courage or the knowledge to dive into untested water, *Computer Resources For People With Disabilities* can teach anyone with any kind of disability how to scan, select and scroll with the best of them." — *One Step Ahead,* A Newsletter by People with Disabilities for People with Disabilities

"This wonderful new book is another example of the power of parents to change the world. Less than 10 years ago, a few parents recognized that technology could help their children with disabilities. They began a collaborative effort which become the Alliance for Technology Access. Today, these centers serve thousands of children and adults with disabilities, parents, and professionals." — *Exceptional Parent*

"This book is a veritable clearinghouse of different technologies available and their applicability to the lives and tasks of people with various disabilities. It strives to be a sort of Whole Earth Catalog of cutting-edge and approaching technologies . . . . [It is] informative and unusually easy to use." — *Booklist*

"This well-organized work is an invaluable and much-needed reference tool for all types of users . . . . In this time of universal ADA compliance, this is a highly recommended reference." — *Library Journal* (starred review)

"Assistive technology can be liberating, creating opportunities and independence for people with disabilities. This comprehensive and clear guide through the often confusing maze of technology can inform people, and empower them as well." — **Joseph P. Shapiro,** Senior Editor, *U.S. News & World Report* and author of *No Pity: People with Disabilities Forging a New Civil Rights Movement*

"This book takes the reader step by step through the process of setting goals, assessing needs, finding the right people to help, and getting funding, through the selection of hardware and software to actual purchase and follow-up assistance . . . . For anyone with a disability or working with a person with a disability, this is probably one of the best starting points to consideration of adapted computer technology. As stated in the book, though, this will only be the start. Where each individual goes will be determined by his/her own needs, desires, and will to succeed and grow." — *Kliatt*

"The authors of this book give `non-techie' people with disabilities (and people who love and work with them) a user-friendly manual for approaching, evaluating, securing, and using computers and assistive devices — all in understandable, simple language." — *Inside MS,* a publication of the National Multiple Sclerosis Society

"The next time someone says, `I think a computer would benefit me (my child, my student, my client) — but I don't know where to start,' give them *Computer Resources For People With Disabilities* . . . . If you can only afford one book, this is probably it." — *Real Times*

Computer Resources for People with Disabilities

A Guide to Exploring Today's Assistive Technology

The Alliance for Technology Access

>   Hunter House Inc. Publishers
>   P.O. Box 2914
>   Alameda CA 94501-0914

Library of Congress Cataloging-in-Publication Data
Computer resources for people with disabilities: a guide to exploring today's assistive technology / Alliance for Technology Access. — 2nd ed.
p. cm.
Includes bibliographical references and index.
ISBN 0-89793-197-1 (spiral: alk. paper)
ISBN 0-89793-196-3 (pbk. : alk. paper)
1. Computers and the handicapped. 2. Computers and the handicapped—Equipment and supplies. I. Alliance for Technology Access.
HV1569.5.C675   1996
004' .087—dc20   96-26423
                                                         CIP

Ordering
Trade bookstores and wholesalers in the U.S. and Canada, please contact
>   Publishers Group West   1-800-788-3123   Fax (510) 658-1834

Hunter House books are available for textbook/course adoptions, and are sold at bulk discounts to qualifying community and health care organizations for resale or for special promotions and fundraising. For details please contact:
>   Marketing Department
>   Hunter House Inc., P.O. Box 2914, Alameda CA 94501-0914
>   Tel. (510) 865-5282   Fax (510) 865-4295
>   e-mail: marketing@hunterhouse.com

Individuals can order our books from most bookstores or by calling toll-free:
>   **1-800-266-5592**

Cover design: Jil Weil, Oakland   Book design: *Qalagraphia*
Cover illustration: Kiran Rana   Proofreader: Lee Rappold
Project manager: Lisa E. Lee   Copyeditor: Mali Apple
Editorial assistance: Jenny Moore   Production manager: Paul J. Frindt
Sales & Marketing: Corrine Sahli   Production assistance: Kim Wallace
Customer support: Sharon R.A. Olson, Joshua Tabisaura, A&A Quality Shipping
                        Publisher: Kiran S. Rana

Printed and bound by Publishers Press, Salt Lake City UT
Manufactured in the United States of America

9 8 7 6 5 4 3 2 1   Second edition

Contents

Contents (continued)

Foreword

This book is about problems of expression and communication, and how to solve them. I am dumb, in the literal sense of not being able to speak. Maybe I'm dumb in the more figurative sense, but we won't go into that here. I, and thousands like me, have been helped to communicate by modern technology. Indeed, the fact that I have been asked to write this foreword is a sign of what technology can do.

This book offers something no other does: a guide to maneuvering the growing world of computers, both the mainstream and the assistive technology, to find what is right for you. Evaluating your needs and finding the technology to fill them is a process. My methods of communication are an example.

The main problem of communicating without being able to speak is what is called the baud rate, the rate at which information can be conveyed. Normal speech is between 120 and 180 words a minute. By contrast, a reasonable typist can produce 40 to 60 words a minute. Thus, if people were equipped with keyboards to communicate, they could do so at half to a quarter of the speech rate.

However, many people like me who cannot speak also have other disabilities. They cannot use a keyboard. Instead, they can use one or more switches, operated by a head or hand movement. This is where a person is really confronted with the rate of information flow. If you take an average word to be five characters and assume that any character can follow any other character, normal speech has an information flow rate of between 50 and 75 bits a second. By contrast, a person might be able to operate a switch at two or three bits a second.

The real information flow in human communication, however, is much less than this. (In the case of political speeches, it is practically zero.) This is because spelling out a sentence letter by letter is inefficient. Most sequences of letters don't make recognizable words, let alone meaningful sentences. It takes a handful of these bits of information (letters) to create meaningful communication (a word). So, communicating by specifying every letter is a lot of redundant effort.

For someone who can use a switch to communicate, it is much more efficient to pick words or even whole phrases from a list of likely ones. Computer technology makes this possible. To translate the press of a switch into letters, words, or sentences requires computers. The development of microprocessors in the last 15 years has meant that virtually unlimited computing power is available at a reasonable cost.

viii

———

Computer
Resources
for People
with
Disabilities

The next step is to find efficient software to translate the input from the switch into phrases and sentences. With the Equalizer program that I use, I can manage about fifteen words a minute. That is not too bad, since an information flow rate of three bits a second corresponds to 25 to 30 words a minute. But obviously there is scope for improvement. And the promise of computer technology is that improvements are always in development.

Having decoded the signals from some input devices, such as a switch, one then has to broadcast it in a form people can understand. This could be visually, with text or diagrams on a screen. But if you want to communicate like others, which is what people in my position would like, you need to be able to speak. Computerized speech synthesizers have improved a great deal in recent years, and this is important: not only does one want to be understood, but one also does not want to sound like Mickey Mouse or a Dalek. My voice may be a bit tinny and American, but it is almost human.

The process I have just described is what this book is all about. I hope others find in this book the inspiration and the technology, hardware and software, that can help them to communicate better—to express their human-ness.

Stephen Hawking
Cambridge University
Cambridge, England

Stephen Hawking *is perhaps the best-known modern physicist since Einstein. When he was twenty-one he was diagnosed with ALS, a degenerative nerve disease. With the use of a voice synthesizer and other computer technology he has been able to communicate his genius to the world. He is the author of* A Brief History of Time *and* Black Holes and Baby Universes and Other Essays.

Preface

The work of redefining human potential and creating a world of access to opportunity through technology has only just begun. It must continue until technology is a regular part of the lives of all individuals with disabilities who can benefit from it. The nonprofit Alliance for Technology Access exists solely to promote this mission, which encompasses millions of people directly and every one of us indirectly.

This book would never have come to be without the vast expertise and boundless passion of the children and adults with disabilities and their families, the professional service providers, and the forward-thinking businesses who make up the Alliance for Technology Access and who contributed so generously and unselfishly to the writing of this book.

We need your help. Please think about joining this terrific and enthusiastic group of people dedicated to improving access to technology for people with disabilities. There are many ways for individuals and organizations to support this compelling mission:

- by volunteering time

- by contributing financially

- by providing in-kind donations

- by establishing new Alliance technology resource centers

To find out more about how you can become part of the mission, vision, and work of the Alliance, or to be added to our mailing list, please call or write us today at:

The Alliance for Technology Access
2175 East Francisco Blvd., Suite L
San Rafael CA 94901
Phone: (415) 455-4575   Fax: (415) 455-0654
E-mail: atafta@aol.com

Important Note to the Reader

The material in this book is intended to provide an overview of the hardware, software, and other considerations surrounding computer resources for people with disabilities. Every effort has been made to provide accurate and dependable information and the contents of this book have been compiled in consultation with a variety of computer professionals and users. The reader should be aware that professionals in the field may have differing opinions and change is always taking place. Therefore the authors, publisher, and editors cannot be held responsible for any error, omission, or outdated material.

The authors and publisher disclaim any liability, loss, injury, or damage incurred as a consequence, directly or indirectly, of the use and application of any of the contents of this volume.

If you have any questions or concerns about the information in this book, please consult your local Alliance for Technology Access center.

Many of the designations used by manufacturers and sellers to distinguish their products are claimed as trademarks. Where those designations appear in this book, and the authors were aware of a trademark claim, the designations have been printed with initial capital letters. The inclusion of a product in this book does not imply endorsement or recommendation.

The people and events described in the personal stories in this book are real. In all but the first chapter, their names have been changed to respect their privacy and that of their families.

Acknowledgements

This book was produced through a collaborative effort of the Alliance for Technology Access, its staff, board, volunteers, friends, and families. The effort that created this book models the Alliance way of doing business. It involves children and adults with disabilities, parents and family members, educators, technology developers, medical professionals, advocates, and friends, all working together to bring the best information and most complete access to interested people everywhere.

The book grew under the loving guidance and tireless efforts of our editor, Mary Lester. Without her skill, leadership, and patience, this book would not exist. While many people provided her with individual stories, perspectives, and expertise, she translated them into a meaningful whole with clarity, passion, and truth.

The Alliance also wishes to especially thank the following people for their significant writing contributions, starting with Bob Glass, without whose help this effort would not have been possible. Although many people participated and are acknowledged in later sections, this group contributed the major writing for the book: Jackie Brand, Amy Dell, Donna Dutton, Bob Glass, Dave Grass, Melinda Harrington, Donna Heiner, Russ Holland, Jane Lee, Steve Mendelsohn, Bridgett Perry, Lois Symington. We also thank Mali Apple for her clarity, knowledge, and expertise, which improved this effort so dramatically.

We are particularly indebted to Bridgett Perry who played a crucial role in making sure that the technical information in Part II was accurate and complete. She coordinated a vast network of contributors, making a tough task seem easy.

We acknowledge with great appreciation the wonderful work of graphic designer Sherry Stoll, who developed the charts in Part II.

Concept Team

Jackie Brand, Greg Burkett, Vicki Casella, Pat Cashdollar, Lynn Chiu, Lisa Cohn, Donna Dutton, Suzanne Feit, Bob Glass, Mary Ann Glicksman, Ann Grady, Hod Gray, Melinda Harrington, Anita Harris, Donna Heiner, Russ Holland, Jane Lee, Helen Miller, Caren Normandin, Bridgett Perry, Dave Salkever, Mary Salkever, Dave Schmitt, John Schweizer, Sherry Stoll, Lois Symington, Lisa Wahl, Alice Wershing

Technical Team

Carol Adams, Francia Baily, Michael Baruch, Jane Berliss, Greg Burkett, xii

———

Computer
Resources
for People
with
Disabilities

Pat Cashdollar, Terri Chastain, Lynn Chiu, Donna Dutton, Charlie Farkas, Suzanne Feit, Pam Frost, Janice Fouard, Ken Funk, Mary Ann Glicksman, Lana Gossin, David Grass, Elaine Hackett, Pam Harnden, Melinda Harrington, Kirsten Haugen, Donna Heiner, Ginny Heiple, Robert Hill, Russ Holland, Roger Holt, Jean Isaacs, Gary King, Patricia Kenyon, Cindy Mathena, Helen Miller, Suzan Murn, Charlotte Nelson, Steve Obremski, Janet Peters, Melody Ram, Dave Salkever, Helen Schneiderman, Cindy Storm, Judy Timms, Leslie Todd, Randy Tompkins, Sally Townsend, Lisa Wahl, Edie Weintraub, Alice Wershing, Peggy Whitworth, Sherrill Williams

Fact Checkers for Second Edition
Marge Adams, Deborah Bauder, Judy Bias, Kathy Bradford, Roxanne Cortright, Janice Fouard, Patricia Furner-Nolan, Margaret Gallaway, Dierdre Geraci, Lana Gossin, Elaine Hackett, Nancy Johnson, Cheryl Klein, Jan Michelson, Kathy Reed, John Schweizer, Lois Symington, Judy Timms

Other Contributions
Carol Adams, Marge Adams, Mike Berkmire, Craig Boogaard, James Francis-Bohr, Michelle Brand, Pat Cashdollar, Diane Coleman, Tony Compton, Amy Dell, John Duganne, Mary Ann Glicksman, Ann Grady, Kirsten Haugen, Dee Hoban, Paul Jakab, Darrell Jones, Cheryl Klein, Laura Leininger, Mary Male, Steve Mendelsohn, Sue Milburn, John Schweizer, Bob Segalman, Tom Shworles, Peter Soloman, Karen Spurrier, Pat Steinke, Pat Stewart, Cathy Synyders, Mary Ann Trower, Terry Trzaska, Lisa Wahl, Rachel Wobschall, Gregg Vanderheiden, Adrian Zackheim

Reviewers
David Clark, Donna Dutton, Bob Glass, Ann Grady, Dave Grass, Donna Heiner, Russ Holland, Don Johnston, June Kailes, Arjan Khalsa, Jane Lee, Bridgett Perry, Dave Schmidt, Sheila Sondik, Lois Symington, Alice Wershing

Most of the people listed above are staff and board members of Alliance for Technology Access centers. The following centers have participated in the writing, editing, or reviewing of this book:

Technology Assistance for Special Consumers, Huntsville AL; Technology Resource Center, Little Rock AR; Center for Accessible Technology, Berkeley CA; Computer Access Center, Culver City CA; Sacramento Center for Assistive Technology, Sacramento CA; SACC* Assistive Technology, Simi Valley CA; Special Technology Center, Mountain View CA; Team of Advocates for Special Kids, Anaheim CA;

CITE, Orlando FL; Tech-Able, Conyers GA; Northern Illinois Center for Adaptive Technology, Rockford IL; Technical Aids & Assistance for the Disabled Center, Chicago IL; Technology Resources for Special People, Salina KS; Bluegrass Technology Center, Lexington KY; Enabling Technologies of Kentuckiana (enTECH), Louisville KY; SpeciaLink, Covington KY; Learning Independence Through Computers, Baltimore MD; Living & Learning Resource Centre, Lansing MI; PACER Computer Resource Center, Minneapolis MN; Technology Access Center, Saint Louis MO; Parents, Let's Unite for Kids, Billings MT; Center for Enabling Technology, Whippany NJ; Techspress, Utica NY; Carolina Computer Access Center, Charlotte NC; Technology Resource Center, Dayton OH; East Tennessee Special Technology Access Center, Powell TN; West Tennessee Special Technology Resource Center, Jackson TN; Computer Center for Citizens with Disabilities, Salt Lake City UT; Tidewater Center for Technology Access, Virginia Beach VA

We are very grateful to Libbie Butler for painstakingly incorporating the corrections for Part III to ensure that the resource and references lists are current and accurate. We are also grateful for the important contribution made by Maggie Morales.

The Alliance is especially and deeply grateful to Lisa Lee, our editor at Hunter House and supporter. Without her vision and energy, this book would never have been started. Without her belief and trust in us, we would not have had this tremendous opportunity to share with you what we have learned. And without her patience, persistence, hard work, and commitment, this book would never have been finished.

We would also like to thank Kiran Rana, Paul Frindt, and Corrie Sahli of Hunter House for believing in this work and for promoting access to it for consumers, family members, and professionals everywhere.

Our work, though utterly fascinating and truly compelling, has rarely been confined to a mortal's time schedule, as all of our wonderful and significant others will unanimously agree. Among the most important contributors have been and continue to be our own families, who often and gracefully handle the personal loads which allow us to follow our dreams.

Most importantly, we thank those people we meet everyday in every center who have taught us so much and who have, in countless ways, contributed to the richness of this book.

The Alliance lovingly acknowledges the invaluable and essential contribution to this book by Jackie Brand, the Founder and first Executive Director of the Alliance for Technology Access. Not only did she see the big picture and keep the vision for this work, and all the xiv

———

Computer
Resources
for People
with
Disabilities

work of the Alliance, she also kept a focus on the little picture. It was her continuous hands-on support of the team, in writing, editing, fact checking, and proofreading, that dramatically strengthened our effort. It was her dedication and devotion that motivated each of us to give not only our skill but our heart to making this more than just a book. It is a reflection of the talent within the Alliance, and a tribute to the passion and commitment to our mission that she has inspired in us all.

Computer Resources
for
People with Disabilities

Introduction

Imagine having a keyboard that changes effortlessly from a standard layout to one that includes only the keys you need for a specific task, such as creating a budget, working on an English assignment, or exploring music composition. Imagine a computer that talks to you, that reads messages sent to you from all over the world. Imagine having the ability to make choices by simply touching a picture on your computer screen. Imagine having the ability to type without using your hands by simply looking at the right letter on a keyboard pictured on the screen. Imagine going to the Library of Congress to gather materials for a research project without leaving your home.

These scenarios are just a few examples of what you *can* do today with computers. For a person with a disability, today's applications offer new promise and excitement. These new abilities level the playing field for all of us.

Why This Book Was Written

If you are a person with a disability, or a parent, other family member, teacher, employer, or friend of a person with a disability, we want to share with you what we have learned about the ways assistive technology is literally changing lives by creating new abilities for children and adults with disabilities—sensory, cognitive, learning, or physical disabilities.

Everyday, in the course of our work, we are asked questions about available technology and its applications. "I have a vision impairment. Which computer should I buy?" "My son has a learning disability, and his teacher said a computer might help him do better in school. Which should I buy?" "I have a girl in my sixth-grade class with cerebral palsy, and the school has agreed to provide her with a computer. Which is the best?" Your questions may be similar.

The goal of this book is to help you begin answering your questions for yourself, and to allow you to take advantage of the incredible new tools on the market today. We won't teach you about the insides of the latest computers or list every computer product ever developed. Our intention is to help you create a purpose and a framework for approaching technology so you can make initial decisions about the role it can play in enhancing your life. We have included many stories about real people who are using technology successfully—people of all ages and all disabilities who use technology for different reasons.

This book is written for a community that has not yet discovered the power of technology. This community includes people with disabilities, but it also includes family members, advocates, and friends of people with disabilities. It encompasses thousands of professionals in the fields of education and rehabilitation who are concerned about quality-of-life issues and options for children and adults with disabilities. It includes the technologists, engineers, and designers who will be the developers of tomorrow's technology. This broad group represents a huge constituency that will be dramatically impacted by technology in this and the next century. We believe this constituency will demand nothing less than a revolution in expectations, making more options available for people with disabilities everywhere.

Throughout the book, we address the audience as "you," in recognition of the important decision-making role played by individuals with disabilities in defining their own futures. Supportive family members, friends, advocates, and professionals should translate the wording as needed, but always remember that choices about technology should be, to the greatest possible degree, dictated by the user.

A Word About Us

We, the authors, are a diverse group of people who have become connected and interrelated by our search for technologies to support our dreams. We are people with disabilities, children and adults, family members and friends, teachers and therapists, employers, service providers, technology vendors, professional organizations, and community agencies. We come from all over the United States, from small towns and urban centers. We cross age, ethnic, and ability/disability lines. We represent a growing community of people across the country and around the globe who are employing the tools of technology and reaching new levels of satisfaction. We did not choose technology because we were intrinsically interested in it; we became users of technology because it allowed us to become what we wanted to be: teachers, communicators, artists, composers, students, engineers.

We are connected by a strong belief in the vast potential of people with disabilities to use technology to achieve their dreams, and by a profound commitment to bring the benefits of technology to people who have historically been excluded from the American dream. We have been through the process of trying to understand a bewildering and complex field. We have searched for expertise and support. And we have created an organization that bonds us to each other and to all people looking for similar answers and support.

The Alliance for Technology Access is a collaborative, energetic community of people redefining what it means to have a disability. Having a disability no longer has to mean that things cannot be done—it means that we can find new ways to get them done. The Alliance is made up of expert advocates dedicated to pushing the limits of convention—people who ask not whether something can be done, but how it can be accomplished. We share your challenges and your frustrations. We believe in every person's right to be productive and independent and to achieve his or her desired quality of life. And we believe the most noble application of technology is to support those rights. The Alliance is a network of assistive technology resource centers and technology vendors whose members share a common vision—and an uncommon commitment to improving the quality of life for children and adults with disabilities through the imaginative application of assistive technology.

The Alliance was created to demonstrate how technology can transform limitations into opportunities. We work toward this goal by providing access to assistive technologies and related services that enable people to achieve productivity, independence, and success according to their needs and interests. Services available at Alliance technology resource centers include

- Guided exploration and consultations
- Hands-on computer demonstrations
- Information and resource services
- Workshops and user groups
- Technical support services
- Professional development

The Alliance has rapidly grown from a small group of parents, consumers, professionals, and vendors to become one of the nation's most effective efforts devoted to enabling people with disabilities to gain access to the full benefits of technology. And public demand for services continues to grow at a rapid rate; the number of individuals crossing resource center thresholds, for example, went from 20,000 in 1987 to over 100,000 today.

People with disabilities must be at the center of the learning and decision-making process. We take a new approach to service, both at our centers and in this book, that varies from the standard, professionally driven model that assumes the "experts" know what's best for you. We believe that we as individuals know what we need; that a team that includes professional resources can help guide us in the right direction; and that, in the end, we must make our own decisions and direct our own lives.

Navigating Through This Book

This book, like the Alliance, represents a collaborative effort, with many voices lending richness and texture to the content. We represent a great diversity of approaches and solutions, each with its own purpose and validity. We will introduce you to a broad and growing community of technology users who are excited and eager to share what they have learned.

You'll find the arrangement of this book somewhat unusual. Many books relating to people with disabilities are arranged according to disability. You can usually turn to a chapter on "visual impairments" or "physical disabilities," and you are likely to read about a particular tool that was designed for a specific disability.

We find that approach restrictive and inappropriate, and prefer to focus on a functional look at a person's needs rather than looking at deficits. If the goal is to have a screen display large letters, it doesn't really matter if you need it because you have a visual impairment, a learning disability, or some other requirement. The question is not what does a person with X disability require, but what are the ways in which we can enlarge print on a computer screen. The assistive technology field is about giving people better access to the environment—through a better designed environment or a set of tools that navigate around barriers.

The Structure of This Book

The book is divided into three parts. **Part I, The Search for Solutions,** will guide you through the process of defining your needs, developing a technology plan, building a supportive team and making technology-related decisions. It offers strategies, first steps, and resources, and it should help you become more confident in your exploration.

Part II, The Technology Toolbox, focuses on the technology itself, offering examples of various assistive technologies. Several guides will inform and direct your search, helping you to zero in on the technologies most likely to match your abilities and goals. Part II can be read selectively as you narrow your search. It is not a compendium of every product on the market, but through it you will learn enough about the categories of products on the market today to feel comfortable taking the next steps.

The search for technology solutions is a lifelong process. As your life changes and as technology evolves, you'll find yourself continuing your search. This is one of the most exciting aspects of this field: realizing that the technology is constantly evolving. Changes are so rapid that information is often out of date before it is printed. We can't predict your needs or the products that will be available in the future, but we can provide you with a plan and appropriate resources for starting and continuing your search.

Part III, Helpful Resources and References, contains lists of resources, references, and organizations that we have found valuable in our personal and professional study of assistive technology. Keep in mind that as quickly as the technology changes, so does the information regarding the players in this newly emergent field.

Much of what we offer are the right questions and some key resources. You will learn how others have faced similar challenges and have developed effective strategies. If you find that, after reading this book, you have a goal in mind, some easy first steps to take, and a range of supporters to help; if you are armed with enough information to talk comfortably with your local computer dealer; or if you are inspired or excited by someone's story, we have accomplished our goal.

In the following pages, you'll hear a lot about journey, process, pursuit, quest, direction, search, exploration, routes, dead ends, travel assistance, places to seek out, places to avoid, rights, and community. We will go over what you should know, where to go, and what to do next; how to handle disenchantment and how to persevere until you find a friendly voice. Do the concepts of pioneering and journey sit well with you? Fortunately, we make every effort to positively reward your pioneering spirit with sound advice and guidance.

Part I
The Search for Solutions

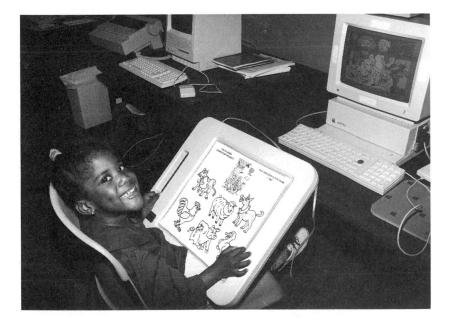

Chapter 1

Real People and Their Success Stories

The success of technology has more to do with people than machines. All the right parts and pieces together won't work miracles by themselves. It is people who make technology powerful by creatively using it to fulfill their dreams.

The evolution of the field of assistive technology is more about the evolution of people and their expectations than it is about circuitry. The story is about challenges, barriers, and solutions; about people wanting to do things and finding more creative ways to get them done. It is about the inclusion of people with disabilities in every aspect of society and how technology can serve as a tool to facilitate that process: in school, at home, on the job, and in the community. From the elementary school classroom to the labs at NASA, people with disabilities are taking their place as full and participating members, and technology is helping to make that happen.

The stories that follow illustrate how a few people have found and used technology to accomplish their goals.

Victor

Victor had a vision. To him it was simple: go to school with his peers, graduate from high school with a New York State Regent's Diploma, go to college, get a job, be independently mobile, and live independently.

Victor had cerebral palsy and was nonverbal. In 1984, his only reliable physical control was his eyes and a single switch he could activate with his head. For most of his younger years, there was no technology to help him. While watching *Sesame Street,* Victor had developed a technique of spelling with his eyes that enabled him to communicate with family, friends, and others willing to take the time to learn his system. Victor had become an effective self-advocate with a vision of what he needed.

The first use of assistive technology Victor encountered was a system that enabled him to communicate by scanning a series of choices as the computer cycled through them and then making a selection by pressing a switch. The system printed out Victor's message on a narrow ticker tape.

In 1984, with the support of the local Optimist club, Victor procured an Express III (Prentke Romich Company), a row/column scanning device activated by a single switch. Using the device was laborious, and little support was available in Victor's community for its programming and use, so Victor continued his search.

He advocated for the development of his own technology support team, which included a counselor in the New York State Office of Vocational Rehabilitation; a technology resource person to assist with programming the scanning device, adding computer components to the system, and helping Victor learn the technology; a high school counselor willing to help make classes and materials accessible; and a tutor to assist Victor in developing his writing skills. In 1989, Victor became the first student using augmentative communication in New York State to receive a Regent's Diploma. Victor received his diploma not because of the sophistication of the technology, but because he had expectations, vision, and the determination to pursue them.

Victor

Victor was empowered by his vision far more than the technology. He *expected* that the technology was there or would be developed. When he went camping, Victor expected to be able to fish. He assembled a team on the spot and had them develop technology consisting of a fishing pole attached to an old helmet. And when it came time to toast marshmallows around the campfire, Victor had the team make a few technological modifications to the fishing pole that soon had flaming marshmallows flying across the campsite.

John

"I was born with cerebral palsy in 1971, and my first public school program was a development center for children with severe disabilities. I couldn't control my movements and couldn't talk like other kids. Teachers said to my parents, 'He's not learning.' The school psychologist tested me and said that I had mental retardation.

John

"Lucky for me, my parents didn't believe it. They believed that I needed friends and support to be able to do things that my body wouldn't allow me to do. My stepfather began making gadgets and switches, and my mother began to advocate for me to be included in everything with kids my age: in school, in playgroup, at playgrounds, at church. I left public school and went to a community playgroup and then to a private alternative school where I was the only kid with a disability and was included in everything.

"However, I was still having trouble learning, and after 2 years the teachers suggested that I return to public school where there were special education teachers to help me. . . . But my IQ test followed me, and people saw my wheelchair and my inability to talk before they saw me. I was again in a class for students with severe disabilities.

"Then in 1978, when I was 7 years old, I got my first computer. This was the beginning of real life for me. There were no adaptive devices at that time, so my family's first invention was plastic wrap over the keyboard so I wouldn't drool on it, and a pencil taped in my hand to touch the keys. We saw the computer as a learning and communication tool. We have been working at making it perform for me ever since."

John makes presentations regularly to large audiences in the hope that, by sharing some of his story, he will have demonstrated "how technology, great expectations, and a support network have helped one person to get around some of the stereotypes and prejudice that block off connections with real life for children who are growing up with disabilities."

Dusty

In 1981, when Dusty was just 6 years old, she visited her friend John (who told his story above) and was amazed at all he was doing with his Apple II+ (an early Apple computer). Dusty saw immediately what power John had. Control was an issue for Dusty, as she had Down syndrome and very little control over things in her life at that time. With John's computer, she could push a button and make things happen. Her parents had to drag her home from that first technology encounter.

Dusty was in a regular kindergarten at the time. Her parents were told that she did not attend well and wouldn't stay on task. Her mother knew the trick would be to find a task that Dusty *wanted* to stay on.

Through her research, Dusty's mother learned that children with Down syndrome tend to be good visual learners. This clinched it for her. At Christmas they bought Dusty an Apple II+ and some early software programs, Hodge Podge (Dynacomp) and Counting Bee (EduWare). Dusty learned the keyboard quickly and began practicing counting without even being invited.

Dusty's mother had had no prior experience with computers and wasn't mechanically inclined. She and Dusty learned together. As a way to get her daughter access to a computer at school, she volunteered to help the teacher. She took the computer to Dusty's class and worked with the other students. As the students played with the computer, it became clear to the teacher that Dusty could be included in activities using the computer, just like everyone else.

Dusty is now attending her local high school. She uses a Macintosh computer with large print; Write:OutLoud (Don Johnston, Inc.), a talking word processor; and Co:Writer (Don Johnston, Inc.), a word prediction program. Using these tools she writes children's books in her English class, which she then reads to the babies in the daycare center in which she works one period a day. (For more information on these and other specific products, refer to Part II, The Technology Toolbox.)

Dusty

As her mother says, "Technology gave Dusty confidence in her ability as a learner. She began to feel good about herself. Her self-esteem improved. She has always been able to do the things without the technology that she does with it. But without the computer, her work appears to have been done by a 6-year-old. With the computer, it looks as if it were done by a high school student. She can easily correct mistakes and participate in the writing process, which before was a catch-22 situation. She would write something and have someone correct it for her. Then she would copy it over, fixing the old mistakes often making new ones in the process. With the computer she can follow a regular writing and editing process and get it right.

"Technology is highly motivating and it can bring out the best in a child. As a parent, I think it can help you find out how your child learns best, because it gives you so many exciting avenues to explore. It's a feel-good thing. Fun for the whole family. It's also a good integrator. For us, it attracted kids from around the neighborhood who wanted to come over and play."

Tammy

Tammy was mainstreamed into the neighborhood school where she was the only student with a physical disability. But, by the time she was 7 years old, school was becoming harder and harder because she could not see to read the board, books, or even her own handwriting.

As computers grew more commonplace, it became obvious that if Tammy could use one in school, it would make a tremendous difference in her ability to participate and learn. Her father brought a computer home and started using it with Tammy. Like most children, Tammy wasn't fearful of or intimidated by the computer.

After elementary school, Tammy enrolled in the state school for the blind—where there also were no computers. Her parents knew that Tammy could benefit from them, but convincing the school to start using them took quite a while. Using a computer for administrative purposes was one thing; making them available to students, it seemed, was a fairly radical notion.

Even when computers were finally introduced, they were mostly kept in a separate room that students could only access once or twice a week, and rarely in the evenings. The school had not anticipated that the students might want to use the computers to do their homework. Compounding this lack of access was the fact that none of the teachers or evening staff knew how to use the equipment themselves.

In spite of the fact that the school had no expectations of Tammy's being able to pass the exams for her high school diploma, she gained her diploma by taking all the required functional tests on a computer.

Early on, Tammy's mother had low expectations for technology because it was difficult to think very far ahead. She knew that computers could assist her daughter in school, but it wasn't until Tammy was out of school that her mother realized the impact technology could have on Tammy's career options. "I have high expectations of comput-

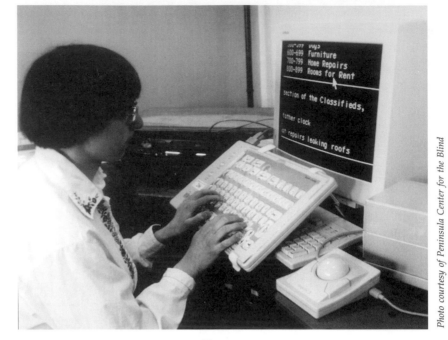

Photo courtesy of Peninsula Center for the Blind

Tammy

ers in terms of her career. In the right environment, technology can really work for my daughter."

Tammy, now in her twenties, has a full-time volunteer job at a music conservatory, and uses a computer with a large-print program called ZoomText (AI Squared) and an abbreviation expansion program, PRD+ (Productivity Software International, Inc.), that increases her typing speed by reducing the number of keystrokes needed to complete a task. As the assistant receptionist, she takes messages on her computer and sends them through the network to people's desk computers or prints them out. Without the computer, she would not be doing this job, which she finds so enjoyable and that holds so much potential for her.

Tony

Tony is an athlete, but he is no longer able to compete professionally in his sport because of progressive vision loss. Just when the world told him his options were narrowing, he told himself that in order to have more options he was going to have to create them for himself.

Tony was in his forties when he went to his rehabilitation counselor with the idea that a computer might be worth exploring. His counselor agreed to enroll him in a local community college where he could take a computer class. Tony started with only an understanding that technology would give him new skills. "Once I was introduced to voice output (the ability of a computer to read text aloud with a synthetic voice), I knew that with a computer I could be employable. I had no real idea of what job I might do because I didn't know what was out there that I would be capable of doing with technology. I just knew it was the key for me."

Tony's first surprise was that he not only had to learn how to operate his IBM computer, but also how to use a screen reader, a software

Tony

program that tells the user what is on the screen and vocalizes every keystroke the user makes. "Use of a computer requires a nonvisual individual to use their memory a lot more in the beginning to be able to learn to use the computer. I have to know what is going to be produced on the screen when I call for it as well as know how to call for it. It required some real retraining for me, because I hadn't exercised my brain that way in a long time. I wasn't really intimidated; I always thought it was exciting, something to have fun with as much as something to use to get work accomplished."

With a computer using a speech synthesizer and a screen-reading program, Tony is able to attend writing classes and build his communication skills, critical preparation for reentering the work world as an equal. "Technology has given me higher goals and hope for greater achievements. It has allowed me to find my creativity and express it through writing—a whole new form of communication for me. Communication is going to be the key for me in any job, and technology is my most critical tool."

Tom

Over 20 years ago, Tom was exploring the possibility of getting a grant to figure out how to employ people with disabilities using technology. His fellow rehabilitation professionals were discouraging, but Tom is not one to tolerate negativism, and he was on a mission to assist a man who had sustained a major spinal cord injury in finding a new occupation. Tom wrote the grant and got it federally funded. As a result of Tom's effort, the man became a computer programmer with a terminal installed in his home.

Tom's project ran successfully for 6 years. It employed occupational therapists and rehabilitation engineering students in helping to match

Tom and his son

people with information-handling occupations such as computer programming and microfilm equipment operation.

Tom's own use of technology did not come until later, when he purchased a TRS-80 (an early Radio Shack computer) to be able to play with his children. The computer immediately gave Tom a feeling of empowerment, as it allowed him to play with his children on equal terms. It changed what it meant for him to have a disability. And it compelled him to look for other people with disabilities in his city who were using technology.

Tom found a few other people, and together they founded a self-advocacy organization focused on increasing access to technology by people with disabilities. Tom felt strongly that if people with disabilities let technology pass them by, they were going to lose out in a very big way. Before long, they had 600 members in their group using technology in new and innovative ways.

Tom, now in his sixties, has a well-equipped office in his home that allows him to carry on his activities as an advocate for people with disabilities in the areas of transportation and technology. "Technology is vital for people with disabilities who want administrative positions. It provides a way to deal with piles of paper, of which there is an abundance in administrative jobs." Tom must interact with public officials on behalf of the organization. In a recent meeting, he was able to lay out a Gantt chart, an organizational chart, and a theme chart, all prepared with the use of assistive technology. "We were able to communicate with the power structure convincingly—*that's* empowerment."

Tom sees himself as a part of all humankind. "What I am and who I am comes from my interaction with the environment. This technology—in spite of some of the problems with it—is enabling. I see young kids with cerebral palsy and speech difficulties in school using speech output. I see technology helping me to be seen as an equal. I am deeply impressed by how much more equal people with disabilities are because of technology. They have the power to communicate and the power to be more accepted and acceptable. People are less different. Technology allows people to be different on their own terms, rather than on society's terms."

Jumping In

If you spend enough time around seasoned users of assistive technologies, you will pick up on an important perspective about incorporating technology into your life—it's a process. It is a journey with a definite starting point for every individual, but it's also a journey with a destination that can be vague at times. You may know which direction to head. It could be a short trip or a long one. You have some expectations. And, though you may not be sure exactly where you will end up, you realize that you, yourself, will be the greatest determinant of what happens to you. All that you may be really certain of at this point is that you are ready for a change.

No one goes into the search for technology access knowing exactly what to expect or fully understanding the power or potential of technology. They just jump in. And that's what we are inviting you to do.

Chapter 2

Setting Your Goals

The Power of Expectations

From day one, you may hear about realistic expectations. It may come first from the medical community telling you that because of an identified medical condition, you must lower your expectations to avoid disappointment. At a kindergarten screening, you may be told that your child does not conform to the norms for her age and that you should reduce your expectations for her academic success or even her participation in mainstream education. At a parent-teacher conference, a teacher may suggest that you be more realistic, that you accept your child's placement in a classroom designed for children who are autistic, along with their notion of the appropriate expectations for autistic children. After a spinal cord or traumatic brain injury, you may be told that you will need to accept that there are things you will just not be able to do any longer. Or, as you grow older, you may be told that you can no longer participate socially or live independently at home.

We have all been told to be realistic in our expectations of ourselves (or others) based on someone else's best guess as to our ability and potential. Every expert has education and experience on which to base an opinion, yet none necessarily knows you or your child well. They may know about a physical or cognitive condition, but know little of who you really are: your personality, ambitions, goals, and drive. Experts are aware of some barriers to goal attainment and may recommend that you modify your goals. If you accept their recommendations for lowering your expectations, those diminished expectations may prove correct.

Most of us perform to the expectation level we and others set. If you are told that your reading level will never exceed fourth grade, and you are placed in a classroom where the expectations for students are just that, your reading level will likely be fourth grade. Your achievement often has more to do with the expectations and environment then with your real potential. We have seen far too many examples of the negative consequences of lowered expectations.

Jennifer came to our resource center in rural upstate New York in 1986 at the age of 18. She was minimally verbal and had been placed in a local developmental center at age 2 at the recommendation of the family physician. Jennifer's family was now exploring community living options because the developmental center was closing. Jennifer was learning the skills of daily living but had few opportunities for learning academic materials. She had written very little

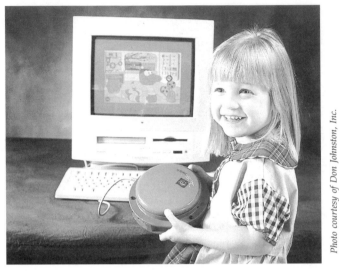

*Discover:Switch allows this child to do anything you
could do with a standard keyboard and mouse
(Don Johnston, Inc.)*

because of her poor fine-motor skills. In the course of her visit, she played with a talking word processor on a computer with a speech synthesizer. (See Part II for more about talking word processors and speech synthesizers.) She was ecstatic at being able to make the computer speak and within a few minutes had demonstrated the ability to make it communicate whatever she wished. Eventually, Jennifer was moved to a foster home and attended special education classes, and in 3 years she was reading at an eighth-grade level.

Most of us aspire to similar goals: to reach our maximum potential, to participate in many aspects of community life, and to pursue gainful employment. Each of us puts different twists on these expectations and generally is free to do so. There are constraints—finances, academic achievement, prior experience—but our society affirms the right of most citizens to aspire to whatever they choose. It is that freedom that lets us think big and achieve big. It is also that freedom that enables us to decide to start all over again, to adopt new goals, to set new expectations, and to follow some paths many times over. The same freedom must apply to people with disabilities.

"Unrealistic" expectations may carry the dangers of disappointment, failure, or lack of fulfillment, but they enable us to apply all of our abilities in reaching our maximum potential. It is in our best interest to encourage them.

Conventional and assistive technologies empower children and adults who have disabilities with new abilities to communicate without speech or sight, to manipulate the environment with little or no physical dexterity, and to demonstrate cognitive abilities in nontraditional ways. The future holds even more promise and excitement for expanding the potential of all individuals. The following sections will help you examine the specific areas around which your expectations are soaring and help you define in greater detail those goals that can be supported by access to technology.

Having a Vision

To have and nurture a vision, we must see beyond externally imposed constraints and give ourselves permission to think freely. This is the key to developing goals to which we want to apply our abilities and to setting our sights high enough so that we are unwilling to settle for expectations based on a limited understanding of our abilities and the available tools.

For a person with a disability, the most difficult part of this process is often feeling free and able to envision a preferred future. How do we give ourselves or others this freedom amidst all the voices of realism? Person-centered planning is one of the processes by which we receive permission to do what everyone else is allowed to do: to develop grand expectations, then employ all possible abilities and tools in their pursuit. In person-centered planning, an individual brings together a group of people to help in imagining a preferred future and thinking through the supports needed to realize that future. This process, like the one described in this book, places the individual with a disability at the center; hence the term *person-centered*.

Setting Goals

Whether or not you are a planner or a goal-oriented person, establishing some specific personal goals and a plan for yourself with technology will be helpful for making the technology discovery process manageable. There is much to consider, and having a plan will help insure that nothing important is forgotten, such as budgeting for training.

Goals provide the foundation upon which you will establish your personal technology plan, which will be examined in subsequent chapters. A technology plan should include the following elements:

1. Goals

2. Resources
   — Knowledge of pertinent legislation
   — Community resources

3. Supporters and advisors

4. Budget

5. Technology tools and vendors

6. Sources of funding

7. Implementation and training

8. Ongoing self-evaluation

Many people begin with very broad goals like "I want a better job," or "I'd like my son to do better in school," or "I want to be more productive." These are fine goals, but technology can only play a supporting role in reaching such broad goals. For example, using a computer for writing is one way technology might help a child to do better in school. Good attendance, a healthful environment, and appropriate related services, such as physical therapy, are also essential. Making good personal choices about assistive technology requires asking the right questions and specifying the tasks and activities in which technology can play a part in helping you attain your broader goals.

Getting specific

The reasons for using technology are as varied as the equipment options themselves. Many adults purchase computers for such tasks as writing letters, keeping up with personal finances, and developing a database of addresses and phone numbers. Parents often purchase computers to help their children in school: word processors can assist with writing, doing a research project, or designing a school newsletter; software can improve skills in reading, math, or spelling. Computers can also provide entertainment and recreation opportunities such as sports simulations, and outlets for creativity through music and art programs. Computers can help people develop social skills by connecting them with others through a telecommunications network through which they can correspond with people around the world.

Some people buy technology because it exists. Some believe it will make life easier. Some recognize its potential. Some realize it is the only way certain tasks can be done. For example, a person with a physical disability can use environmental controls to turn on lights, radios, and other electrical devices; a person with a learning disability can use a computer rather than a pencil and eraser as a writing tool. Computers sometimes provide the only means a person with a disability has for reading, writing, or speaking.

You should develop goals that will guide the decisions you have to make, whether you plan to use technology for pleasure, school, work, recreation, communication, learning, or activities of daily living. Important questions to answer in developing goals for the use of technology are:

- Who will be the primary user, and who else will be using it?

- What do you want to do? What do they want to do?

- What do you need to do? What do they need to do?

- What are the personal issues, such as the hearing and vision levels, cognitive ability, physical ability, and mobility?

Multiple users often pose interesting challenges.

Sarah, a young woman with autism, used a Macintosh PowerBook (a portable laptop computer) as her communication device. However, other family members wanted to use the PowerBook when Sarah was not using it. Sarah protested vehemently: this equipment was her *voice* and should be available for her at all times; use by others was an invasion of her privacy.

Multiple users can also be an issue in schools. When a student needs access to a computer for writing or other school work, the computer might become a dedicated machine for that student, off-limits to other students. If the family has purchased the equipment, they have some control over who uses it and when; if the school or others purchased it, the school would probably have more control over its use.

Identifying Your Goals

Among your expectations for assistive technology, you can probably categorize your goals into five areas:

- Education

- Employment

- Communication

- Living independently

- Recreation

An individual may have technology-related interests in all five areas. In which area or areas do your interests lie? In a specific area of interest to you, what are your immediate goals? Near-future goals? Long-term goals? The following sections discuss each area and give examples of immediate, intermediate, and long-term goals.

Education

Technology can help you achieve success from preschool to graduate school.

What are your education goals?

- Full inclusion for your child in your neighborhood elementary school?

- Independently attending a university and majoring in math?

- Vocational training to help you reenter the workforce?

Can you imagine ways in which technology might help you to accomplish those goals?

- Using a computer, could your child complete homework assignments?

- With a low-vision aid, could your child read the same textbook the rest of the class is using?

- Could the computer serve as your pen and paper if you cannot use your hands?

- Could you use software to simulate your frog dissection?

- Could you read instrumentation if it was magnified or produced audible feedback?

James is a 6-year-old with cerebral palsy, and the ultimate goal for him was inclusion. An early step toward this was a simple game, Red Light/Green Light, that involved his entire classroom. Using Ke:nx, a special interface device, we set the computer to alternate between a large square on half of the screen, labeled Red Light, and a square on the other half, labeled Green Light. (For more information on Ke:nx see Interface Devices and Switches in Part II). These squares lit up one after the other. When James made his selection by pressing his switch, the computer would say either Red Light or Green Light. The class, assembled in a circle, responded to James commands. (In the traditional Red Light/Green Light game, students line up and try to reach the finish line first. The computer version was designed to be noncompetitive so students of all abilities could enjoy it.) The simple game soon had everyone laughing, and James was ecstatic. The computer had empowered him as a leader. Red Light/Green Light was particularly successful for James because it was something he really enjoyed doing, it made technology part of the curriculum rather than a separate activity, and there were no wrong answers since the class responded to whatever choice James made.

Education is a lifelong series of learning opportunities, including post-secondary education, continuing education, informal education, self-improvement, and professional development. The common theme in educational endeavors is that an individual acquires and demonstrates new learning. Technology can be used for instruction; for written, artistic, and verbal expression; for reading, calculating, and simulating inaccessible or dangerous activities; for gaining basic reasoning and higher-level thinking skills, and for making the transition from school or from the ranks of the unemployed to the workplace.

Technology can play an important part in your education goals. In a post-secondary program, using assistive technology to earn a degree in architecture might be a long-term goal. A short-term goal might be having an instructor make reasonable accommodations to computer-aided design (CAD) courses, permitting a person with a disability to have access to the technology and materials used by the rest of the class.

John, whom we met in Chapter 1, discussed his goals in a personal essay written as part of his admissions application to the California Institute of the Arts:

I want to work in the entertainment business. I want to be part of a team working on animation projects: films, interactive videos, commercials. I want to be a background artist for animated films. I need to learn all that I can about how movies are made. Animators I have met, and who have mentored me a little, say that I should get a good liberal arts education, and then, really focus on art.

My educational story is different from most students. Because of cerebral palsy, I had to struggle my way into regular education classes, with the support of my friends and family. Starting out in classes for severely handicapped children, by the time I was in high school I was in regular classes and majoring in art. Because I cannot use my hands, the computer became my tool. With it and my HeadMaster, I do with head movements what other people do with their hands. (The HeadMaster is a head pointing system that uses ultrasonic signals and allows a person to operate a computer without using the standard keyboard or mouse. For more information, see Electronic Pointing Devices in Part II.)

I graduated from high school in 1990. I took a year off from school and used the time drawing, learning to use state-of-the-art graphic programs. I worked 6 to 8 hours a day on my Macintosh IIsi.

My goal is to learn how to do with my HeadMaster and Macintosh what other artists do with paint brushes and pens in their hands. All my work is done using a computer as my production tool.

After a good year of doing what I wanted to do, working at home, I started Santa Monica College in September 1991. I use my computer for written work and oral presentations, but since I don't use a communication device, I have always used an assistant, who also serves as an interpreter for me.

Cal Arts is the school that I think would best help me to develop my talents and to prepare me to achieve my goals. I would love to have the opportunity to be around creative people, to be a part of production teams working on different projects and film assignments, and to add my perspective to the creative process.

Employment

Technology is redefining the work place for everyone. The possibilities today are limitless.

What are your employment goals?

- To reopen your accounting firm after sustaining a spinal cord injury?

- To attain an entry-level position in a local bank?

- To start a home-based business on the Internet?

- To return to work after being on leave with a repetitive stress disorder (such as carpal tunnel syndrome)?

Can you imagine ways in which technology might help you to accomplish those goals?

- Could a computerized address book and automatic dialer help you place calls?

- Would the capacity to send and receive faxes from your computer reduce your physical exertion in a helpful way?

- Could a hand-held, closed circuit television system enable you to read instruments?

Photo courtesy of IntelliTools

*The world is becoming more accessible since products like
IntelliKeys, originally designed for people with disabilities,
are increasingly used by others as well (IntelliTools)*

• Would a portable computer with built-in cellular telecommunications capabilities allow you to work away from your office desk?

• Would speech output provide you with access to customer account records?

Perhaps you tend to think of employment in terms of a career, such as investment broker, lawyer, small-business owner, printer, public servant, broadcast announcer, accountant, journalist, engineer, poet, or teacher. Even from such a career perspective, there are specific job-related functions to be performed and that can be identified.

With the advent of the Americans with Disabilities Act, jobs are frequently described in terms of the functions required of the employee. This functional perspective is particularly well-suited to identifying specific tasks in which conventional and assistive technologies can play an important role. For example, a particular job might require placing and answering telephone calls, accessing a computer database, visually inspecting an assembly-line product, or manipulating a set of controls at a power plant. Setting goals for employment involves selecting the job and identifying the essential functions required to perform it. Once the functions have been specified, technology can be identified to help support them.

Shenita is a social worker who needs to type many reports. She is a one-handed typist because of her cerebral palsy. The trouble is she now has developed carpal tunnel syndrome. Surgery has been ruled out for her so she needed to find another solution. She tried an alternate keyboard, IntelliKeys (IntelliTools). The angle and the sensitivity of the keyboard allows her to type without pain. She also added a word prediction program that allows her to type using fewer keystrokes. These accommodations are making it possible for her to go about her business.

The strategy for achieving an employment goal consists of developing a list of essential job functions and developing access to those functions using technology where appropriate.

Nick is an engineer, recently retired from the Army Corps of Engineers. His job involved monitoring flooding and protecting homes, commerce, and traffic along the river. While attending a training seminar, he contracted Legionnaire's disease. He developed multiple sclerosis and became legally blind within a year. Keeping the job he loved and remaining productive required him to find some new ways of doing business.

Working with his state department for the blind, and later with his local Alliance for Technology Access center, Nick gained screen access to the IBM computers and software used at his previous position. He needed access to the Lotus 1-2-3 spreadsheet program to monitor readings and to perform calculations, and to a word processor to report findings. With access to technology, Nick was able to remain a fine engineer and to reach retirement with the Corps after 9 more years, and he has also established an engineering consulting business in his home.

Communication

Everybody has something to say. Technology offers new ways to communicate when the old ways are not effective.

What are your communication goals?

- To establish a more effective written communication system?

- To expand your oral communication in a work environment?

- To improve your social interactions with friends?

Can you imagine ways in which technology might help you to accomplish those goals?

- Using a spell-checker and a word prediction program to speed up the process of typing, could you write more effectively?

- If important phrases are programmed into a portable communication device to "speak" at work, would communication with colleagues be enhanced?

- With specialized presentation software and a voice synthesizer, could you make training presentations?

- Could you share information with sighted colleagues using a printer that prints both letters and braille dots on the same page?

The ability to communicate is a worthy goal for assistive technology, which opens channels of communication through print, symbols, and synthetic speech. For example, devices are now available to allow individuals with severe hearing impairments to converse over the telephone. (See the section on TTYs in Part II.)

Technology can also provide a synthetic voice for individuals who are unable to articulate their thoughts verbally. This application is often referred to as employing an augmentative or alternative communication (AAC) aid, which range widely in complexity and price. (Refer to "Assistive Communication Products" in Part II for more information on these devices.) If access to these aids is part of your technology goals, we recommend finding a qualified speech therapist with experience in this technology to assist you in selecting the right solution for you. Together you will consider many important factors, such as hearing characteristics, cognitive abilities required to use the device, and the ability to connect the device to a computer.

People who have lost their ability to communicate in either print or speech due to degenerative physical conditions or diseases can benefit from alternative forms of communication.

Sidney has multiple sclerosis and no longer has the ability to control any movement from his neck down. He lives in a nursing home around the corner from the church where he is a visiting minister. The church wanted to take up a collection to help Sidney realize more independence and gave him a choice between a motorized wheelchair and a computer. Sidney chose the computer.

Writing to friends around the country and even in town was not possible until he received his computer. Now he "surfs the net," plays everything from Wheel of Fortune to bridge and feels that the computer has saved his sanity. Turning the pages of books was not possible for Sidney. The CD-ROM collection that he has now accumulated includes the Bible, an encyclopedia, and a wide range of books on great works of art and even how to learn Spanish. Before getting his computer, Sidney used to wait for someone to bring him the phone and hold it for him while he spoke. Now he easily communicates online. No more answering machines, busy signals, or waiting for assistance. Sidney is able to carry on private communications when and how he wishes.

Sidney uses a Headmaster system (Prentke Romich Company) and an on-screen keyboard developed with Ke:nx (Don Johnston, Inc.). He uses a puff switch to replace the mouse click. The keyboard was custom designed by Sidney. If he needs a new key, he adds it. The camera key in the middle of the keyboard was added so he can take snapshots of the screen and import the graphics into his letters

Customized keyboard layout

to his grandchildren. He uses a Power Macintosh with a built-in CD-ROM. The monitor is on a hospital table and is wheeled in front of him on the bed. The CPU stays on the dresser next to the bed.

Living in a nursing home generally means access to a very limited amount of space. Technology has afforded Sidney a level of independence that he had thought he would never retrieve.

Ben, a 7-year-old with autism, was trying to use a regular keyboard with the assistance of his teacher. He was not having success. He was bouncing around a lot, missing the keys, and making too many mistakes for his meaning to be communicated. The standard keyboard was replaced by the IntelliKeys keyboard (IntelliTools). An overlay was used on the keyboard that had large letters, providing targets big enough for Ben to strike. His pointing suddenly became much more accurate and his communication was clearly understandable.

Julia is 14 years old and very suddenly lost her hearing because of a drug she was taking to treat her cystic fibrosis. This quick and dramatic change in her life was difficult for her. So her mother started investigating technology and went to her local Alliance for Technology Access Center to see what they had. She borrowed a text telephone and a Closed Caption Decoder so that her daughter was again able to talk on the phone and watch TV. Julia is now excited about investigating other possibilities, like the Phone Communicator (IBM), so she can carry on private conversations with her boyfriend without having to use the phone company's relay service.

Finding technology solutions is an ongoing process as your goals and needs change.

Living independently

Many goals consist of performing tasks that facilitate living more independently, such as reading mail with an optical device that converts text to large print, synthetic speech, and tactile symbols. An environmental control system can manage a home security system, control thermostats and lighting in the home, operate an intercom system and front door lock, place and receive telephone calls, send out an alert for help, and run a home entertainment system. Other goals for daily computer use might include the ability to keep a database of favorite recipes, monitor some aspect of a health indicator, use an alarm clock, or shop and bank from home. To apply assistive technology to living more independently, create a list of the specific, essential functions you require, and identify those that may be made accessible with the proper tools. (For more information on environmental control units see Part II.)

Technology does extraordinary things. It can also do very ordinary things like open the door, turn on the lights, and dial the phone.

What are your independent living goals?

- Do you want to be able to live alone?

- Do you want to move into a shared living arrangement?

- Do you want to be able to function more independently in your current living situation?

Can you imagine ways in which technology might help you to accomplish those goals?

- Would an environmental control system that is operated by a single switch and controls kitchen appliances, the lights, the television, and the automatic door opener enable you to live more independently?

- Do you need an emergency alert system?

- Would a closed-circuit television help you to read and write messages and pay your bills?

- Would using a computer to shop on an on-line telecommunications system increase your independence?

Jim sustained a spinal cord injury over 16 years ago and, using his computer, writes, "Because of the high level of my injury, I am unable to use my hands and arms in a functional manner. A few years ago I learned of a person who could help me in getting a voice

Photo courtesy of Prentke Romich Company

*Vanessa accesses the computer as well as online services with a
Delta Talker augmentative communication device from Prentke Romich
(Prentke Romich Company)*

operated system to control my environment. What he did was to customize my MS-DOS computer system using a Dragon Systems voice input card and X10 Powerhouse environmental control module which allows me to turn lights on and off, answer and originate phone calls, control a television set, open and close my garage door, and unlock my back door, all by voice commands. A microphone is mounted on my wheelchair, as well as a speaker through which I get voice feedback from the system. In this way, I can be anywhere in my home and still can use the voice input system to control my environment. There is also a microphone and speaker mounted by my bed, so that I can respond to any emergency during the night. This particular aspect has given me a much greater peace of mind than I have ever had since my injury. I greatly enjoy the independence I have gained from this environmental control system."

Recreation

Computer technology holds great promise for entertainment and other forms of recreation. Hundreds of popular games, such as poker, chess, television game shows, and board games, have been adapted for computers, providing access to games that may otherwise be inaccessible. Many commercial telecommunications services allow users to enter into games with people in other locations or to follow sporting news around the world. Using a computer for an environmental control can also provide access to common electronic entertainment devices and appliances like the television, videotape recorder, and CD player.

Determining recreation goals consists of identifying the activity or functions in which one wishes to participate, and then selecting the devices, software, or technology services required to support the goal. For example, a young adult may wish to learn to play chess with a live opponent. Once the software for the game is identified, the next task would be to identify any additional devices needed to allow each player access to the software program.

Just because you might not be able to get down on the floor with your kids doesn't mean you cannot play with them. Technology can help make the games accessible to everyone.

What are your recreation goals?

- Do you want to become a champion chess player?

- Do you want to be able to play games with your children?

- Does your child want to be able to play with the children next door?

Can you imagine ways in which technology might help you to accomplish those goals?

Through computers and an environmental control unit such as LIAISON, anyone can control their environment—from turning on the lights to dialing the telephone (DU-IT Control Systems Group) computer work station, an environmental control unit

Photo courtesy of Du-It Control Systems, Inc.

- Would your neighbor be interested in learning to play computerized chess with you?

- Could access to your child's adapted computer enable you to play their favorite video game together?

- Would a talking computer be fun for kids, whether or not they needed the speech device?

At the Center for Accessible Technology, the ATA center in Berkeley, California, parents bring their children to the play groups with the goal of developing social and other skills. Children come with the goal of having fun with their friends. Of course they also learn. With battery-operated cars attached to large brightly colored switches, they develop switch skills that they can later use to operate a computer. By attaching marking pens to these cars and running them over huge sheets of butcher paper and watching them crash into each other, they experience the joy of creating and playing together.

Setting New Goals

Just as your reasons for purchasing different items change with your personal circumstances, experience, and budget, your technology needs will change over time. Six months or a year after your computer purchase, you may be anticipating a career change that would require number crunching, recalling huge amounts of information, or networking with other agencies via a telecommunications system, and want a machine with a faster processing speed. You may be dealing with a disability that will require a different configuration in the future: addition of speech recognition, alternate keyboards, or screen enlargement programs. Or you may find that your growing technology experience allows you to develop more sophisticated skills and requires more sophisticated tools.

Technology is continually changing: becoming faster, more powerful, and more versatile. It is often hard to decide when to purchase. What if I buy this computer today, and tomorrow they drop the price or discontinue this machine? Technology is an investment in the future, and no one can afford the luxury of putting the future on hold. Future achievements depend on planning, practice, and finding the right tools to work toward chosen goals.

Chapter 3

A Review of the Technology Tools

Much of what individuals with disabilities want is simply access to conventional technologies. You want to be able to write with a word processor. You want teachers to be able to read your writing. You want to publish a newsletter. You want your child to be able to draw and experience the process of creating pictures. You want to be able to create and perform music on a synthesizer. You want to play the latest computer games. You want to work a cash register. Your daughter needs access to a patient tutor for learning her multiplication facts. Your search for technology will have much in common with the process everyone goes through to become proficient in using technology—assistive or conventional—for a specific purpose.

The similarity of assistive and conventional technologies revolves around aspects common to both. That is, all computing involves three things: input, processing, and output. *Input* refers to how you give information to a computer. *Processing* relates to the electronics that operate on, or process, the information you provide. *Output* refers to the way you perceive what the computer is doing and producing with your information.

The ways in which assistive technologies are different from conventional technologies involve these same three aspects. In the pages ahead, you will have an opportunity to determine in what ways your search will be similar to the process everyone goes through because you are selecting some conventional technology components, and in what ways your search is unique because you have some unconventional considerations.

As you put a computer system together, individual needs—your own or those of someone you know—will determine if selections will be made from conventional or assistive technologies. Individuals with disabilities who venture into technology will usually select a combination of conventional and assistive technologies and rely heavily on the conventional, especially when universal access features are part of the product's design.

The jargon of technology can make a discussion about the specifics of input, processing, and output sound intimidating, but don't worry if some terms don't mean much to you at this point. You will gradually learn more of them in the pages ahead and in the experiences you will have during your quest for technology.

Conventional Technology

The term *hardware* is used to refer to the computer components—the actual pieces of equipment—such as the computer box or CPU (central processing unit), the monitor, and the disk drive. The term *software* refers to the electronic instructions that tell the computer what to do. *Application* and *program* are other common words that refer to software.

The following list organizes categories of conventional hardware and software by function.

Input

- Keyboard
- Mouse
- Trackball
- Microphone
- Disk drive (external and internal)
- CD-ROM drive
- Modem
- Scanner

Processing

- Computer or central processing unit (CPU)
- Disk operating software (or system software)
- Cable
- Software program (or application program)

Output

- Monitor
- Printer

Conventional input

Conventional input devices—devices that give information to a computer—include the keyboard and mouse. Keyboards are usually patterned after traditional typewriter keyboards in terms of key size and placement, and they contain several additional keys that make a computer do operations traditional typewriters never could. They may also contain a separate or attached numeric keypad that makes entering numbers and performing calculations easier.

The mouse, invented long after the computer keyboard, made computers easier to use because it allowed the user to point to things seen on the screen. By pointing to icons and words, you can make a computer do many things without ever touching the keyboard or memorizing commands. The mouse contains a ball that rolls around inside a small device with a button or buttons, and is usually connected to the computer by a short cord.

There are many other ways to provide input to a computer. Conventional peripheral, or add-on, devices, such as scanners and modems, carry information through cables that are connected to ports (small plugs or outlets) on the back of the computer. Scanners are something like photocopying machines. They put an image of the page you are scanning into your computer, and the image can then be seen on the computer screen. Some scanners have the ability to decipher and read the print that appears on the scanned page. Once you have scanned the page into your computer, you can change or add to the text. Modems are devices that allow you to connect your computer through telephone lines to other computers and information services around the world.

Conventional processing

Processing, in conventional terms, refers to the electronics commonly used to process, or operate on, the information you provide to the computer. The key to processing is the operating system. The *operating system* is the complex programming that tells your computer system millions of mundane—but extremely important—things every minute. It tells your computer what to do when a key is pressed, what kind of electronic dots to put on the screen, how to save a piece of information, when to access the disk drive to retrieve data, and all of the other functions your computer must perform when it is turned on. The operating system gives different brands of computers their different characters.

Computer companies invest millions of dollars in developing operating systems they think will appeal to you. Which devices and software you want to use will help you determine which operating system and computer you should purchase. All of these components must be compatible with one another for your system to work.

There are many computer manufacturers in the world, but in the United States, the majority of personal computers can be divided into these groups: IBM, Apple Macintosh, and IBM-compatible computers (or IBM clones).

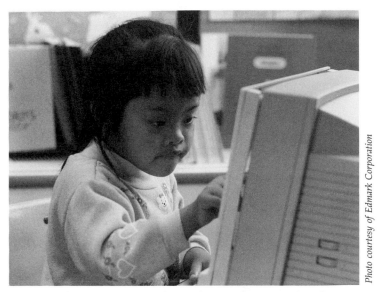

Photo courtesy of Edmark Corporation

This young girl is making a direct selection using the Touch Window in place of a mouse (Edmark Corporation)

In a Macintosh computer (made by Apple Computer, Inc.), the operating system is referred to simply as the *System* or *System Software*. Apple pioneered and pushed the limits of the intuitive, graphic user interface, which allows the user to point at menus to select commands and to click on pictures to open files. This interface eliminates the need for the user to remember and type in a series of complex commands, as is usually the case with text-based operating systems such as MS-DOS.

For IBM and IBM-compatible computers, the most popular operating systems include MS-DOS (Microsoft Disk Operating System) and Windows software. Windows is a program that runs along with MS-DOS. It creates a graphic user interface, much like that of Macintosh computers, that makes the machine much easier to navigate. Microsoft has developed Windows 95, an operating system designed to replace both Windows and MS-DOS. OS/2 is an operating system developed by IBM to replace MS-DOS. OS/2 will run programs written for MS-DOS, but MS-DOS cannot run programs written for OS/2. There is a special feature of OS/2 that gives the screen of IBM computers the feel of a Macintosh computer.

The way a user interacts with a computer is very different in the graphic user interface (GUI) and the text-based operating system models. With the emergence of Windows software, it appears that the world of personal computing is moving toward GUI as the common model. Many people welcome this change because it simplifies computer use. But for many other people, especially those with visual impairments, this change presents significant challenges.

Operating systems are continuously being upgraded (revised and improved) and released in new versions. Numbers after the program title indicate which version it is, such as MS-DOS 6.2 and Macintosh System Software 7.5. However, the most recent version of Windows is called Windows 95 and IBM now has OS/2 Warp on the market.

The computer you choose will most likely be a Macintosh, IBM, or IBM-compatible computer. Your choice will reflect your opinion of which operating system you find easiest to use or which is required for the software and assistive technology you need. We don't recommend one manufacturer over another, because the choice is a personal one and depends on a great many variables. The fans of each type tend to be loyal and vocal in their praise of their particular brand and model. You will probably develop the same devotion after you make your choice.

ROM (read only memory) and RAM (random access memory) are two more acronyms you will frequently encounter. The terms have to do with computer memory—how much and what kind of information it can work with at one time. Both ROM and RAM store information in computer chips. ROM is built into your computer and contains information that tells your computer what to do when it is turned on. RAM is short-term storage and holds information that is being processed and manipulated, like your database application when you are entering new data. When you turn off your computer, RAM is cleared. *Storage* relates to how you can save the information that you have processed in RAM when you turn the computer off.

Floppy disks are small diskettes of magnetic material—much like recording tape—on which you can store and retrieve information. You insert floppy disks into the disk drive. Hard disk drives are for storage and are also made of magnetic material and can hold well over a hundred times as much information as a single floppy disk. Hard disk drives are often built into computers, but can also be purchased and connected to your computer separately or in addition to a built-in drive. In business environments there are other types of storage devices that are commonly used.

RAM and storage capacity are measured in kilobytes (K), megabytes (MB), and gigabytes (GB), commonly called "K's," "megs," and "gigs." To give you a sense of size, 1 K equals approximately 170 words. One meg is 1024 K, so one gig (1024 megs) is an enormous amount of storage.

How much storage space and RAM is in a computer is significant information and will be included in any advertising. An ad in the Sunday paper for an IBM-compatible computer might read something like this: "Features a Pentium 100 processor, 1.2 GB HD, 8 MB RAM, with built-in 4X CD ROM." What this means is that the hard drive (HD) will hold 1.2 gigabytes, and there are 8 megabytes of RAM.

Software

A computer can do nothing without some kind of program telling it what to do. These programs can be short and simple or huge and sophisticated, and are commonly referred to as *software*—electronic instructions, stored on computer disks or computer chips, that tell the computer what to do after you turn it on.

Computers are different from any tool you have ever owned because of the software developed for them. Unlike a toaster—which is always a toaster—a computer can become any tool a particular piece of software tells it to become: a typewriter, an encyclopedia, an alarm clock, a paintbrush, a stock broker, a musical instrument, your mail and message system.

Software programs provide the instructions that make the hardware do the work you need done. Software is created by programmers and, as you might expect, has a cost that reflects the time and effort that went into creating the program. A program that lets your computer behave like a stopwatch may cost little or nothing; a program that allows you to produce an animated, full-length cartoon feature or the special effects used in *Star Wars* may require a second mortgage.

You must consider the cost of software in your planning. An individual may well spend more on software in the first couple of years of computer ownership than was spent on the computer hardware itself.

Further, there is no "best" piece of software, or for that matter, no "best" piece of software for someone with a disability, just as there is no best book or best vehicle. Your individual needs and resources will determine your software options, just as they do your choice of books and vehicles.

A note about copyright: If you are going to use a piece of software, you must be licensed to use it. Every program on your computer should be registered in your name. Unauthorized copying of commercial software is theft. For software publishers to remain in business, they must be properly compensated for their products. If you are unsure about the rules, check the manuals and other documentation. Software companies always make the laws clear. There are programs called *shareware* that you may try for free before you decide to use them. They always include information on how to pay the developer should you decide to keep and use them. *Public domain* software programs are free to anyone who wants to copy and use them.

The range of software titles is phenomenal and growing. The following list, which is not exhaustive, is one way to group the types of software tools available. These programs are all available through local computer and software retail outlets, and through good mail-order sources.

Education and Training

- Early language skills building

- Early learning

- Keyboarding

- Reading

- Writing

- Math and science

- Problem solving

- Language arts

- Social studies

Business Applications

- Word processors

- Desktop presentations

- Databases

- Charting, graphing, and statistics

- Spreadsheets

- Desktop publishing

- Finance and accounting
- Project planners

Games and Recreation

- Sports simulations
- Chess and other board games
- Mysteries and adventures
- Interactive novels

Graphics and Design

- Computer-assisted design or engineering (CAD/CAE)
- Clip art
- Digital photography
- Drawing
- Animation
- Painting

Communications

- Telecommunications
- On-line services

Music and Sound

- Training
- Composing
- Recording

Utilities

- Security/anti-virus
- Screen savers
- Back up
- Macros

Conventional output

Conventional output devices—devices that let you know what the computer is doing and producing with your information—include monitors and printers. Although they may resemble them, computer monitors are more sophisticated than television screens and produce a higher-quality image. Monitors can be black and white, gray scale, or color. Gray-scale monitors use dozens of shades of gray, which improve the picture considerably over black and white images; some color monitors can produce millions of different colors. Monitors are available in many different screen sizes. Some computer systems include built-in monitors, but most are separate from the CPU. Many computers—portable models, for example—have built-in monitors and may allow you to attach an additional, larger monitor when you are at home, at work, or making a presentation to an audience.

Printers generally fall into three categories: dot matrix, ink jet, and laser. Dot-matrix printers form letters and graphics from a pattern of dots, generally created by small pins striking against an inked ribbon. Ink-jet printers are usually specified as *near-letter quality*, meaning that they print well-defined letters and images that are almost the quality of those produced by laser printers. Laser printers use a laser beam to form characters and images. They produce the highest-quality printing and, as might be expected, are the most expensive of the three dominant types of printers. Color printers are available in all three types.

It is standard for computers to play sounds that have been incorporated into software programs. Some computers require added equipment to play sounds. Some computers also have the capacity to record and play back sounds while some machines require additional equipment and software to accomplish this.

Assistive Technology

The distinction between assistive and conventional technologies is becoming less clear as the concept of universal design is incorporated into conventional technology. Universal design is an approach to the design process that results in products that are usable by the greatest number of people. Both assistive and conventional fields are broadening and converging. What is a necessity for some is convenience for all. Touch screens, for example, are used as alternatives to the mouse for people with disabilities, and in tourist-information booths at airports and theme parks. Voice-recognition systems, which allow you to control a computer through verbal commands, are used by people who cannot use a keyboard to provide input and, in many parts of the country, by telephone users. By the end of the '90s, voice recognition may eventually become the most common form of input for everyone, and keyboards may become obsolete.

As the plea from the community of assistive technology users has gone out for universal access, companies have responded. The worlds of assistive and conventional technology are blending, and a new generation of products is emerging—products designed to be used by *all* people. A number of companies are aware of the need and are designing products with universal access in mind. One company in particular, Brøderbund Software, recognizes the need for designs that provide the greatest function for the greatest number of users. Brøderbund, a successful educational software publisher of such popular and acclaimed products as Kid Pix, Print Shop, and the Carmen Sandiego games, has become educated in access issues for individuals with disabilities through training and consultation.

Brøderbund contracted with the Alliance for Technology Access to test the compatibility of their products with assistive technology devices and has published the data in product catalogs. They have established an internal bulletin board to which information related to access is posted for everyone's use. And engineers, product managers, and sales staff are collaborating with other vendors in the field to create solutions that mean greater access to Brøderbund software. By assessing the needs, addressing the issues, and identifying the steps that need to be taken, Brøderbund is making its products universally accessible and leading the way for other mainstream software developers.

Several companies are now working together to achieve greater accessibility and applicability of their products. Especially in the area of alternate keyboards, software developers such as Edmark, Brøderbund,

Photo courtesy of CITE

This man uses the enlargement capabilities of a CCTV to read a pamphlet

and Hartley, are teaming up with hardware developers. Together they are developing overlays (customized keyboard layouts that slip onto the surface of the alternate keyboard) for specific software programs so they can be easily accessed with alternate keyboards like IntelliKeys (IntelliTools), Key Largo (Don Johnston, Inc.), and Ke:nx On:Board (Don Johnston, Inc.). These are important collaborations in furthering the goal of increased access by making both conventional and assistive technology products that are clearly designed to work together.

The following list categorizes assistive technologies in the same way conventional technologies were categorized: according to input, processing, and output uses. Part II describes in detail dozens of products in each category. The page number following each item indicates where you can find more information about each category in Part II. In the remainder of this chapter, we will briefly discuss a few representative items in each category and help you formulate disability-related questions relevant to your needs.

Input

- Access utilities (p. 169)

- Arm and Wrist Supports (p. 198)

- Alternate keyboards (p. 163)

- Interface devices (p. 179)

- Joysticks (p. 194)

- Keyboard additions (p. 172)

- Electronic pointing devices (p. 188)

- Pointing and typing aids (p. 190)

- Switches and switch software (p. 175)

- Optical character recognition and scanners (p. 186)

- Trackballs (p. 196)

- Touch screens (p. 192)

- Voice recognition (p. 183)

Processing

- Abbreviation expansion and macro programs (p. 200)

- Menu management programs (p. 211)

- Reading comprehension programs (p. 204)

- Writing composition programs (p. 207)

- Writing enhancement tools
  - Grammar checkers (software features, p. 159)
  - Electronic reference tools (p. 209)
  - Spell checkers (software features, p. 161)
  - Word prediction programs (p. 202)

Output

- Refreshable braille displays (p. 218)

- Braille embossers (p. 216)

- Monitor additions (p. 228)

- Screen enlargement programs (p. 226)

- Screen readers (p. 223)

- Speech synthesizers (p. 220)

- Talking and large-print word processors (p. 213)

Assistive-style input

Everyone needs an input method. If standard methods don't work, you must find an alternative. For example, someone with a learning disability or with complete blindness can usually use a conventional keyboard. But what if you need to protect the keys from being pressed accidentally? Someone with limited dexterity may benefit from one of the many keyboard devices available, such as a clear plastic keyguard that is placed over the keyboard, with holes over each key to help guide and support the fingers. One option for people with little or no ability to move their fingers is an electronic pointing device with an on-screen keyboard. An on-screen keyboard is a software program that displays an image of a keyboard on the computer screen. Using an electronic pointing device, you point to the key you want and activate it by pressing a switch. Someone with use of only one hand may prefer to use a miniature keyboard designed for use with a single hand; another person may benefit from a very large keyboard with picture symbols in place of letters.

Arjan Khalsa from IntelliTools, the company that produces the IntelliKeys keyboard, explains how modern-day keyboard layouts came about: The QWERTY (and most common) keyboard was developed in

Photo courtesy of IntelliTools

Adults with disabilities may find programmable keyboards useful for a variety of purposes—employment, productivity, communication

the 1860s and first sold by a small-arms manufacturer, E. Remington & Sons, in 1873 as a typewriter. "The keyboard was designed to slow down the typist so the keys would not jam," he says. "We say that computers are great for youngsters, but they use keyboard technology developed in the 1860s. Computers feature 1990s data processing, 1990s graphics and sound, and 1860s keyboard input." The IntelliKeys keyboard, a touch-sensitive customizable keyboard, was designed to be more flexible and appropriate for all children and adults, and is especially useful for people with disabilities.

It is time to discard your preconceptions about keyboards. Do you want a keyboard with 8-inch-tall keys? With tiny keys that you can operate with very small movements? With keys arranged in alphabetical order? With large keys today and small keys tomorrow? All of these options are possible. Why should each keystroke give you only one character? Why not assign whole sentences to a single key?

Switches and scanning are a tremendous input option for many individuals. With scanning, the computer automatically and repeatedly cycles through the alphabet and other common characters on the screen. As the computer highlights the desired letter or character, the user selects it by clicking a simple switch, then moves on to selecting subsequent letters. Many things can be scanned, such as word lists, pictures, arrow keys, and menu choices.

Mouse modifications and alternatives provide access to conventional computer functions normally controlled with a mouse. A mouse requires the user to point to, click on, and/or drag objects seen on the screen; mouse alternatives accomplish the same tasks in other ways. An electronic pointing device is one mouse alternative that enables people who cannot use their hands to fully operate a computer system.

Assistive-style processing

Processing considerations deal primarily with how you plan on using your computer and how you can interact more effectively with the machine to best accomplish your goals. For example, an individual with a disability may require a computer that is small, lightweight, portable, impervious to constant vibrations, and has a number of important built-in applications that are available whenever the computer is turned on.

Other assistive technologies related to processing are designed to speed up the computing process or to make it more effective. For example, if you hold down a letter key on most keyboards, the letter will repeat itself until you release the pressure. For people with dexterity problems, this key-repeat feature of conventional technologies can be terribly annoying. A small program or option can tell the operating system to ignore sustained pressure on the keys.

Assistive-style output

Access to technology for individuals with disabilities must include access to computer output. What is needed for an individual to reliably perceive output from the computer? Conventionally, the individual views print or images on a monitor or on a printout. Several options provide output when these conventional methods are inadequate.

People with visual impairments or learning disabilities may benefit from specialized software and speech synthesizers that read aloud characters appearing on the screen. (Many of these products are classified as screen readers and are discussed in Part II.) People with vision impairments may benefit from options that enlarge characters on the screen or allow color and contrast adjustments to the text and background. Braille displays constantly translate what is happening on the screen into tactile output, and embossers can be connected to computers to produce brailled documents.

By using a combination of conventional output methods and assistive technology options, you can easily work with technology in a typical environment, such as an office or classroom.

A Word About Other Technologies

Some stand-alone products on the market involve all three functions: input, output, and processing. Many of these helpful devices are described in Part II and include products like hand-held, closed-circuit television (CCTV) systems, which aid individuals with low vision in reading print and instruments. Reading machines use synthetic speech to read books or other print materials fed into the system. Other devices in this category include text telephones (also known as teletypewriter devices), which provide telephone access for individuals who are deaf or require printed communication.

Augmentative and alternative communication (AAC) devices, also called assistive communication products, provide speech for people unable to communicate orally. Some are designed for a single use and thus are called *dedicated systems.* They may be as simple as a board with word choices that a user selects, or as complicated as an elaborate computer system. The computer devices usually include voice synthesizers that vocalize what the user chooses to say. Depending on the type of device, voices may sound very real because the sound is recorded (digitized) or robotic because the sound is synthesized. The AAC field has expanded enormously over the last decade, and interested individuals should thoroughly investigate the options and consult with a speech

Photo courtesy of Don Johnston, Inc.

*Co:Writer is a powerful word-prediction tool that lets
you write almost as quickly as you can think
(Don Johnston, Inc.)*

and language therapist skilled in AAC devices before making an investment. (See Part III for more references and resources. See Part II,
Assistive Communication Products, for product information.)

The following is a description of one individual's transition into
effective communication through the use of AAC devices:

Melinda is a different young lady today than she was three years
ago. When we first met Melinda, she was a youngster with a lot
to say, but no way to express herself. She had learned in her short
life that screaming in frustration was the quickest way to get attention. Unfortunately, this method of communication had become her
biggest barrier, and her family, friends and the professionals who
worked with her were as frustrated as she was. Fortunately,
Melinda's family devoted themselves to exploring alternate means
of communication for her.

Melinda first visited an augmentative communication clinic
when she was nine. She had begun to use sign language and gestures as her main form of communication. During this visit it was
suggested that she use a portable communication device. The occupational therapist and speech therapist suggested that the pictures
in the book be color coded, and provided ideas for how to use the
book. Melinda's mother took these ideas and improved on them,
attaching the book with suspenders, laminating it and personalizing it for Melinda. Teachers and staff at her school added their ideas
as well. At first, Melinda didn't use the book and the challenge
became one of how to facilitate her interest in this method of communication. Again, more frustration.

One night Melinda was very upset and could not calm herself
down. Her mom lay in the bed next to her and tried to help by asking Melinda what she wanted for breakfast the next morning. As
she listed her daughter's favorite foods, Melinda became increasingly upset. She had a specific food in mind, but she couldn't communicate what it was. They went to the kitchen to try and find what
Melinda desired, but she indicated it wasn't there. Then suddenly,
Melinda remembered her communication book. She quickly
retrieved it and pointed to the picture of a person eating a donut.
They went out and got the donuts that night and Melinda slept
peacefully, as did her mom.

What resulted from these efforts was an enjoyable and functional
method of communication. Melinda began actively communicating
with her peers, friends, and family, and showed much less frustration. Using her signs, gestures, and verbal expressions along with

her new book, Melinda became excited about communication and began making tremendous gains in school as well as at home.

Melinda returned for a follow-up appointment to see the augmentative communication specialists. School personnel, family, and the team believed it was time to add speech output to her communication repertoire. A school visit was made to survey the school setting and talk to relevant professionals and friends of Melinda in her new inclusion setting. In the end, several different devices, all with voice output, were loaned to Melinda for trial periods of 1 to 3 months. She and her family determined the appropriate device. "The Wolf has a voice that her classmates do not understand but we like the overlays; the Cheaptalk 8 doesn't have enough space for messages but we like its ease of use." Finally, a device called the EasyTalk (The Great Talking Box Co.) was tried. It had portability, lots of spaces for messages, and was easy to use.

Mom reports that Melinda is enjoying her EasyTalk but that the learning process is never ending. She explains it is difficult to keep on top of the programming because Melinda's communication needs are dynamic and always changing. She says she often feels frustrated by not being able to identify all the messages her daughter might need, and Melinda sometimes cannot find what she needs on her board when she needs it. But, we all laugh as we discuss this because we know that it is the *process itself* that has transitioned Melinda from a very unhappy girl to one who enjoys communication. We also know that no device is the only means of communication and that Melinda will continue to rely on the total communication approach.

Setting Off in the Right Direction

The questions that follow will help you specify some of your general areas of interest and disability-related considerations. The questions are grouped around issues related to the input-processing-output technology model. By answering the questions, you will begin to focus on many of the specific options and solutions described more fully in following chapters and in Part II that will be important in your particular quest for access to technology.

Questions About Input

- What parts of your body and what abilities can you use consistently?

- Is there at least one set of muscles you can move reliably? For example, can you blink, move your chin, use your fingers, or turn your head whenever you wish?

- Do you think you can use a regular computer keyboard very well, OK, somewhat OK, poorly, or not at all?

- Do you think you can use a regular computer mouse very well, OK, somewhat OK, poorly, or not at all?

- How might input devices be positioned to make the input process as comfortable as possible?

Some Input Solutions

- By using a switch with scanning, you can operate a computer with any reliable muscle movement.

- There are keyboards that can be altered to create keys of any shape, position, size, and color.

- There are devices that replace the mouse, and there are ways you can use the keyboard instead of the mouse to accomplish the same tasks.

Questions About Processing

- Would it be difficult for you to hold down more than one key at a time?

- Are you aware of any aspect of using a computer that could be annoying to you, such as the key-repeat feature of many keyboards?

Some Processing Solutions

- There are access utilities that allow you to press keys sequentially rather than simultaneously.

- You can turn off the key-repeat function with a software access utility.

- Word-prediction programs allow the computer to finish words that you start.

Questions About Output

- If it's not possible for you to see the screen, do you know that a speech synthesizer can be used to read the screen for you? Would speech output interest you?

- Do you want to be able to produce output and materials that can be used by people both with and without disabilities?

- Do you need brailled output?

- How might output devices be positioned to make their use as comfortable as possible?

Some Output Solutions

- Words you create with a computer can be spoken with synthetic speech, translated and embossed in braille, seen on the screen, and printed on paper.

- There are several devices that can pass braille dots beneath your fingertips.

These questions and answers, and the information proceeding them, provide a framework in which to think about technology, both conventional and assistive. At this point you should begin to see, at least in a broad sense, how technology can help you fulfill your goals.

Chapter 4

Current Laws and Legislation

Many people have taken this journey before you and have forged the way. The most significant trails blazed have been through the Congress. What follows is a review of the pertinent legislation enacted through the hard work and persistence of people with disabilities and their families across the nation who understand the growing importance of technology.

This legislative summary will give you a sense of the rights and protections afforded individuals with disabilities. The passage of these ground-breaking laws clearly indicates that technology is gaining recognition at every level of our society, and that advocates for its use are developing more clout in every arena.

Legislative Mandates: A Brief Overview

Congress has passed four important laws that have the potential, when enforced, to greatly improve the civil rights of people with disabilities. Among many other benefits, these pieces of legislation provide access to assistive and conventional technologies for individuals with disabilities in certain situations. The mandates are

- Individuals with Disabilities Education Act (P.L. 101–476)

- Americans with Disabilities Act (P.L. 101–336)

- Technology-Related Assistance for Individuals with Disabilities Act as amended in 1994 (P.L. 103–218)

- Rehabilitation Act as amended in 1992 (P.L. 102–569)

By contacting the office of your congressional representative or senator, you can obtain copies of these laws and related background materials. Call (202) 225-3121 for the U.S. House of Representatives, or (202) 224-3121 for the U.S. Senate, and an operator will connect you to the right office. Materials on all of these laws are available in braille, large print, audio tape, as computer files from the appropriate government agency, and on the internet in a variety of locations. There is a list of some of these resources on pages 59 and 61–62. In this section, we briefly summarize each law.

Individuals with Disabilities Education Act (IDEA)

IDEA is the amended version of the Education for All Handicapped Children Act of 1975 (P.L. 94–142). The law encompasses and expands upon several earlier education initiatives and guarantees four basic rights and two protective assurances for infants, toddlers, children, youth, and young adults with disabilities:

- All children with disabilities are entitled to a free public education appropriate to their needs.

- To the maximum extent possible, children with disabilities should be educated with students without disabilities, as close to home as possible, and in the least restrictive environment.

- Children with disabilities must be provided supplementary services that permit them to benefit from their education, such as physical therapy and assistive technology services.

- With the parents' informed consent, a fair assessment must be completed to determine the student's educational needs.

- Due process rights require prior notice be given to parents before changes are made in the child's program and a method provided for resolving disagreements.

- Students who have been identified or who are perceived as having difficulty learning in school must have an Individualized Education Program (IEP) prepared annually for them by a team that includes the child's parents. The IEP must clearly spell out what services a student will receive and how and where the student will receive them, and set forth specific educational goals and the tools to be used. An example of a specific goal would be, "John will write a well-organized, grammatically correct paragraph, free of spelling errors, using word processing software on a Macintosh computer equipped with IntelliKeys and a large-print overlay."

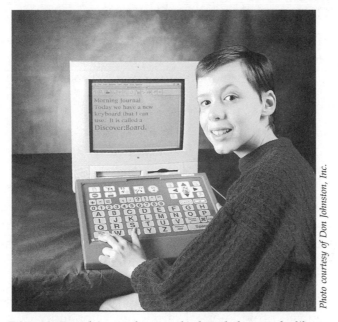

Photo courtesy of Don Johnston, Inc.

*Discover:Board is an alternate keyboard that works like
a standard keyboard and mouse. (Don Johnston, Inc.)*

In addition to provisions for the school-age population, the law includes the preschool level of ages 3 to 5 years and provides for the Early Intervention State Grant Program for infants and toddlers from birth to age 2. For infants and toddlers, assistive technologies may be specified in the individualized program and include toys and other devices that develop readiness for computer-based technologies that the child will need to participate in the environment and to learn. IDEA also mandates the inclusion of transition services in the IEP beginning no later than age 16. Assistive technology can serve a vital role for youth with disabilities who are making the transition from secondary school to higher education or work or greater community involvement.

Once assistive technology has been included in a student's IEP, the school system must provide it, as is true of any services included in an IEP. The Office of Special Education Programs (of the U.S. Department of Education) has issued a series of administrative letters over the years interpreting IDEA. One such letter stated that a school district or other local education agency may not maintain a flat policy barring the inclusion of assistive technology in IEPs. Rather, they must make a determination based on the facts of each case. Other letters have upheld the student's right to use assistive technologies purchased with school funds at home and away from school, when the IEP specifies that the devices are needed to maintain educational goals and learning.

Americans with Disabilities Act (ADA)

Modeled after Section 504 of the Rehabilitation Act of 1973 and the Civil Rights Act of 1964, the ADA provides civil rights protection against discrimination for individuals with disabilities similar to the protection provided in other legislation on the basis of race, gender, age, nationality, and religion. The ADA defines *disability* functionally as any condition that impairs major life activities such as seeing, hearing, walking, or working, and it covers nearly 900 specific disabilities. Under separate sections, it mandates accessibility and accommodation requirements in public facilities, employment, state and local government services, transportation, and communication. For example, one of the protections afforded by the ADA that is not commonly discussed covers parents and guardians with disabilities wishing to participate in their child's school environment. PTA meetings, parent-teacher conferences, and other school events are required by law to be accessible. The law intends to break down the barriers that exist in these five areas and to provide equal opportunity for individuals with disabilities.

Among the many important rights and protections addressed in the ADA is the requirement that an employer with 15 or more employees may not discriminate against an individual with a disability because of the disability when the person is qualified to perform the essential functions of the job, with or without a reasonable accommodation. The ADA defines *reasonable accommodation* as some modification in a job's task or structure, or in the workplace, that will enable the qualified employee with a disability to do the job. The modifications or changes, which can include the use of assistive technology and technology access, must be made, unless the change creates an undue hardship for the employer. Many employers and consumers (before doing their research) make the assumption that most modifications are going to be very costly and therefore qualify as undue hardships. This is not proving to be the case.

Preliminary findings of the President's Committee on Employment of People with Disabilities indicate that the majority of accommodations cost less than $500 and many have little or no cost at all. This committee, a small federal agency, is working with businesses and groups representing people with disabilities to promote the successful implementation of the ADA.

Through the Attorney General's Office and the Office of Civil Rights, the U.S. Department of Justice places a high priority on fair, swift, and effective enforcement of this landmark civil rights law. Contact the following agencies to receive lists of publications, location of the state or regional office nearest you, and information about people's rights and responsibilities under the law. They can also provide information about how and where to file a complaint.

Disability and Business Technical Assistance Centers
(see list in Part III for locations)   (800) 949-4232

U.S. Equal Employment Opportunity Commission
1801 L Street NW   (800) 669-3362, voice
Washington DC 20507   (800) 800-3302, TTY

Access Board
Architectural and Transportation Barriers
Compliance Board
1331 F Street NW, Suite 1000
Washington DC 20004-1111   (800) 872-2253, voice/TTY

Office of Program Management of Federal Transit Administration
U.S. Department of Transportation
400 Seventh Street SW   (202) 366-1656, voice
Washington DC 20590   (202) 366-4567, TTY

U.S. Department of Justice
Civil Rights Division
Public Access Division
PO Box 66738   (800) 514-0301, voice
Washington DC 20035-6738   (800) 514-0383, TTY

Technology-Related Assistance for Individuals with Disabilities Act (Tech Act)

The Tech Act provides federal funds to assist states in developing easily available, consumer-responsive systems of access to assistive technology, technology services, and information. First signed into law in August 1988, the Tech Act was the first piece of U.S. legislation ever to use the term *consumer responsive*. The law requires that state-developed systems must, at a minimum, have in place a process for evaluating and responding to the concerns and suggestions of citizens with disabilities.

The Tech Act provides a definition of assistive technology that became the standard definition used in all subsequent federal legislation and regulations. In the Tech Act, assistive technology includes devices that are not necessarily computer-based. The definition is broad enough to include "any tool or item that increases, maintains, or improves functional capabilities of individuals with disabilities" in such areas as seating, mobility, daily living, and environmental control. In addition to "high-tech" devices, it includes "low-tech" and "no-tech" devices such as mechanical page turners, custom-molded seats, single-switch-activated toys, and hand-held magnifiers.

All states are funded to implement the Tech Act. States have primarily used their federal funds for providing technology services such as information and referral, and for creating statewide programs that provide access to assistive technology to individuals with disabilities. The Tech Act focuses on eliminating barriers that prevent consumers of disability services from gaining access to assistive technology. You can obtain information related to the Tech Act from the lead agency in your state. See Part III for a list of State Tech Act projects.

Rehabilitation Act Amendments of 1992

"In 1973 the rehabilitation act was passed. It was enacted to prevent discrimination against people with disabilities and covered employment and government services. The 1973 act primarily constituted a reauthorization of existing federal aid programs for people with disabilities. The act provides a statutory basis for developing and implementing comprehensive programs of vocational rehabilitation and independent living through such means as research, training, services, and the guarantee of equal opportunities.

"In general the rehabilitation act covers both public and private employment. The basic goals of section 501, 503, and 504 are to prohibit discrimination against individuals with disabilities and to increase the employment opportunities within society." (Minnesota Star Program, ADA/ADR Pilot Program, January 1996.)

The Rehabilitation Act Amendments represent a dramatic departure from the practices that evolved in the rehabilitation system under earlier laws. Particularly for individuals with severe disabilities, the 1992 amendments abolish many barriers to gaining access to rehabilitation services. The former system evaluated individuals for their "employability," "feasibility of employment," and "rehabilitation potential." It served in many ways as the gatekeeper of opportunity for hundreds of thousands of people with disabilities. The new law is built on the presumption of ability to achieve employ-ment and other rehabilitation goals regardless of the severity of disability.

Under the new law, "individuals with even the most significant disabilities should be presumed capable of gainful employment and provided the needed supports to do so." Vocational rehabilitation agencies are now required to focus on solutions and the attainment of employment outcomes. In a 180-degree shift in perspective, vocational rehabilitation agencies must provide services unless the agency can "unequivocally demonstrate" that no possibility of employment exists for a particular individual, even after careful consideration is made of every option for training, assistive technology, reasonable accommodation, and other supports.

Additionally, all state vocational rehabilitation agencies are required to provide a broad range of technology services on a statewide basis, and the technology needs of every client of a vocational rehabilitation agency must be addressed in the Individualized Written Rehabilitation Program (IWRP). Conceptually similar to the IEP required in educational settings, the IWRP for every client must contain "a statement of the specific rehabilitation technology services to be provided to assist in the implementation of intermediate rehabilitation objectives and long-term rehabilitation goals."

More References and Resources

In addition to obtaining copies of the laws and related supporting materials from your congressional representative, there are other resources available at the community and national levels. Parent training and information centers, as well as consumer groups and independent living centers, can be especially helpful. (See Part III for a list of these organizations.)

Parent centers can fully inform you about your options under IDEA and assist you in advocacy efforts. Consumer groups and independent living centers can furnish you with a great deal of information related to ADA and the Rehabilitation Act Amendments. Your state's department of vocational rehabilitation can provide materials related to the Rehabilitation Act Amendents, and public schools are required to distribute information on IDEA to families who have children with disabilities. Some other resources are:

> RESNA
> 1700 North Moore Street, Suite 1540
> Arlington VA 22209-1903   (703) 524-6686

RESNA is an interdisciplinary association for the advancement of rehabilitation and assistive technologies. They produce many materials—some available at little or no charge—that relate specifically to providing technology and technology services under IDEA, ADA, the Tech Act, and the Rehabilitation Act Amendments.

National Association of Protection and Advocacy Systems
900 Second Street NE, Suite 211   (202) 408-9514, voice
Washington DC 20002   (202) 408-9520, TTY
email: hn4537@handsnet.org

Protection and Advocacy, Inc. (PAI) is a network of organizations that provide legal assistance and information to individuals with disabilities and their families. PAI is also included in the Tech Act as amended in 1994 to provide information and assistance in the area of assistive technology. For the PAI office in your state contact their national office.

The Internet is a growing source of information on these issues. There are many online resources currently available that can provide you with the text of laws, legislative updates, and alerts. Internet resources and how to locate them change on a regular basis. But, with that in mind, here are a few places that can provide valuable information. There are more references included in Section III, Telecommunications, along with information about using the Internet, what the World Wide Web is, and how to get on various "mailing lists."

The Disability Mall
http://disability.com

Starting from here you can connect (or "link") to a wide variety of resources for people with disabilities, including a whole group of "Disability Related Legal Resources," and "Government Resources."

EDLAW, Inc.
http:www.access.digex.net/~edlawinc/

This group provides basic legal information for educators, parents, and their advisors about state and federal requirements for the education of students with disabilities.

EASI (Equal Access to Software and Information)
gopher://sjuvm.stjohns.edu//11/disabled/easi/easilaw

Look here for information, fact sheets, and bibliographies on the ADA and the Rehabilitation Act.

Justice For All

This is a list serve (see Part III, Telecommunications, for the definition of a list serve and information about how they work) that provides alerts about pending legislation and regulations. To subscribe send email to majordomo@mailbot.com with the following in the body of the message: "subscribe justice username@hostname." Substitute your email address for username@hostname.

There Is More To Be Done

Much has been accomplished, but there is still much to do. These laws form a good foundation for including technology as a regular part of the lives of people with disabilities, but none of them guarantees access to technology.

Laws are only as good as we make them. They need to be enforced. If laws are being violated and complaints are not filed with the authorities responsible for enforcement, the violations will continue. Learn more about how the law applies to you or your child. Follow up on the resources presented here. If you feel your rights have been violated and you need advice on how to proceed, there are many community-based advocates who can help figure out what next steps to take.

In spite of what the law says, there is still a strong tendency in these days of budget-cutting for technology to get dismissed as a costly luxury rather than an essential tool for education, employment, and independence. It is everyone's responsibility to make sure that this does not happen. We all need to take action to help ensure that the new generation of technology products will be designed with universal access in mind. We all need to assure that people will have lifetime access to technology.

Chapter 5

Exploring Your Local Resources

Assistive technology is still a new enough field that it can be difficult at first to discover working partners in your area. Geographic isolation has been a formidable barrier for years; overcoming it is one of the primary reasons this book was written.

Part III covers many types of information resources that you may contact by telephone, mail, or a personal visit. Information resources are also available in more common community settings, such as the public library. Developing natural supports in the community will do more than anything else to ensure your success with assistive technologies.

Your First Steps: Where You Can Go to Learn More

Conventional and assistive technologies can be very seductive, appealing to your impulsiveness to purchase immediately. If possible, identify a place where you can get hands-on experience with computers and assistive devices before making purchase decisions. Be patient. It is easy to overbuy or underbuy assistive devices when you are operating with incomplete information. We frequently hear stories that speak to this. One father spent a great deal of money on a sophisticated computer system that tracks eye movements, when a simpler touch screen would have been the more appropriate tool for his child. A family that bought a secondhand TRS-80 (an early Radio Shack computer) at a yard sale because they heard it say "Die Earthling!" had assumed that, because the computer had some speech capability, it could function as a talking word processor for a child with complete blindness. At the time they did not understand the nature of the technology, the task, or the options. This is where community-based technology resources can help.

Many types of places and groups can be good resources in technology and disability, and some may be in your community. As you make your initial contact with them, here are some questions you might ask:

- Is there anyone in your group or on your staff who knows about assistive technologies for children or adults with disabilities?

- Would this person know about specific assistive technologies for people with particular needs?

- What computers and assistive devices are you using now? How are you using them?

- Would it be possible to see your equipment?

- Do you know, or can you recommend, anyone else in town who can show me more about assistive technologies?

When you contact information sources, don't be afraid to ask questions and to keep asking them until you feel you know what you need to know. Most people in this field love to share what they know with others.

The Alliance for Technology Access

One of the most important resources is the directory of Alliance for Technology Access centers (see Part III for more information). Call, write, or visit one of them as soon as possible. The staff and volunteers provide hands-on opportunities to explore assistive technology in an environment free of architectural and attitudinal barriers. There are no eligibility requirements, and everyone seeking assistance is served. Alliance centers take an approach that places the potential technology user at the center of the process as the evaluator of the equipment and software, rather than as the object of evaluation. The centers are committed to helping you develop the expertise you will need to make the best decisions.

Alliance centers are dedicated to serving people of all ages with disabilities of all kinds and have comprehensive, multifaceted programs that reflect community needs and local talents and resources. Although each center is unique, all provide services that help parents, teachers, employers, children, and adults with disabilities explore computer systems, adaptive devices, and software. Once connected to an Alliance center, you are in touch with a large network of individuals with disabilities, parents, educators, friends, and vendors who are glad to share their expertise.

Libraries

Every library has a number of resources that will be useful to you. Libraries stock a wealth of books and periodicals that cover conventional computing, and you will find reference books cataloged under the topic of computers. The reference librarian can suggest current periodicals such as *MacWorld, PC World, InfoWorld, T.H.E. Journal, Electronic Learning, Technology and Learning,* and *MacUser.* A bit technical for the novice, these periodicals are still useful sources of new product information. Most of these publications are also available at local bookstores and computer stores.

In the beginning of your search, avoid books on computer programming; focus on computers with commercial programs instead. It is a common misconception that everyone who uses a computer must know how to program one. That's a little like thinking you can't ride on an airplane unless you know how to fly one. The fact is you can use computers every day and never need to write a single line of computer code. If you later find yourself interested in computer programming, you may decide to learn programming in order to create tools that do not currently exist.

Check out the journals, available in college and some public libraries, that regularly discuss aspects of assistive technology and that can refer you to other sources. Some of these journals are *Closing the Gap, Exceptional Parent Magazine, Journal of Special Education Technology, Journal of Vision Impairment and Blindness, A.T. Quarterly,* and *Journal of Disability and Technology.* They contain a variety of articles on new products, strategies for using assistive technology in the classroom, resources, and personal stories. (See Part III for a listing of these publications.)

Libraries can also be a good source of information about local organizations, as libraries are often on mailing lists to receive newsletters and brochures.

Computer dealers

Visit a local computer dealer to learn about conventional technology. Keep in mind that dealers have generally not been exposed to the field of assistive technology and will probably not be able to answer your questions related to access and assistive technology.

Parent groups

Parent groups provide information and support to family members of children with disabilities. The types and strengths of parent groups vary greatly.

In the mid-1970s, a federal program to establish a national network of community-based parent training and information centers was created. These centers inform parents of their child's educational rights and assist them in their advocacy efforts. Parents and family members are always welcome to join an environment in which they can share and contribute from their own experience. Some of these centers are good resources for assistive technologies.

General information about parent training and information centers in your area can be obtained from the Federation for Children with Special Needs (voice/TTY: (617) 482-2915). The parent training and information center in Billings, Montana, called Parents, Let's Unite for Kids (PLUK, (406) 657-2055), is the federally designated source for parent and family information specifically related to assistive technology in public education. PLUK is also an Alliance for Technology Access center.

Many communities have parent support groups focused around specific disabilities. Families of children with disabilities can be rallied and reinvigorated around the banner of assistive technologies. Consider joining the effort and introducing technology into programs and groups that have not yet given the issue the attention it deserves.

Photo courtesy of CITE/Florida

A keyboard personalized with muppets provides an exciting alternative for kids

Consumer groups and independent living centers

If you enjoy individualism and taking personal responsibility for making your life all it can be, you will find many kindred spirits at independent living centers (ILCs) and other groups that are led primarily by adults with disabilities. ILCs and other consumer groups have many missions, but they primarily exist to support individuals with disabilities in reaching self-defined goals. Like parent groups, ILCs and other consumer groups have many levels of knowledge about assistive technologies. Some are disability specific; some are open to any adult with a disability. Since they are community-based programs, they reflect the needs and resources of the individual community.

Independent living philosophy upholds certain beliefs and values:

- a person with a disability has the right to self-determination

- a person with a disability has the right to access and to participate fully in the environment

- a person with a disability has the right to tools that enable full participation

- a person with a disability has the right to direct the process through which tools are procured

Consumer-driven groups and models of disability services such as ILCs have emerged as important alternatives to the traditional medical model of disability services. You can obtain a directory of independent living programs by contacting ILRU (Independent Living Research and Utilization, 2323 South Shepherd, Suite 1000, Houston TX 77019; (713) 520-0232, voice; (713) 520-5136, TTY). The cost for the directory is about $10.

Disability agencies

Most communities have several agencies serving children and adults with disabilities. Some are government agencies, such as the Department of Vocational Rehabilitation (which may have a different name in your state, such as the Department of Rehabilitation Services or the Department of Rehabilitation); some are private for-profit or not-for-profit organizations, such as Easter Seals, United Cerebral Palsy, and The Arc (formerly Association for Retarded Citizens); some may provide opportunities for hands-on computer testing. Disability agencies usually have restrictions regarding who they can serve, which may vary by age, disability, and geographic service area. Although they may not serve people with your disability or zip code, they may be happy to discuss or share with you the assistive technologies they are using.

Persevere in your search through the bureaucracy. Some agencies are staffed by highly trained professionals and are extremely well equipped with assistive devices, software, and hardware; others have yet to discover technology.

Public schools

Infants, toddlers, children, youth, and young adults with disabilities, up to the age 22, are entitled by law to a free public education. Every public school system in the U.S. has a special education department or some cooperative arrangement for providing special education and related services. You may find teachers, therapists, or other individuals in your special education department with expertise to share. You may also find many regular educators who are well versed in technology and able to provide assistance.

A school system will often have only one individual who coordinates all or most of the assistive technology resources for the entire district. Although these people may be busy and difficult to contact, they can often provide you with valuable information. You may be able to schedule time to explore their equipment and to observe students using it. Call the special education department to identify the people on the staff who are most knowledgeable in assistive technologies.

Teachers' colleges

The college of education at your local university trains educators. Teacher preparation programs for special education and related services often have a faculty member who is knowledgeable in assistive technologies and who may be able to provide you with access to equipment and information resources. You may want to inquire about taking an introduction to assistive technology class.

University services

Most colleges and universities have an office dedicated to coordinating services for students with disabilities and to providing access to college life through technology. Facilities and expertise may be located on campus, or you may be referred to local community resources such as ILCs. These offices have many concerns—housing, transportation, physical access to facilities, curriculum adaptations—and so may not be completely knowledgeable about assistive technology. However, with so many legislative mandates in place, colleges and universities should be models of access by the end of the decade.

User groups

Many communities have well-developed user groups of computer enthusiasts who enjoy getting together to share new technologies and practical tips to improve their performance with existing technologies. Some groups are so large that they are subdivided into special interest groups, such as educators, accountants, and dentists. Some groups are dedicated to specific disabilities, such as Bay Talk, a group of people with visual impairments in the San Francisco Bay Area. (For more information about this group, contact the Rose Resnick Lighthouse at (415) 431-1481.) User groups are usually focused around a particular type of computer or operating system such as Windows, MS-DOS, Macintosh, or Commodore.

To find out how to contact user groups in your area, call the User Group Connection in Scotts Valley, California at (408) 461-5700. You may find announcements of user group meetings in the computer section of your newspaper's classified advertisements or in computer magazines.

The main benefit of connecting with user groups is learning about conventional technologies. For example, if personal financial management software is of interest to you, a user group member can probably teach you everything you need to know about the topic. Members of user groups tend to be knowledgeable, helpful, and enthusiastic. What they may lack in assistive technology experience they will make up for with motivation, commitment to helping others, and ingenuity.

User groups are outstanding places to obtain public domain software, demonstration programs, and shareware programs. Public domain software is free; shareware requires you to send a small fee to the programmer if you decide to keep and use the program. Demonstration programs are copies of software that the publisher has made available for people to test out to see whether the software is suited to their needs. They are usually missing a crucial function, like the ability to print or to save work, or are fully operational but only for a limited period of time. In addition to user groups, a number of on-line computer services have forums focused on the use of technology by people with disabilities. The people who participate in these forums and use on-line bulletin board services can also provide good and up-to-date information. For more about on-line services and telecommunications see Part III.

71

Exploring
Your
Local
Resources

Friends and neighbors

Don't overlook friends and neighbors who are computer users in your quest to become one yourself. They can be valuable resources for keeping you current and for good advice. Technology can be so energizing and contagious that you may discover a new friend or two. Friends who use technology at work or at home should be able to advise you about places to shop and things to avoid. They can be enlisted to help you carry boxes, hook up your computer, or help make telephone calls to your local resources for support and follow-up.

Disability newspapers and newsletters

Like regular newspapers and newsletters, those related to disabilities contain both articles and advertisements that may offer valuable information. Many disability newspapers have regular features on conventional and assistive technologies, plus space for vendors of conventional and assistive technologies to reach their markets. In the classified advertisements and small print, you may find components you need at a lower price or announcements of meetings and events to help in your networking efforts. (See Part III for a list of publications.)

Lead offices of the Tech Act

Part III lists, by state, the lead offices coordinating the implementation of the Tech Act. By contacting the lead office in your state, you can obtain information about devices and funding options. Your state may also have demonstration centers established for technology exploration. Be sure to inquire about placing your name on the mailing list to receive newsletters and publications.

Vendors of assistive technologies

When you contact some of the resources above, such as an Alliance center, state Tech Act office, disability newspaper, special education department, or independent living center, you can gather names and addresses of vendors of assistive technologies, services, and information resources. A list of vendors is included in Part III. Vendors can provide you with information about their products and may be able to furnish names and phone numbers of additional resources in your area.

Making Sense of It All

If you have been talking to friends, neighbors, parent or consumer groups, your Tech Act office, dealers, and a few users, you have no doubt heard differing viewpoints on the best computer, the best software, the best place to shop, and the best people with whom to work. It is natural to be confused by all this input.

You may be able to reduce confusion by realizing that technology decisions are very personal. There is no one best computer, no one best software title, no single universal access device. There are only tools to be found that work well for you in your circumstances. The decision-making process is analogous to a personal automotive decision: pickup trucks are the most popular vehicle in the nation, but they are not right for everyone.

Take time to interpret what you find, read, and hear, and to seek additional advice from the helpful people you have discovered. You are exploring tools that have changed what it means to have a disability, and you are going places and doing things that have been inaccessible to people with disabilities throughout history.

Take a moment now to record the next three to five steps you need to take, the types of questions you have, and who in your community you think can help you answer them.

Chapter 6

Building a Circle of Support

Once you have identified key resources in your community, it is time to enlist their help in your personal search. You need to find a few good thinkers, people who can work with you on imagining a preferred future. In this chapter we present a range of individuals who represent the kinds of people you might want to involve in your effort to help you solve problems and explore potential solutions.

We take a collaborative approach to the subject of technology exploration, knowing from experience that the most effective efforts are those tackled by a team, a circle of support made up of people who can help you think through all of the possibilities. Your personal support team might be informal, including only one or two trusted friends, or it might be formal, like an Individualized Education Program (IEP) team, including parents, teachers, therapists, and school administrators.

Whatever its size, at the center of the team is the person who will eventually use the technology: you, your son or daughter, or your student or client. Even if an agency will be funding your technology, you—regardless of your age or the nature of your disability—are the ultimate authority on what is the most useful for you. We all have preferences and can express them in a variety of ways: through speech, gestures, actions, attitudes, or a twinkling in the eye. In any case, it is the ultimate user who must be heard by all others involved in the process.

Choosing technology is a complex process. Working collaboratively with a team of supportive people with various types of expertise is the most effective and comfortable way to proceed.

The Talent Pool

In building your team, you might want to start with a generalist, someone you trust who has a broad knowledge of assistive technology. This person may help you identify a few other people to involve in your effort.

You will find plenty of people who want to help you once you start to look for them. Some will have more time and energy than others. You need not necessarily ask people to make a major time commitment; it may be that you only need someone to attend one meeting, to make a couple of fact-finding phone calls on your behalf, or to refer you to a community agency or an advocate. Use the resources discussed in the previous chapter to locate help in areas you haven't yet covered. Here are some of the people you might want to consider to be a part of your personal support team:

- parents

- partners

- friends

- advocates

- professional service providers

- other people with disabilities or their parents

- computer-using children

- computer enthusiasts

- rehabilitation counselors

- job coaches

- employers

- teachers

- funders

Consider people with a good knowledge of

- you

- your environment

- funding resources

- relevant legislation

- community resources

- assistive technology and the vendor community

Your parent, partner, or friend

This team member is someone who is already a support in your life and who knows you well enough to offer sound advice. He or she can help you consider all the areas in which you might benefit from using technology in your life and can also help you sort through your financial position.

Someone who knows your environment

You may spend most of your days in a classroom, on the job, or at home. Someone familiar with the environment in which you will use your technology—a teacher, job developer, job coach, an employer, or someone with whom you live—may be very helpful.

Someone who knows about funding resources

If you are hoping to secure funding from an outside source—for example a school district, the Department of Rehabilitation, Social Security, or medical insurance—you will want to involve someone who can advise you about such resources.

Someone who knows the law

Provisions in federal legislation—Americans with Disabilities Act (ADA), Individuals with Disabilities Education Act (IDEA), the Rehabilitation Act, and the Tech Act—regarding assistive technology and the rights of persons with disabilities may be helpful to you. You need to know how they can directly benefit you, and a person who knows about the law as it relates to the provision of assistive technology will prove very useful. (See Chapter 4 for more information on these laws.)

A trained advocate

If you are concerned about challenges from a potential source of funding, you may want to use the services of a trained advocate. This person may be a member of an organization that frequently deals with the implementation of laws and public policy relating to people with disabilities, such as a self-advocacy group, a parent advocacy center, or a disability-related organization. In extreme situations in which there is concern regarding a person's rights, you might want to seek counsel from an organization that specializes in disability rights, like Protection and Advocacy (P & A). P & A is a system of federal programs mandated to provide legal and other advocacy services in each state to protect the rights of individuals with disabilities. (See Part III for additional information on the National Association of Protection and Advocacy Systems.)

A professional with relevant expertise

An occupational therapist or physical therapist who can help with seating and positioning may be of benefit to you. A speech pathologist can help if augmentative, alternative, or facilitated communication is needed. Other professionals can provide assessments and evaluations when needed. If you anticipate the need for customized equipment, you may want to consult an engineer. Rehabilitation engineering centers around the country provide formal evaluations and specialized service.

Other consumers or parents with similar interests or experiences

It is often extremely helpful to ask someone ahead of you on this journey to act as your mentor. The person may be a current user of assistive technology or have had experience working with one of the organizations involved. It is wonderful to be able to call someone to ask whether you are on the right track or if you are considering all of your options.

Children who are accomplished computer users

Some of the most remarkable mentors we have encountered are young people who are avid computer users. This especially applies to youngsters with disabilities who use assistive technology effectively in their daily lives.

> *Joshua*, age 15, has a learning disability and has found energy, excitement, and academic success with his Macintosh computer. His computer has changed his life and empowered him as a leader. He has become a model and a mentor to many young people he meets. He is programming with sophisticated multimedia tools and creating programs on disability awareness. He is focused on the issues of access and making sure that every student's needs for access are considered.

Photo courtesy of IntelliTools

Combine IntelliTalk with IntelliKeys, Overlay Maker,
and your computer to create a powerful and flexible
communication and learning system (IntelliTools)

Someone who can provide technical support

It may be helpful to include a friend or acquaintance with technical expertise at the beginning of your search. Computer user groups can be good sources of people you might need to get your computer up and running.

> *Jerome*, a parent of a son with cerebral palsy, knew he would need assistance with setting up his son's new computer. He involved a staff member from his local Alliance center in his plan right from the beginning, so that when he was ready to connect the cables he would have the help he needed. When the time came to open the box, set up the machine, and install the software, the staff member was there to assist.

Your state's office of rehabilitation

If you are seeking employment with the support of assistive technology, you may wish to work with your state agency. Counselors can assist you with your job search and the acquisition of the assistive technology.

> *Angela* brought her rehabilitation counselor with her to her local Alliance center to try out equipment and software so they both could begin to construct a mental image of Angela working in a

business office with a computer. Prior to this experience, the counselor had ruled out several potential positions in offices because she had assumed Angela would not be able to see the screen well enough to do the necessary tasks. After their visit, she and Angela both had ideas about how to magnify images on a computer screen so Angela could adequately see the text. They left with more clearly defined goals and the information they needed to meet with an employer to discuss with confidence specifics of job accommodation.

An agency providing supported employment

Agencies that provide support for employment for people with developmental disabilities can help with employment needs.

Andre needed his job developer and his job coach to see that he could enter data accurately and quickly using a computer. At a community center, Andre copied information from cards into an electronic database with almost compulsive accuracy. Seeing this, the job developer was able to convince a community college library to hire Andre in a data-entry position. In the library, Andre's job coach knew what to expect, and was able to tailor support strategies and eventually turn over his supportive role to Andre's employer and coworkers.

An employer

Potential and current employers can be valuable resources.

Ron, who has autism and was unemployed, holds a degree in math. A public agency serving people with developmental disabilities wanted to hire someone with a disability to run a complex database using the Windows operating system. Ron got the job. His new employer needed to learn what accommodations Ron needed to use the necessary software and sought assistance in the planning process from his community resource center. Working together, the team—Ron, the employer, a coworker, and a technology access specialist—determined what computer equipment and software was needed.

A teacher, administrator, special education program specialist, or technology coordinator from a district might be of tremendous assistance to a family planning for classroom technology for a student. It is not uncommon to discover that there is one overworked technology expert for many schools, with little or no budget. A lack of understanding about technology on the part of many administrators, combined with ongoing budget crises, have led some administrators to allot zero dollars for technology purchases. When district or school staff are resistant, cautious, or apprehensive, it is important for you to involve them from the start and to work on convincing them of the wisdom of what you are doing. It won't be easy, but it will be worth it.

When working with a school, it is helpful to have basic information about the school:

- What kind of computers are used at the school?

- Are they in the classroom or in a lab?

- Will a portable computer be necessary to meet the needs of a student who moves from classroom to classroom during the day?

- Is a printer available?

- In what ways is the IEP team willing to provide support and follow-up for the student if assistive technology is purchased?

- Will the school provide a computer for use at home?

- Is compatibility an issue?

- Will disks be shuttled between home and school?

With older students, the issues can be somewhat different.

Gloria is about to finish high school and move into a transition program that her district provides for students 18 to 22 who are not going to become full-time college students and who need special education services as they move to adult life. Gloria has been using a laptop computer and switch access hardware and software in lieu of a pencil and paper to complete work in high school. The equipment and software were provided by the district through the IEP process. Gloria's current goal, articulated in her Individual Transition Plan (ITP) as mandated by IDEA, is to have a full-time job by the time she is 22. She wants to work in an office and would use a computer system similar to her current setup. As she moves into the transition period, these questions must be addressed:

- Will the laptop computer she has been using work in the transition program?

- Will she use it in the workplace?

- Will she need to consider new equipment?

- Who will help her find a job?

- Who will provide support in the workplace?

- Who will help the employer understand her needed accommodations?

- Will she have a job coach?

- Will the Department of Rehabilitation play a role?

- Will other agencies be involved?

- At what point should they become involved?

- Will independent living skills be an issue?

- Who will provide help?

- What are Gloria's long-range dreams, and what nightmares does she seek to avoid?

- Who will be a part of her circle of support as she moves into adulthood?

At this point in her life, technology is playing an integral role in Gloria's transition process. Her technology support people will need to advise the rest of her transition team to ensure that technology is integrated into Gloria's life where appropriate.

A dreaded scenario is one in which Gloria is forced to leave her computer at high school because it was purchased by the school district and belongs to them. Separated from her writing tool, she enters into a limbo transition period. No one understands that she is capable of writing well and can use her skill capably in a job if she has the right tools. Gloria starts to spend most of her days at home and becomes more and more socially isolated. No one knows who to contact for help.

A brighter projection is that Gloria is allowed to bring her computer with her into the transition period. A job developer works with her over time to find her a wonderful job where she can use her assistive technology. A community agency provides job coaching and links her with the supports she needs within the company. The Department of Rehabilitation commits to providing an upgrade to her hardware and software along with training in their use. Gloria links with an independent living center to help her in finding her own apartment. Gloria meets regularly with her circle of support to iron out problems and takes her place as a contributing member of her community.

Who might Gloria enlist for her technology team? Members might include her high school English teacher, who fully understands her current use of the computer; the counselor from the school district's transition program, who has an interest in and responsibility for continuing the use of assistive technology; Gloria's prospective Department of Rehabilitation counselor, who will help with employment planning; a staff person from a supported employment organization, who can explore emerging technology with Gloria and help her envision herself using it in her future; the technical resource person from the local Alliance center, who can provide Gloria with opportunities to try out new technology before choosing what she wants to use; and her sister, who will help coordinate the process and advocate for Gloria. With all or some of these people included, Gloria has a much better chance of achieving her goal.

Private organizations

Representatives from the following agencies might be helpful to you in your journey: your local Alliance center; your local center for independent living; a disability organization to which you belong, such as United Cerebral Palsy or your Retinitis Pigmentosa Support Group; a parent training or advocacy center; a self-advocacy group; and a service organization. If you have close ties with anyone from any such groups, they might play an advocacy role for you or help you to sort through all of the information you will uncover along the way.

Mabel just completed her GED using computer technology for all of her written work. Mabel is 93. She is a participant in a social model day program in an independent living center, which is designed to assist individuals to live independently. She became interested in the technology program at the center at the same time she became determined to finish her high school education. With support from a peer mentoring program at the center, she learned word processing and used a computer for all of her written school work.

Song is the leader of a self-advocacy group for young adults with developmental disabilities who are learning how to stand up for themselves and to be full participants in their communities. At one of his monthly meetings, Song learned from a fellow member that he could visit his local Alliance center and use a computer to work on his agendas and print them out for the meetings. He began making regular visits and brought his independent living coach along to help him. His coach works with him several times a week as he acquires the skills he needs to become an independent adult living on his own. Together they are becoming proficient at using word processing software and are beginning to think about how Song might acquire a computer for use at home.

A potential funder

If you will be seeking funding from an outside source, you will want to learn all you can as early in the process as possible. You may want to turn to someone with a good understanding of funding resources who can help you assess your financial resources and make optimal use of your options. Perhaps someone from Social Security, Medicaid, or your private insurance company will figure into the equation. Consult with these experts throughout your process, and make no assumptions about what they will or will not be able to do for you.

Gary is a pediatrician and has been a dedicated scientist all of his adult life. A traffic accident and spinal cord injury were not going to stop him. After his initial rehabilitation, it was clear that Gary would not be able to use his hands, but he was determined to continue his work, perhaps with the assistance of a computer and an aide to help him physically. He had read about devices just coming on the market that would provide computer access for people with little or no hand use. The team he assembled included a staff person from the local Alliance technology resource center, a counselor from the Department of Rehabilitation, and himself. He brought to the table an excellent knowledge of emerging technology, gained through his personal efforts. The Alliance center staff person brought a variety of devices Gary could try out. The rehabilitation counselor brought the ability to provide funding by negotiating a complex system. After Gary made his choices, the stressful process of securing funding began. Various agencies turned him down, as is often the case, until finally one agreed to provide him with a portable computer, a HeadMaster (a head pointing system by

Prentke Romich Company), and an on-screen keyboard. Patience and perseverance had been extremely important, as were the people that helped Gary negotiate the maze. Today Gary is working as a geneticist in his chosen field.

Moving Ahead

Ask the following key questions of yourself as you begin to develop your personal support team:

- What information do I still need before I can make a choice?

- Who in my community can help me find the information I need?

- Will I need a formal assessment to help me sort through my choices, meet my needs, and provide documentation to a funder?

- Do I simply need an opportunity to try out and evaluate a range of equipment and software before making decisions?

- Who can help me find a place to try the equipment or software?

- Who do I know, that knows me well and whom I trust, to help me consider and evaluate my options?

- Will I be paying for my new equipment or software, or will I need assistance from a funding source? Do I know which source? If yes, would I want to include that person on my team from the very beginning?

- Do I anticipate a challenge from my potential funding source? If yes, would it be helpful to include a trained advocate on my team?

How many people you have on your personal support team is entirely up to you. It is important for you to feel comfortable and confident, so choose people who will enhance those feelings. Most of all, choose people who will support the idea that *you* are the person who ultimately must make the decisions, based upon the best information available.

Once you have chosen your team, you will need to consider how it will function. Some people find that informal consultation with individual team members is all that is needed, but others use their team members more extensively.

Alicia is an 18-year-old in a regular high school. She has been using technology since she was 6 years old, and her current and primary educational goals focus on developing her skills to communicate appropriately with peers and adults and learning to write fluently. Alicia's family has put together a team that includes Alicia, a speech pathologist expert in augmentative and alternative communication, a rehabilitation engineer, two special educators, her English teacher, the special education director, and a technology specialist from the local Alliance center. They use the outside consulting services of an occupational therapist and a physical therapist when appropriate.

Their goal is to put together a communication system that can be mounted on Alicia's wheelchair and that she can access using a switch with her chin. The family is at the center of the process, which has been long and involved. Together they are brainstorming ideas, testing proposed solutions, preparing computer setups with Alicia's choices of words and phrases, and troubleshooting technical problems that arise. They are currently using a program called Speaking Dynamically (Mayer-Johnson Co.) to design the communication boards on the computer screen.

In addition to providing technical assistance, one of the key roles team members can play is to help you financially plan for computer acquisition. Knowing funding sources is one support role; helping you budget is another. As you come closer to knowing what products you will need, you can begin to develop a budget that includes the conventional and assistive technologies and reflects a knowledge of the cost of things. You will revise your budget many times, but it is good to have a plan in mind, especially as you prepare to approach funders. Your team can help you make sure that you are accounting for such things as software and training in addition to your equipment needs.

Teams may not be as elaborate as some of those mentioned here, but they should be as collaborative. Think about what you will need in terms of expertise and creativity. What are the key access issues that are emerging for you, and who can best help you address them? If you don't already know who can help you, who should you contact for a referral? As you begin to locate your personal resources, be prepared for the enthusiasm you will very likely encounter.

Chapter 7

Developing Your Funding Strategy

By now you may have a clear plan for identifying and working with the resources you need. Inevitably, though, your ability to implement your choices and achieve your goals with assistive technology depends upon the availability of financial resources.

Just as you need to formulate a plan for choosing and using technology, so must you develop a strategy for funding it. You must begin to plan the financing when you start your selection process.

Few established funding sources exist for assistive technology. For the most part, funds still need to be taken from sources designated for other purposes. This can mean hard work, but it rewards persistence, assertiveness, and imagination in extraordinary ways. Remember, the vast growth in technology devices, awareness, and use over the past decade has occurred largely as the result of grassroots efforts by people like you—people who wanted the equipment and found ways to get it.

You may encounter physical or attitudinal barriers in your search. A third kind, systemic barriers, are more treacherous and difficult to understand. They usually relate to administrative and bureaucratic obstacles. Systemic barriers are exemplified by agencies that provide access to technology, but only for certain people; or agencies with the potential to fund the acquisition of assistive technology, but only for specific or limited activities. The funding landscape is filled with systemic barriers; working to remove them is an important effort for advocates and consumers of assistive technology.

Approaches

The best starting point for developing your funding strategy is to answer this series of questions.

- What do you mean by funding? Do you need all or some of the cost in the form of a grant?

- If you need only part of the cost in the form of a grant, will the grant be a down payment, funds for subsequent installment payments, or resources for specific components of your computer system?

- Are you eligible for services from a program which has the authority to provide technology, but which must be persuaded to provide it?

- Would a loan for some or all of the cost meet your needs? Would the technology be used to facilitate repayment?

- Do you need your entire system—hardware and software—at once, or can acquisition be spread over a period of time?

- Can you modify your component selection if substitutes are cheaper or more readily fundable?

Other considerations concern what we call comfort levels. For instance, if you have a fear of debt, or if you are doubtful of your ability to make payments, a loan may not be the right strategy for you, even if one is available. The issue of comfort level, and even of integrity, comes up in a number of settings. For some funding sources, one's desperation is unfortunately an important criteria for support. In other settings, capabilities and potential are the keys. Your chances of getting people or organizations to do what you want increase with your ability to meet their criteria, to follow their procedures and use their language. Research it. Find out what they need to know.

Revisit your budget throughout your search, and review and adjust it according to the information you are gathering. Having a clear idea of what kind of computer system you would ideally like and how much it would cost, along with what it will take financially to get a system that will at least get you started, is very important.

Your goals for technology will determine your selection and prioritizing of potential funding sources. As early as possible, you will find it useful to begin collecting information on all potential sources. Generally speaking, funding sources can be organized according to their criteria, which may include:

- your purpose for using the technology (such as vocational, educational, communication, quality of life or independent living issues, or medical care)

- the nature of the equipment
- your age
- location requirements
- financial circumstances requirements

In reviewing eligibility criteria, don't dismiss a potential source until you are certain it will not work for you. For instance, many programs use means testing (a way of determining eligibility for a program or service based upon income, resources, or other measures of individual or family economic status), but certain resources or income items may be exempted in making the eligibility determination. Until you know exactly what goes into a particular agency's calculations for the means test (such as family size and amount paid for rent, food, or health care), you should not assume you are ineligible.

The language you use with different sources should reflect their orientations. In medical settings, stress the therapeutic nature and "medical necessity" of the equipment. In vocational settings, the goal and potential for self-sufficiency are crucial elements. Again, it is important to research and understand the language the potential funder prefers. Sometimes vendors (those who supply the goods and services you want) can help you understand what is needed to obtain authorization from an agency or insurance company.

In many instances, particularly when several components are involved—including the computer itself, peripherals (such as printers and modems), and assistive devices and software—your funding will probably not come entirely from one source or all at one time. For this reason, your funding plan must prioritize, as well as identify, potential resources so that you will approach them in the best order. Prioritizing and order of approach are also important because a number of sources consider themselves "payors of last resort," meaning, they won't pay until all other sources have either paid up or refused to pay anything. Sometimes it seems there are so many contenders for this status that one wonders who is left to ask first. It is critical to find out what prior rejections, by what other sources and within what time frames, will be required for you to meet their particular definition of "last resort."

Major National Programs

People throughout the country have used an enormous range of funding resources to meet their assistive technology needs. We will focus on sources that are relevant to the largest number of people. Because many adults and children with disabilities qualify for services under federal entitlement programs of nationwide scope, we will start with the technology funding potential of vocational rehabilitation, special education, and Medicaid.

These three programs are called *entitlement programs* because anyone who meets their eligibility requirements automatically has the right to receive their assistance. But saying someone is *entitled* to services is not saying what those services will be. Services vary according to decisions the state has made concerning the implementation of the program, to the availability of funds in relation to demand, and to individualized assessments of need and potential. For example, an individual might be receiving Medicaid but not be entitled to a particular medical procedure unless the state provided it and it was deemed "medically necessary" for the individual.

Vocational rehabilitation

Operating through state agencies under the auspices of the Federal Rehabilitation Act (U.S. code, title 29, sections 701 and following), the vocational rehabilitation program (called by a variety of names, such as VR, DVR, OVR, or DR, depending on the state) provides assessment, training, placement, and other services to people with physical or mental disabilities who could benefit in employability or other identified goals. Services are planned and provided according to a kind of annual contract between the agency and the recipient, called the Individualized Written Rehabilitation Program (IWRP). Assistive technology can be written into the IWRP in two ways: first, rehabilitation technology may be designated as one of the services that must be provided; second, technology may be deemed to be an element of another service, such as job placement.

Tony, whom you may recall from Chapter 1, is an example of someone who benefitted from this program, to a point. Tony was contacted by his rehabilitation counselor about a training position at a technology service center that might be appropriate for him. It seemed like a good fit, and Tony went to work as the intake counselor for a technology service program. His job required a lot of interviewing and record keeping. Because of Tony's limited vision, he needed a computer system to accomplish the required tasks. The Department of Rehabilitation agreed to purchase a computer system equipped with a speech synthesizer, large print program, screen reading program, and a scanner. The system allowed Tony to take printed forms, scan them into the computer, read them, fill them out, and print them.

The technology was very effective. However, adequate training in how to use the system was not given, and Tony had to learn through trial and error along with some help from his coworkers. And, because the system was purchased by and belonged to the Department of Rehabilitation, it had to stay behind when Tony relocated out of the state.

Although an IWRP is required by law, many adults dealing with the rehabilitation system are unaware of this requirement or of the fact that one of the documents they may have signed represents their acceptance of a proposed IWRP.

In the VR process, you have three technology-related goals:

1. To ensure that all eligibility determinations take full account of technology's potential to help achieve program goals.

2. To ensure that provision for technology is incorporated into the IWRP in sufficient time to be available when it is needed for employment or other life events.

3. To identify and resolve any problems that might prevent the VR agency from acquiring the technology you need (one particular model of a device may be approved for state purchase, but the version you need may not be).

Special education and related services

Administered under the Individuals with Disabilities Education Act (IDEA; U.S. code, title 20, sections 1401 and following), the special education program lists a variety of assessments and services that school systems must provide so students with disabilities may receive a "free and appropriate public education." Using a model similar to the IWRP, school placement decisions and goods and services to be provided are written out in the Individualized Education Program (IEP) according to the annual determinations of a student's IEP team.

Assistive technology devices and services must be provided when appropriate, but once again, the determination of when this is, and exactly what technology to use, is highly individualized and far from simple. A person is on strongest ground when able to argue that, based on the school system's own assessment of student needs, technology represents the best or the only effective means for dealing with the barriers that have been identified. Schools have often effectively limited access to general classrooms for students with disabilities based upon an inability to speak or to use a pencil when, in fact, technology can easily provide an effective alternative. Parents have important rights in the process, including the right of participation, the right to have experts of their own choosing at the IEP conference, the right to administrative appeal, and even the right to court appeal if dissatisfied with the administration's decision.

> *Judith* and her family knew the importance a computer could make in Judith's life, but were worried they would not be able to convince the IEP team. Despite having a strong team of educators and support staff, none were particularly well versed in technology, let alone assistive technology. And, given the workloads they all faced, they were not likely to find time to adequately research assistive technology.
>
> So Judith and her family began the search on their own. They made calls, asked questions, and even tested some equipment borrowed from another school. When they finally had a good sense of what they needed, they borrowed a video camera and recorded Judith operating the computer to accomplish a simple but important task. They realized that a good picture of Judith effectively using the technology would be worth a million IEP words.
>
> They were right. A largely inexperienced team could easily see the potential and added the necessary assistive technology to Judith's IEP for purchase by the school district.

Medicaid

Established under title 19 of the Social Security Act and administered by state agencies, Medicaid is a national program of medical assistance for the poor, including people with disabilities. When assistive technology comes within the arena of Medicaid, it must, with a few exceptions, do so under one of two headings: it must qualify as Durable Medical Equipment (DME), an optional service offered by some states; or, in the case of children, it must arise under the Early Periodic Screening, Diagnosis, and Treatment (EPSDT) program. Durable medical equipment tends to be narrowly defined, and EPSDT, while it has resulted in the availability of important medical treatment for children who might otherwise go without health care, has been of limited value in facilitating access to computers or related technology.

Many procedural and technical barriers continue to make Medicaid an extremely limited source of assistive technology support. To date, augmentative and assistive communication devices probably constitute the computer technology that has made the greatest progress under Medicaid because they have a better capacity to be described as a medical necessity and because they are dedicated systems for the primary purpose of communication. In the long run, a national health insurance program is likely to affect the availability of technology in the health care sphere far more than changes to Medicaid itself.

Though all these programs have appeals processes, both from up-front ineligibility determinations and from decisions relating to the scope of services, the systems often move slowly. When the appeals process is taken into account, eventual success may be delayed far too long to be meaningful for time-sensitive equipment needs, such as accepting a job offer or taking a school course.

Other National Programs

Several other national entitlement programs deserve brief mention. The program of early intervention for preschool children of ages 3 to 5, and the program for infants and toddlers of up to age 2, can include technology in appropriate cases, as can the older Americans programs at the other end of the age spectrum. Developmental disabilities programs, also operated through designated state agencies, now include provisions for assistive devices.

In fact, over the past decade, references to assistive technology have been added to most of the major federal disability-oriented programs as they have come up for renewal. Within any benefit program, consumers should be aware of the possibility for the inclusion of assistive technology among the goods and services authorized. If the program includes any flexibility in the nature of the goods and services it provides, you have a plausible case for arguing—unless something in the governing statute or regulation excludes the technology you need—that it should be provided.

Social Security work incentives

People with disabilities who receive Social Security Disability Insurance (SSDI) or Supplemental Security Income (SSI) are ever mindful of the risk that small amounts of work or tiny increments in income will jeopardize their benefits. SSDI is indirectly means-tested. The ability to work determines eligibility for benefits, and income is a major factor in assessing that ability. SSI, by contrast, is strictly means-tested, with payments reduced proportionally as income or resources rise above specified levels.

Among work incentives, several relate directly to the ability to obtain assistive technology. An SSDI recipient's income will be considered to have demonstrated the ability of the recipient to work or perform "substantial gainful activity" (SGA) if it exceeds certain monthly levels. But to the extent that this income is used to meet impairment-related work expenses (IRWEs), it will not count for purposes of the SGA determination. Assistive technology devices, services, and training needed for work are a prime illustration of IRWEs. Another example would be a sign-language interpreter's services.

The same holds for SSI. Although income above the individual's benefit level will result in reduction or eventual elimination of the monthly payment, the IRWE concept (and in the case of recipients who are blind, the blind work-expenses provision) will serve to exclude income from being counted. For SSI recipients, the Plan for Achieving Self-Support (PASS) can be used for shelter income and resources for use in obtaining education or training, as well as for the purchase of technology that will contribute to or be necessary for work. PASS benefits are subject to approval requirements, and must be something that furthers the self-sufficiency goal. Good examples would be assistive technology for use in training or work, tuition costs in some program leading directly to self-sufficiency, and the costs of a van-lift for a vehicle to get to work or job training. All efforts to use Social Security work incentives require fairly detailed record-keeping. However, provisions such as these can be used to leverage a fair amount of work- or training-related technology for people who could not otherwise put together the sums necessary to provide it without relinquishing their benefits.

Rights and accommodations

The Americans with Disabilities Act (ADA) is described as the greatest legal landmark in the history of civil rights and equality of opportunities for America's estimated 49 million people with disabilities. Its impact upon the availability of assistive technology will be substantial. The ADA requires employers, governmental and nonprofit service providers, and businesses providing public accommodations to take reasonable steps to accommodate persons with disabilities. In the provision of "reasonable accommodations" or of the "auxiliary aids and services" sometimes required in public accommodations settings, equipment is clearly included among the strategies for meeting the law's requirements. While no business or organization can be made to provide accommodations that would create an undue financial burden or hardship, there are many occasions when assistive technology represents the most appropriate and cost-effective method for meeting the need.

> *Kendall* had been researching the sex lives of fish for the Department of Environmental Conservation for 12 years when he sustained a traumatic brain injury in an automobile accident. Kendall became legally blind and developed problems with balance and significant memory difficulties. He had a strong desire to return to work and an employer eager to have him back. His job involved field work, data collection, and statistical analysis, and it seems Kendall was the only one able to manipulate the appropriate files.
>
> Kendall began working with people at his local independent living center who helped him develop strategies to compensate for some of his memory and sequencing issues. Working with the staff of his local Alliance center, he found he was able to read print at 8x magnification as well as work with speech output on a computer. Working in collaboration with the Commission for the Blind and Visually Handicapped, he was able to test several projection and large-screen devices. One system was rejected because the office modifications needed would be too great, but they succeeded with a screen enlargement program working with the spreadsheet on a 37-inch monitor. The system was integrated into his workplace with the support of the employer, and Kendall returned to work with the aid of a job coach. He is currently working almost independently in all of his former duties, and any necessary job-description modifications were negotiated by his employer with the civil service bureau.

Where an accommodation or auxiliary aid/service is needed to meet the requirements of the law and no other defense applies, such as the cost constituting an undue hardship, the organization or business must provide it. This means that the business is obligated to pay for the technology, although the technology user may not become the owner of the equipment. One example of such an accommodation is the assistive listening devices used at public meetings. There are many applications in employment where accommodations will be required, or where what is needed is the appropriate assistive device to access an existing system.

The tax system

A number of provisions in the tax laws can translate directly into financial assistance for those trying to acquire assistive technology, whether an individual or a small business. For example, the tax law gives important subsidies to small businesses in meeting their ADA compliance goals, whether in the employment or public accommodations spheres.

Among a number of pertinent Internal Revenue Code provisions, the Disabled Access Credit (IRC sec. 44) gives small businesses a tax credit for 50 percent of their first $10,000 of ADA compliance expenses per year, above the first $250 spent. This means that an eligible small firm (one with 30 or fewer full-time employees, or with gross revenues under $1 million per year) that spent $10,250 to accommodate persons with disabilities could claim a tax credit of $5,000, dramatically reducing the real cost of its efforts.

Favorable tax laws can lower the net cost of technology for individuals, families, and businesses. In fact, with attention to the details of justification, documentation, and expenditure timing, much of the cost of assistive technology—and virtually all of the cost of items designed or modified for use in the context of a disability—can qualify for tax deductibility either as medical expenses, impairment-related work expenses, or architectural or transportation barrier-removal expenses. Consult with a tax specialist about what your specific rights may be. *Tax Options and Strategies for People with Disabilities* contains valuable information on this topic. (See Part III, Books, for reference.)

State telecommunications equipment programs

Earlier in this chapter, we mentioned situations in which the nature of the equipment sought will determine the best source. No better example can be found than telecommunications access equipment programs that provide the devices needed by people with hearing, vocal communications, motion, visual, or other disabilities so that they may use the telephone network. Examples of the kind of equipment available include speaker phones, TTYs, phones with large buttons, and amplified phones.

Funded by fees of a few cents a month, charged to all telephone users, these programs vary from state to state in what disabilities and what types of equipment they cover, in their use of means tests, and in other respects. So far, these programs have been largely limited to basic telephone access. Whether, as our definition of basic and universal telephone service evolves, these programs will be extended to technology that permits use of the expanded capabilities of the telephone system, only time and advocacy will tell.

The simplest way to find out if your state has such a program is to check a phone bill for a few cents charged for something that sounds relevant. In California, for example, it is called Communication Devices Funds for Deaf and Disabled. Contact your local phone company to inquire about their programs.

Grants

If you need a grant to purchase technology, you may wish to look to the private sector. In many communities, service, religious, or fraternal organizations (such as the Elks and the Lions) provide equipment to individuals under particular circumstances. Small, case-by-case grants of this sort are hard to categorize, but tend to hinge on the community ties of the applicant and do not necessarily reflect established giving patterns or long-term funding priorities.

> *Paula* was 8 years old when her family, knowing that the school district would be difficult to convince, decided to try to put together a system at home to give Paula the chance to become proficient in its use and, ultimately, her own advocate. They knew it would be difficult to find financial resources, so they explored other avenues.
>
> Because of Paula's visual impairment, they approached their local Lion's Club, knowing of the Club's interest in visual impairments. They discussed their needs with the Lion's Club, and they even borrowed the equipment they had identified, long enough to demonstrate it to some key members. The members were captivated by Paula, and by her technology, and worked with the family to help them purchase the initial equipment Paula needed. As a thank-you, Paula demonstrated her new computer system to a packed crowd at the next Lion's Club meeting.

Related resources

Foundations and corporate grant programs exist that concern themselves with disability-related needs on an ongoing basis. A number of directories of foundations and corporate donors, such as the *Foundation Directory* by the Foundation Center, can be found in many public libraries.

A number of barriers must be addressed when pursuing foundation funding. Foundations are far more likely to give grants, and sometimes loans, to organizations than to individuals. When their work does extend to individual recipients, higher education, followed by medical care and the relief of destitution, are their predominant reasons for giving. Think of these restrictions as creating opportunities. For example, by working with a consumer-directed organization, donors can create an environment in which more than one person can use and benefit from a particular equipment setup. When access to technology rather than its possession will meet the need, this can represent a good strategy.

A network of libraries connected with the Foundation Center maintains collections of books, articles, and reports related to foundation and corporate giving. For information about the Foundation Center library nearest you, call their headquarters in New York at (800) 424-9836.

When applying for scholarships or other educational aid, remember to include assistive technology when you compile your needs. It is significant that the newly enacted National Service Program, which is reminiscent of the old VISTA volunteer program, will provide educational funding to its participants and includes provisions for accommodating individuals with disabilities.

See Section III, Books, for a list of several directories of funding for individuals and organizations.

Loans

Commercial credit, the source of so much of the capital for business and personal purchases in our consumer society, has not been widely available for the purchase of assistive technology. For the many people who would eagerly accept the opportunity to pay for their own equipment, this situation has proved especially frustrating and harmful.

There are a few strategies that will improve the odds in dealing with commercial lenders.

- First, research what loans are available through your local lending institution and be sure to apply for the right kind.

- Second, deficiencies in credit-history reports, sometimes arising from interruption of earning power due to the onset of disability, or from other, nonwillful causes, must be pointed out and explained to senior officials of the lender.

- Third, when the acquisition of equipment is directly linked to income enhancement, as in the case of a job offer or a return to work, this fact should be emphasized.

Sometimes even these strategies may not make a difference, so a number of nonprofit loan programs have been established in the disability community. These include programs set up by consumer and membership groups, efforts conducted by major nonprofit organizations, and joint efforts between device vendors and banks. If a loan is a viable funding strategy for you, make it a point, through networking and inquiry, to investigate the existence and applicability of any loan programs of this sort. Some state rehabilitation agencies and state Tech Act projects have loan programs or loan guarantee programs. Check them out. Your state Tech Act program, local independent living center, or Alliance center should be a good starting point for your inquiries.

Cutting costs

Naturally, every penny you can save on the cost of technology is important. For that reason, opportunities to cut costs should be sought. You will want to evaluate product features in relation to cost and to the willingness of the vendor to extend credit if needed or to cooperate by providing timely information and documentation to third-party funders.

Another important cost-saving strategy is the purchase of used equipment. Particularly in the computer field, fast-changing technology and user obsession to upgrade often result in the availability of good-quality used equipment at attractive prices. Several state Tech Act programs have established recycling programs.

The Tech Act

The Technology-Related Assistance for Individuals with Disabilities Act (discussed in Chapter 4) is the first major federal legislation addressing assistive technology devices and services as worthy of federal attention and as public policy deserving of federal support. Funded through the National Institute on Disability and Rehabilitation Research (NIDRR), the Tech Act programs now operating in every state under Title I of the act show diversity in program design and use of funds. States are granted some discretion under the Tech Act as to which of a number of programs they adopt.

As part of their information-dissemination activities, several state programs have compiled statewide funding resource directories which should provide you with valuable suggestions. (See Part III for the location of the Tech Act program in your state.)

Community organizations

As a source of resource information and expertise in navigating the bureaucratic maze, independent living centers can offer insight, guidance, and advocacy and technical assistance. Though not primarily direct funders, independent living centers are a vital link in the funding chain, particularly as a source of networking—which is so essential to learning what is out there and how it works. Local and national nonprofit organizations, such as the Alliance for Technology Access, can also be a source of valuable resource information. United Cerebral Palsy Associations, Inc. operates the Assistive Technology Funding and Systems Change Project which provides information to individuals with disabilities, family members, community-based organizations, and others. For project materials contact them at (202) 776-0406. For individualized information and technical assistance call (800) 827-0093 (voice) and (800) 833-8272 (TTY). You can email them (atfscpc@aol.com) or visit their web site (http://www.assisttech.com/atfsc.html) for more information about this project.

Organizing Your Search for Funding

As important as the funding sources are the imagination and energy you bring to your search. While recognizing that it may not be easy and that there are no simple answers, you must believe you can find a way to fund your technology dreams.

We recommend that you document your contacts and progress as you proceed. Your records will be very useful, especially if you are working with more than one potential funder.

Chapter 8

Selecting Your Equipment

Computer technology is constantly changing, which can create a little anxiety about deciding when is the best time to buy. There are a number of steps to take and ways to think about technology acquisitions that will make the selection process manageable.

It is time to start asking yourself very specific questions about what kinds of access to technology you need. What pieces of information are you missing that would help you make your decision, and how can you get the information you still need? In this chapter we will focus on the selection process.

Hands-On Consultations

When starting your search in earnest, there's no substitute for hands-on demonstration and testing. Hands-on consultations to explore technology will also be important further down the road and at any point when you need new ideas, strategies, or equipment. The process is most effective when it involves the people who will be a part of the implementation of any plan.

Julia was going to begin first grade. Her mother, grandmother, first-grade teacher, and special education teacher were almost as excited as Julia, yet concerned about how to make inclusion work for her. A Macintosh computer and a switch had been purchased for Julia, but she was not motivated to use the system. Julia's computer would be available to her in the classroom, as well as a Light Talker communication device (Prentke Romich Company).

Julia's mother and teachers visited the local Alliance center to explore computer technology as it might relate to Julia, and to see how technology had been used in other classrooms to enhance the inclusion of students with issues like Julia's. They came seeking

100

Computer
Resources
for People
with
Disabilities

ways to motivate Julia to use technology; they left with many ideas about how to customize the first grade environment for her.

While visiting the center, Julia and her team explored Kid Pix (Brøderbund), The Writing Center (The Learning Company), I Can Play Too! (Mayer-Johnson), and Gateway Stories (Don Johnston, Inc.), all excellent software to help her begin to read and become motivated to use her switch. With these programs, she could electronically turn pages and leaf through whatever content her teachers entered to interest her. Using a Jelly Bean Switch (AbleNet)—a large, flat, colorful switch—and Ke:nx (Don Johnston, Inc.) as an interface, she could get her hands on the technology. She tested various switches and software programs, giving feedback to those on her team through her gestures and expressions.

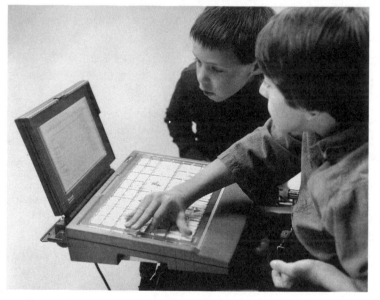

Photo courtesy of Don Johnston, Inc.

Ke:nx On:Board is specially designed as a portable alternate keyboard for use with a laptop computer (Don Johnston, Inc.)

Julia's teachers participated in the exploration and acquired ideas about how to use the software in class to promote Julia's participation. One challenge was to find ways to work on early math concepts; Kid Pix stamps turned out to be a fine medium. Another challenge was to find a way Julia could practice matching sight words. A talking scan was devised that read words using Ke:nx Create; when the computer voiced the word Julia wanted, she pressed the switch.

Julia's outlook improved because of a better switch, Ke:nx as an access tool, and exciting software. She was motivated to use her switch to show what she had learned. And the system gave her access to all other software programs, not just to those written specifically for a switch.

The experience had given the teachers ideas about how to use software to enhance curriculum. Julia's mother was integrally involved, right from the initial contact, and the team came away with a plan. Julia's mother would buy the new switch, and the teachers would find more software. Julia left so excited about the switch that she didn't want to stop playing with it. Her chances for successful inclusion were certainly boosted.

It is time for you to visit a place where you can test out your options. Two of the best places to start are your closest Alliance center and other resource centers in your community. Contact your state's Tech Act office to find the nearest centers. Other options include a variety of federally funded programs, such as Rehabilitation Engineering Centers. Schedule an appointment to try out some of the options you are considering (find out if there is a cost associated with the visit), and be sure to allow yourself plenty of time for exploration.

Another place to have contact with products is at one of the many national and regional conferences that focus on assistive technology and feature exhibits where vendors display their products. Two national annual conferences on disability and technology are Closing The Gap, held each October in Minneapolis, and the International Technology and Persons with Disabilities Conference in Los Angeles, presented by the Center on Disability at California State University, Northridge. These events provide an opportunity to compare different products. (See Part III for a list of conferences.)

Should these options not be feasible, vendors of the devices of interest to you might provide you with demonstrations or product loans. If equipment loans are not possible, try to find another option for testing the device—perhaps visiting a nearby customer of the vendor. (For help with finding vendors, refer to Part III for a list of the key vendors in the field of assistive technology.)

Retailers of conventional technologies may allow you to try out products in their stores. Depending on the nature of the device and the setup required, it may even be possible to have a retailer cooperate with you in trying out a bit of conventional technology with your loaned access devices.

102

Computer
Resources
for People
with
Disabilities

Focusing on Software

Software falls roughly into two categories: open-ended and close-ended. Open-ended programs, such as word processors, have infinite numbers of uses and possibilities and allow the user to define the parameters. Close-ended programs, like math drill programs, have a predefined purpose and set contents. Both types should be considered, depending on the tasks at hand.

Word processors, databases, spreadsheets, graphics or drawing programs, music programs, and address book or scheduling programs are all software programs that have an infinite number of uses. These kinds of open-ended software come with a basic framework or design, but you, the user, add the contents. You can remove, delete, or change the contents whenever you wish. There is a wide range of features to choose from among software programs of the same type. Word processors, for example, come with or without a dictionary or thesaurus and with or without speech, among many other features. Open-ended programs offer teachers greater options for integrating technology into existing curricula. If you want a program for writing letters or for managing your coin collection with a database, you want to be able to control the contents and would need an open-ended program.

With the more structured, close-ended programs, the contents have been defined. Many programs designed for young children fall into this category. Some programs—such as drill and practice programs for spelling and math or writing programs—have some predetermined content, but allow the user to add to it within parameters set by the developer. If your goals include having your children improve their math skills, or become more automatic or have faster recall, a drill and practice program might be appropriate.

A few software programs fall in between these two types. For example, some programs help users learn the process of writing, from simple sentences to complex paragraphs, by modeling the writing process and providing the student with prompts along the way.

You need to decide where on the continuum your goals lie and select software accordingly. You will probably want a variety of software programs for your different goals.

With the above in mind, return to your prioritized list of goals. What patterns of tasks emerge? What kinds of software tools are commercially available to perform those tasks? For review, return to the list of software categories in Chapter 3. As you examine the list, within what software category or categories do your goals lie? Most adults will have goals that require, to varying degrees, access to word processing, database management, graphics, spreadsheets, and telecommunications. You might want to consider *integrated programs*, which include as part of a single package a word processor, a spreadsheet, a database, and sometimes drawing and presentation programs, e-mail and telecommunications components.

Once you have decided on the categories your interests fall under, there are a number of features to look for when selecting software that provide greater access for people with disabilities.

One example is built-in access methods. Some programs are more friendly in their design to a variety of needs. Millie's Math House (Edmark) can accept input from a single switch, as well as from the standard keyboard and mouse. Part II contains a detailed description of these features and may help you decide whether some features would be important for you. For example, would you benefit from an uncluttered screen, where there is limited information and the choices easy to identify and interpret? Would it help if certain things always appeared on the screen in the same place? Do you want to be able to control the difficulty level, speed, or other features of instructional programs for your student or child? Do you need the option of using the keyboard, rather than the mouse, to control computer functions?

Make sure the software you are considering will run on your computer with any needed added devices and that it will comfortably address your goals.

A number of sources—most notably, technology magazines—offer comparisons of software features, and you can get excellent suggestions from them. (A list of publications is included in Part III.)

You can't always tell by reading a software box what features are included in the program. Before you purchase software, ask to try it. If that isn't possible, take a look at the instruction book (the documentation) that comes with the software. If it is readable and easily understood, you have a better chance of being able to load your software, learn what it will and won't do, and find out how to troubleshoot problems on your own. Some manuals are available on tape for users who would benefit from listening, rather than reading, the instructions. Nothing is more frustrating than new software that promises to write, draw, paint, do spreadsheets, databases, and slide shows—but you can't figure out how to use it.

Compatibility issues

Programs are written to run on specific types of computer systems. Be sure the software you are considering will run on the computer and

104

Computer
Resources
for People
with
Disabilities

other devices you are thinking of getting or already have. Many companies are reluctant to take back software after it has been purchased and the box has been opened. If you have an IBM computer and the software box says Macintosh version, you have a problem. Very often a program will come in a variety of versions to run on these and other systems, but you must be sure you buy the right version.

You can learn many things from reading software boxes and catalogs. The box will often tell you what the system requirements are—how much memory you need to run the program and what type of monitor and operating system you need—as well as the age range of the audience for which the program is intended. Look for other small words, such as disk size. If you have a 3.5-inch disk drive, make sure the package holds 3.5-inch disks, not 5.25-inch disks. Also, some older computers cannot read disks designated as high density. Ask a salesperson for assistance.

Considering Hardware

When it comes to computers, memory size, storage capacity, speed, and the quality of sounds and images are constantly being improved. An individual who spent $3,000 a few years ago to acquire an Apple II with 64K of memory, a 5.25-inch disk drive, and a monitor that put green text on the screen, today owns a notebook-size computer with more than 100 times the memory, 1,000 times the storage space on a hard disk drive, and a color monitor, all weighing one-tenth of the original computer and costing less!

Given the one dependable constant that everything changes, here are five guidelines to consider in your planning process:

- Buy the most memory (RAM) and the largest hard disk you can afford.

- Look for the greatest expansion capability so you have the option of adding memory and peripheral devices later on.

- Expect to upgrade, at least partially, either hardware or software in 3 to 5 years.

- Don't delay entering the world of technology because something more powerful may be available 6 months from now—something more powerful is usually on the horizon.

- Understand that pushing the limits of your potential with assistive technology will be rewarding and that you may outgrow your first system as you attain your initial goals and set new ones.

Above all, it is important to get a system that works best for you. The fact that there is something new on the market does not necessarily mean that you need to purchase it. Your decisions need to be based on whether the system you are considering or are already using is working well for you and will continue to meet your needs. In determining your memory (RAM) and storage capacity needs, look at your list of software prospects. How much RAM does the box say they require? If you are thinking of running more than one program simultaneously—for example, having your word processor and spreadsheet program open at the same time so you can transport figures from one to the other—you will need enough RAM for both, so plan accordingly. Likewise, be generous with hard disk storage space, because programs are requiring more and more storage all the time, especially those with sophisticated graphics and sound.

Photo courtesy of Arkenstone, Inc.

*Mickey Quenzer, Technical Support Specialist at
Arkenstone, uses a braille display, notetaker, and
scanner to read and write business correspondence*

106

Computer
Resources
for People
with
Disabilities

Jose, a man in his mid-20s, sustained a severe head injury in an accident that left him with memory, attention, planning, and organizing problems. Jose's first priority was to get a computer equipped with software that would help him keep track of appointments, addresses, and phone numbers. His second priority was to have a system that would enable him to check the spelling of the letters and other communication he wanted to write, since he had difficulty remembering how to spell. His third goal was to start drawing again, since he had designed and built houses before his accident. He also wanted to be able to go from his computer directly to a telephone, and to a dictionary, encyclopedia, and other sources of information.

Fortunately, Jose had an opportunity to test various options, and soon realized that his immediate need was for a computer with a modem, color monitor, and small printer. An important decision he made was to spend an extra $300 to double his hard disk space, since graphics take a lot of storage space. Jose also learned that with a flatbed scanner, he could scan in drawings and print information that had already been created. He knew that at some point in his future, it would be beneficial to add this to his computer system. Other future needs he identified were a more sophisticated drawing and graphing program and a higher-quality printer. His important first decision, however, was to select a computer system that would enable him to add components in the future, with enough memory for the drawings he wanted to do, and equipped with software that would give him the support he needed to write, communicate, and create.

The Important Tools of Access

Once you clarify the types of access you need to conventional technology, your choice of computer system will become clearer.

Thousands of devices on the market fall under the umbrella of assistive or adaptive devices, ranging from tiny keyboards to speech-input or voice-activated computer systems. Take another look at the list of common assistive technologies on pages 46 and 47. Look up in Part II the ones you think may be relevant to you. Which categories of assistive devices may provide access to the conventional types of software and hardware you need to meet your goals?

Making Choices

It's time to focus on making some preliminary choices so you know what products to investigate in depth. You may want to refer to the charts at the beginning of Part II, which pose a series of questions that provide one way to think about access. The charts will guide you to descriptions of products you may then choose to explore.

First, ask yourself: *what is it I really need assistive technology for?* Consider your strengths and weaknesses. Think about all of the component parts of a conventional computer system. Think about how you might interact with them. What are your needs? Then, consider again the components of input, processing, and output.

In terms of input, do you need

- an alternative to a regular keyboard?

- a smaller, larger, or changeable keyboard?

- an alternative to using a mouse?

- a machine that talks?

- a hands-free operating mode?

- a way to operate the system by voice?

In terms of processing, do you need

- to use as few keystrokes as possible?

- to increase the rate at which you can input information?

- help with skills development, either writing or reading?

- to find a way around some standard computer features—such as repeating keys or commands that require more than one key to be pressed simultaneously?

In terms of output, do you need

- braille output?

- large-print output?

- auditory output?

- a larger monitor?

Make a list of all the things that would help you use a computer system, and review it with your supporters. Figure out which needs are

108

Computer
Resources
for People
with
Disabilities

the most critical and start there. Look at the product description pages in Part II (organized by input, processing, and output) for products that address the needs you have identified. The product descriptions include information on what kinds of things people use the product for and some of the features available. If you are looking for a feature that is not listed, it does not necessarily mean there aren't products with that feature. Ask the vendor. It could be that the feature is available or will be soon.

Getting to specifics

Once you have identified the general technologies of interest to you, you can begin to research specific products. Use your team of supporters as a source for information. Refer to Part III for the names and phone numbers of product vendors. Contact them and have them send you their brochures. Take that information to your team members to review, and compile a new list of questions based on what you now know. As you research, ask yourself:

- Which products are most likely to help you do what you want to do?

- What features are most important?

Once you have located the products you are interested in and located the vendors in Part III or in other resource guides, ask the vendors about compatibility and device requirements. Here are a few good questions to ask vendors:

- On which computer system does your product operate?

- What version of the operating system does it require?

- How much memory (RAM) is needed?

- Are there specific monitor requirements?

- Does the device need a computer card that provides the interface between the computer and the device? Does the computer I am considering (or own) have the capacity for such an interface card?

- Does the device need an external port on the back of the computer to which it would connect by a cable? If so, what kind of port does it require?

- Are all of the components I am considering compatible? For example, will the screen reader I am considering work with the speech synthesizer I have in mind?

- What are the key features of the product?

- How is this product different from other similar products on the market?

- Do you have a distributor in my area, or do you handle your own distribution? (Keep in mind that for the most part, assistive technology vendors do business through the mail rather than through retail stores.)

Conventional Hardware Selection with an Eye on Access

Many of the questions we posed earlier for vendors of assistive technologies are also relevant for vendors of conventional technologies. Ask the dealer from whom you are planning to purchase your computer whether the company plans to continue the particular model or brand you are considering. The answer to this question might be very important in deciding what to purchase, including software. The general rule is that you can put old software in new machines most of the time, but you usually can't put new software in old machines. Ask the dealer about the version of the operating system the machine uses, and make sure that the software you want will run under this system. Be sure to check with your support people to confirm that all of the hardware and software you are considering, both conventional and assistive, will operate together.

Returning again to your prioritized list of goals, what types of hardware considerations emerge? One thing to consider if you are buying a machine for home use is whether you will want to have equipment that is compatible with what you use at school or at work. In many families, adults are using IBM or IBM-compatible computers at work; children are using Apple computers at school; and families are looking for a machine that bridges the gap between school, home, and work. Many manufacturers are making versions of their software for each of the major operating systems: MS-DOS, Windows, and Macintosh.

The field is rapidly moving toward a single standard. New equipment is regularly coming onto the market that is blending the differences between the different computer types. However, most computers

110

Computer
Resources
for People
with
Disabilities

still require their own software versions. And there is usually a time gap between the onset of new computer models and the availability of compatible assistive devices.

Reviewing your prioritized list of needs will also help you think about conventional equipment purchases. Here are some things to consider that can increase the usability of your equipment.

Hard disk drives. A hard disk is a good way to store programs and files to eliminate the need to constantly manipulate floppy disks. Given the size of most computer programs, a hard disk is an essential part of any computer system.

Printers. You can eliminate the need to continually handle paper by using a printer with a paper cassette or one that can accept continuous-form paper.

Monitors. Large-screen monitors are commonly available. Standard screens today are 14 to 15 inches. Screens range up to 21 inches, making it possible to view a full page or two pages side by side, or to use large text and graphics. A color monitor might be important because you can alter the background or text colors to increase the contrast, or because the programs you plan to use require color.

On/off switches. The placement of the on/off switch might seem a trivial matter, but if you have limited mobility, you may want the switch obvious and accessible. With young children or infants around, you may want the switch out of sight. Some computers have separate switches for the computer and the monitor, although many machines—such as portables and laptops—have monitors that automatically come on when the computer is turned on. You can also connect the system to a power strip and turn all the connected devices on with a single motion. For persons who will be using the computer independently or for persons with arthritis or mobility difficulties, you might want to select a computer and monitor with on/off switches on the front or top. Several of the newer computers turn themselves off automatically when not used for some predetermined amount of time and are turned back on by simply touching a key.

Operating system software. Another important consideration for hardware is the access features that are part of the operating system software, often called *utilities*. One such utility, CloseView (Apple Computer, Inc.), enlarges all the images on a Macintosh screen and lets you change from black characters on a white background to white on black.

Other utilities, included in Windows 95 and Macintosh operating systems and available for other Windows and MS-DOS systems, allow you to adjust your computer in various ways. For example, you can delay the key-repeat function or turn it off completely. A key-latching utility will notify the computer that keys will be struck sequentially rather than simultaneously, a useful feature for people with arthritis, muscular dystrophy, poor coordination, or weak hands who aren't able to use the three fingers required by many software programs to execute a command. Another utility lets someone who has difficulty using a mouse to control the cursor on the screen use the keyboard instead. You can replace audio cues with visual ones, like a flashing menu bar or other signal. Another utility slows down the reaction of the keys so that when a key is pressed, it won't be entered as data unless it is pressed for a certain length of time. If a key is pressed twice quickly, you can eliminate the entry of the unwanted key stroke. (See Part II under keyboard modifications and access utilities, for more information about these utilities.)

CD-ROM technology. More and more software programs and electronic reference materials are being put out on compact discs in a format called CD-ROM. This format provides easy access to encyclopedias, atlases, dictionaries, and other major reference works. The capacity of each disc is enormous and can accommodate graphics, sounds, and video, which are being incorporated into many interesting and highly motivating programs.

A few final questions to ask yourself include the following:

- According to your priorities, what hardware must you have to get started?

- Can you rank these individual items according to their priority?

- How are you doing in terms of your budget? Do you need to acquire your system in stages and, if so, do you have a plan for how that can work?

Personalizing a system of technology and access that is right for you and your goals can be complex. Identifying your human resources and gathering information should simplify the selection process. You need to take your place among them as an expert in your own right and as the one who drives the process of technology access. After all, who knows better about your circumstances and ability than you? When you engage in dialogue about technology products and disability, you already know more about the important considerations than you may realize.

Chapter 9

Tips on Buying Your Equipment

Your range of options for software, hardware, and access technology is probably broad, perhaps even overwhelming, but now you and your support team can begin to make informed choices and narrow your options to specific components according to your priorities. As you focus on specifics, you can further test your plans by questioning and examining the components in greater detail.

Finalizing Your Purchase Decisions

After having reviewed vendors' catalogs and product information, you are ready to ask the next round of questions—questions related to previewing products and trial periods, technical support, and upgrade policies. You will also want to consider accessories and the possibility of purchasing used equipment.

Previewing products

Businesses may be willing to place their products with you for a short period of time on either a rental or short-term loan basis. You may be expected to pay for shipping or to provide the supplier with product information related to your use. These are some of the questions to ask vendors:

- How do the various types of these products differ?

- With what features am I most concerned?

- What are my options for previewing this product to learn more about it?

- Is it possible to obtain a short-term rental or loan of your product so that I can explore it further before deciding if it is right for me?

• If not, is there some other way I can try out the equipment?

The technology industry is very competitive, so expect to find sources willing to respond to your questions positively. Some vendors will fall short of actually placing the device in your possession, but a good supplier should be able to direct you to a setting where you can explore your questions in greater detail. Many software suppliers offer demonstration or preview copies of their products (which often only work for a short period of time, or perform all essential functions but won't let you print or save your work).

Technical support

For most users, technical assistance is crucial. Product manuals offer a great deal of information, but you will occasionally encounter a difficulty or want to perform a task you cannot find described in the manual. Fortunately, most software and hardware companies have technical support people on staff who work every day to make sure customers are getting the most from their purchase. Vendors in the technology field offer support ranging from little to phenomenal. It is important to know what to expect in terms of service after the sale. There are a number of important questions to ask vendors:

• What kind of technical assistance is available to users of your product or service?

• What kind of support do you offer after the sale?

• Do you offer telephone support—a toll-free or other number a user can call during regular business hours?

• Is there a charge for technical assistance?

• Do you have a product newsletter?

• What are your policies on refunds, exchanges, repairs, and replacements?

• Is training needed to use the product, and is it available?

Vendors that provide a full range of support may charge a little more for their products. You may encounter a situation in which one vendor offers a better price, while another provides better service. Ongoing vendor support can be crucial, and we recommend dealing with vendors that provide good support even if they charge more than a competitor that offers little or no support.

Upgrade policies

Another important question to ask vendors is:

- How do you handle upgrades of your product for users of earlier versions?

Most designers periodically release improved versions of their technology, and you will want to take advantage of the advances. It's important to know what costs and ordering procedures are involved when upgrades are released. Registered users of a product or service will often be able to receive upgrades with little effort or cost. However, dramatically improved software products may require an upgrade fee of $50 to $100 or more.

Accessories

Be sure to examine accessories—such as blank diskettes, disk storage boxes, power strips, security devices, and carrying cases—and include those you want in your planning and budget. You will find accessories in computer stores, department stores, catalogs, and magazines.

The table or desk you will use is also an important consideration. You don't need a fancy computer desk, but the ability to adjust the height, for example, might be important to you.

You will also want to explore products that can protect your system from a variety of ills. Power strips, for example, give you the flexibility to move the on/off switch to a location that improves access. Surge protectors, often part of a standard power strip, can eliminate the threat of surges or spikes in the flow of the electrical current to your equipment. You may want to contact your insurance agent to determine whether your homeowner's or renter's policy will cover the computer. If your general insurance does not cover computer equipment, check the phone book for companies that specialize in insuring personal computer equipment. We encourage you to consider this protection.

Used equipment

Should you consider used equipment? The answer to this question depends on your circumstances. If a warranty and support are important to you, you may not want to buy from an individual but might consider a used-computer store. As with all manufactured goods, every once in a while you find a lemon—which is why computer warranties are important. Some manufacturers offer a warranty on new computers. It is commonly believed, however, that if you are going to have electronic difficulties, you will probably have them within the first 3 months. Most stores that sell used equipment will include warranties. Make sure you are getting the warranty protection and level of support you require.

If you are buying a used computer from an individual, plug it in and make sure it is working properly before you close the deal. Try to find out why the owner is selling. Good news—the seller is upgrading to a faster system. Bad news—a cup of coffee was accidentally dumped on the keyboard, and it's never been the same since.

If you are not sure whether the computer will work for you and think there is a possibility you will return it, don't buy used equipment or make sure you can return it. If you have done your homework, have checked prices in your local stores or discount catalogs, and hear about a used computer for sale that is very close to what you have in mind, it might be a real cost-saver for you. Computers are electronic rather than mechanical devices and usually become outdated before they wear out. If the circuitry goes bad—which it can, particularly when not protected with a surge protector or if it gets wet or dirty—it can be replaced at a cost (with the warning that you might lose information you have stored on your hard drive).

Approach buying a used computer in much the same way you would approach buying a used car. If it all works except for the trans-

Photo courtesy of Edmark Corporation

Millie's Math House, a fun and educational learning program, comes from a company that incorporates access into their software programs (Edmark Corporation)

116

Computer
Resources
for People
with
Disabilities

mission, price a new transmission and determine if it is still a good deal. If parts of the computer system need to be replaced, find out what they will cost before you make your decision.

Computer user groups are often a good source for used equipment because their members tend to upgrade frequently. You can find ads for used equipment in the back of many computer magazines. Stores selling used computer equipment can often be found in the yellow pages of your phone directory.

If you decide to buy a used system, use the following checklist of standard components to make sure you have everything you will need in terms of conventional equipment. The checklist will also be handy if you are inheriting a system from someone else.

- CPU or central processing unit (the main computer box)

- CPU power cord

- Monitor

- Monitor cable (connects monitor to the CPU)

- Monitor power cord (this cord may be permanently attached to the monitor)

- Keyboard

- Keyboard cable (connects the keyboard to the CPU)

- Mouse (most computers come with a mouse)

- Printer

- Printer cable (connects the printer to the CPU)

- Printer ribbon or cartridge

- Printer power cord

- Manuals for CPU, monitor, and printer

When you have gathered enough information to satisfy all of your questions, you are finally ready to purchase. Do it! Order what you need from the sources you have identified as appropriate for you.

Setting Up Your Equipment

When you get all the components together and are ready to set up your system, consider the following suggestions.

First things first

Fill out the warranty and/or registration cards and send them in. These register you as a customer and set a purchase date. Most warranties cover products for one year from the date of purchase. Registering your product may put you on the manufacturer's mailing list to receive information regarding updates or recalls. Some warranty cards register you for technical support services. Keep a copy of the cards in case you encounter problems later. It's also a good idea to keep the original packaging in case you need to return products or have them serviced.

Virtually every piece of equipment contains a serial number. Record your serial numbers and store them in a safe place.

Read the installation information

Read the manual, especially if it says Read Me First in large red letters. If you have some knowledge of computers, you may want to go to the "quick start" portion of the manual to get your basic computer system up and running. Have the manual available in case you run into something you don't understand or have questions during the setup. If you are a beginner, do yourself a favor and read through the manual step by step. Despite reputations to the contrary, most manuals are now fairly easy to follow, jargon-free, and do help people start using their equipment quickly.

Read the manuals for your assistive devices thoroughly. You will be better off spending a little more time making sure everything is set up correctly, and it could save having to go back and troubleshoot later.

Hook up your equipment

The manuals that came with your computer and assistive devices will have diagrams that show how to hook up everything. Many systems have matching icons on the cables and hardware to make connections easier. Most equipment cables now have connectors that can be tightened by hand, although some require an ordinary screwdriver.

Get the computer running with its basic component parts first. Once that system works, add your assistive technology pieces one at a time. This will help you in troubleshooting a problem should there be one.

Environmental considerations

A few environmental considerations should be kept in mind as you establish a home for your equipment. Some environments are

118

———

Computer
Resources
for People
with
Disabilities

unfriendly to computers, particularly those that are too hot or cold, too dusty, or have the potential to be moist. Placement too close to a window will not only create temperature-control problems, but might interfere with the visibility of the monitor because of glare.

A computer system needs air to stay cool, and you will need space to connect cables easily. Make sure there is plenty of space for the CPU; do not push it against a wall or tightly enclose it. Here are other general cautions to consider when you are working with computers and assistive devices:

- Keep your system away from moisture—like drinks and high humidity—which can affect the tiny circuits of the computer. Moisture guards are thin, plastic keyboard covers that provide extra protection if necessary. (For more information on moisture guards, see Keyboard Additions in Part II.)

- Magnetic fields create problems. Keep all magnets away from the computer. Some common sources of magnetic fields are speakers, telephones, radios, and paper clips that have become magnetized by a paper clip dispenser.

- Static electricity may be annoying to you, but it is dangerous for your computer. If you have problems with static electricity, purchase a grounding strip, which is available in most hardware stores and allows static electricity to be harmlessly eliminated.

- Smoke can be damaging to the disk drives and circuits in the computer.

- To avoid damage to any of the components, turn your computer off before hooking up or unhooking any devices.

- Store floppy disks with caution. Magnetic fields can erase disk information. Storing disks in a box, away from extreme temperatures, will help ensure their safety. Don't bend 5.25-inch floppies or place heavy objects on them. The metal clip on 3.5-inch floppies can become bent or jammed if not handled carefully. You can buy inexpensive disk holders in any computer store.

Positioning the elements of your system

The science of ergonomics focuses on the effects of computer use on the human body.

It is important to take preventative measures to avoid problems down the road. For example, take frequent breaks from the computer. It's good for the body, eyes, and mind.

Make your computer setup as comfortable as possible. Easy access and comfort are the top priorities. The table surface on which you put the computer should be low enough so that when you sit you are looking down slightly at the monitor. If you are using a standard keyboard and mouse, your hands should rest comfortably on the desk and keyboard. Wrist rests and arm supports can help make your computing environment more healthful and comfortable. (See Arm Supports in Part II for more information.)

If the computer must accommodate several different users or must be moved around from home, school, and work, use tables with adjustable height and tables on wheels. For very young users, consider a table close to the ground, where children can stand to work on the computer or sit on small chairs. Office furniture stores and catalogs are sources for these types of tables and other computer furniture. Furniture does not have to be expensive, but it is something you need to think about carefully. Computers and assistive devices can take a fair amount of space on a table top or desk.

Monitors can be placed on top of or alongside the CPU. We have even seen monitors placed on the floor to provide access to young children. If more than one person or someone with a physical disability will be using the computer, consider a floating monitor arm. This is a mechanical arm that connects to a table and allows the monitor to move up, down, in, and out with ease, thus allowing people to change positions during the day and move the monitor into a position for best access. (See Monitor Additions in Part II for more information on mounting devices.)

Keyboard placement is also flexible: place the keyboard and other input devices where they can be used comfortably.

Be creative. It is not necessary to set up your computer to look like an ad in the Sunday paper. Some, but not all, CPUs can be turned on their sides. You can put the CPU on the floor or another place to provide easier access to the disk drive. Keyboards can be mounted on trays, angled, or padded to fit the user.

Positioning can be a complex issue for some people. You may choose to consult with an occupational or physical therapist who could help determine the best arrangement for you. If you need a customized setup—such as a way to mount a laptop computer on a wheelchair and use the chair's battery to run the computer—you might want to consult with an engineer or someone with the expertise to work with you. Many things can be fabricated to meet your needs. One resource for

120

Computer
Resources
for People
with
Disabilities

this type of expertise is the federally funded Rehabilitation Engineering Centers. (Contact RESNA at (703) 524-6686 for more information on these centers.)

Powering up

Rather than plugging your computer directly into the wall, we recommend using a power strip, which comes in many styles and prices. Some have filters, and some provide protection against power surges or significant current fluctuations. Unless you have a special requirement or a power problem in your area, a simple power strip with a surge protector should meet your needs inexpensively.

If you cannot activate the small toggle on the power strip, there are a number of alternative ways to get electricity to the power strip. There are power modules that can be activated by a switch and mounted anywhere. A tread switch is an on/off switch that can be activated by rolling a wheelchair across it. There are many solutions that can be individualized to meet your needs.

If, when you press the switch on the power strip, it whirs and beeps and you get a DOS prompt, a Windows menu, or a "happy Mac" icon, you may want to let out a cheer. You have successfully powered up!

Troubleshooting

If, however, you press the switch and nothing happens, you need to investigate or troubleshoot the problem. Your problem could be something simple like a loose plug or cable, or something technical such as a conflict among special utility programs within your system. If you suspect the latter to be the case, it's time to make some calls.

If you bought the equipment at a local computer store, call there first. You can call the vendor of your assistive technology. You can also try the toll-free support number that came with your computer. All major companies have support staff who answer questions and troubleshoot problems. But don't expect them to know anything about your assistive technology. When making these calls, have the model numbers of your equipment, the version of the operating system you are running, and, if possible, your computer turned on and near the telephone so you can test the suggestions offered. If you can't resolve the problem, call on your support team. Remember, they are there to help.

Once you get started, we recommend you use your computer as much as possible during the warranty period. If anything is going to go wrong with the machinery, it will most likely happen during this period. You will become comfortable with your new tools more quickly if you spend time with them right from the beginning.

Alternative Resources

What if you cannot physically handle your computer, or if you feel uncomfortable setting it up and connecting the assistive devices? Some computer stores offer to set up the computer in your home for a nominal fee if you purchased the machine from them. If you bought your computer by mail order, however, you will need to find another source of help. Computer clubs and user groups can be excellent resources, as they are filled with people who enjoy setting up computer systems and may be happy to show off their skills. For the most part they will know conventional technology, but may or may not be able to help you figure out the assistive technology. You might contact the assistive technology vendor about setup support. They may have other customers who would be interested in providing some assistance to you.

Once you have got your system up and running, it is time to develop proficiency with your technology.

Chapter 10

As You Become an Expert…

Throughout this book we have been asking, "What are your dreams?" Now it's time to make those cables, boxes, chips, and disks fulfill them. With your first steps, aim for projects that will give you a lot of positive reinforcement and success.

Your supporters have had an important role to play in helping you get up and running. You may want to bring in some new players to help you develop skills and strategies for using your assistive devices, learning new software programs, and getting connected to the vast world of online services.

Learning and Training

The disks are spinning, the lights are blinking, the beeps are beeping, and now you need to make something productive happen. What you need to learn can be divided into four categories: the computer, the conventional software, the adaptive software and hardware, and online information resources. You only need to know as much as it takes to run them appropriately; you don't have to know how to build or program a computer. It is easy to get overwhelmed by all there is to learn. Keep your focus clear and start with the minimum. Operate, at least initially, on a need-to-know basis, learning what you need when you need it.

Learning on your own

Personal computing is getting more intuitive all the time. You can learn a great deal on your own or with the help of a friend or two.

Begin by going through what you received with the computer. Many computer companies include good step-by-step tutorials on disk, which cover using the mouse, opening and closing files, saving data, printing, and other basic skills.

When it comes to learning software, do not underestimate your ability to train yourself. Many technology users are self-trained and enjoyed every minute of the process. Everything you buy will come with instructions, and many software programs have on-disk tutorials. If you purchased a computer with some software already installed, get to know those programs first. There is nothing like learning to use the mouse with a few hundred games of solitaire. Install one program at a time, learn how to use it, then move to the next program on your priority list. This way, installing your software doesn't become a huge tedious task, and as your confidence builds, you will look forward to experimenting with the next piece of software.

A number of training videotapes and audiotapes with disk activities for popular software titles are available, as is a growing assortment of introductory books on the major computer systems. All are available in local book and computer stores. Check with your sources for their favorite titles.

Whenever you are experimenting or troubleshooting a problem, do one thing at a time and keep track of what you did. Make one change at a time, especially when you are testing assistive devices. If you make a mistake, it will be easier to fix—and if you get it right, you'll be able to do it again.

Don't be afraid to try things. Many new computer users believe they can bring about disaster by pressing the wrong key or making the wrong choice at the wrong time. You really can't blow up a computer by pressing the wrong key. Disasters can be avoided fairly easily. Here are a few suggestions to help eliminate both the fears and the disasters.

Save your work. Learn how to save your work before you learn how to do anything else. Get in the habit of saving your work on a hard disk or on a floppy disk. If the project you are working on is important, save it! Save often. Save compulsively. In the case of a power failure or a system error, you will lose anything you haven't saved to disk. A system error—also known as a crash—happens to everyone at one time or another. A crash indicates that there was a temporary problem with your operating system. The treatment for a crash is to turn off your computer and restart, or reboot your computer. If the problem persists, seek advice.

Back up your work. Keep copies of your work and your applications (your software programs) on disks, and store them in a safe place. Making a copy of your data can save you a great deal of time and frustration if anything happens to the hard disk or a floppy disk.

Experiment. Once you are in a program and your work is saved, look around. Make choices, push buttons, pull down the menus. You

124

Computer
Resources
for People
with
Disabilities

usually can't do much harm if you have saved your data. And you can always reload the program if something really goes wrong.

Sherry shared her experience experimenting with computers:

I first learned about the ATA center from a newspaper article in the 1980s. I visited them then one time but did not really get involved with them until 1992. At the time, I had an IBM typewriter but wanted a new typewriter with a screen so I could see what I was typing, and a word speller to check my spelling. I have cerebral palsy, and can only type with my left index finger bent. I use a keyguard that fits over the keyboard, which allows me to hit one letter at a time without tripping over other keys.

The folks at the ATA center tried to talk me into trying a computer, but what did I need with a computer? I just wanted to type. My friend eventually talked me into trying a computer, but without a keyguard it was hopeless. We tried different devices. I don't have very much control of my head, so I couldn't use a head stick to hit the keys. Then they put a trackball in front of me, and I tried to hit a letter with the ball, but again the lack of control in my hand would not let me. "I need a keyguard." So, my father made several keyguards out of plastic and metal, like the one I used with my typewriter.

The biggest problems then became moving the mouse around, and getting the word processor up to type. Even with my keyguard, the palm of my hand would hit the wrong key while I tried to move the mouse with the arrows keys. Later, I received a donated IBM computer through my friend. The IBM is a lot easier and faster for me, because I don't have to use the mouse keys except once in a while.

I went and bought a Laser 46DX with Windows a few years ago. I use a program called "Staydown" in DOS and Windows. This allows me to hit the shift key to get a "?" or anything else that I need, with one finger. I have a speech problem due to the cerebral palsy and I use a BBS to stay in touch with my friends and as a learning tool to chat with others. It helps sharpen my mind. I can also dial into public libraries, and look up books and reserve them, if I wish to. I have several Print Shop programs that I enjoy. I make cards, posters, and calendars using a color printer. The computer also lets me check my spelling. I spend two or more hours a day teaching myself more about my PC by pushing buttons. The computer world has changed my life. I didn't know that so many interesting things exist out in the world, just by pushing a key. And I'm always ready for a *new challenge!*

Learning more about conventional technologies

There are times and situations that call for a more structured approach to learning computing. Everyone has their own learning styles, and awareness of your own style should guide you in selecting a teaching method or instructor to meet your needs. Private teachers can tailor their approach to match your style and preferred pace. Check your community resources and contacts for referrals.

Should you want to explore them, quite a few options for learning how to use conventional technologies exist. Community colleges, computer user groups, adult education programs of local school districts, computer stores, and even copying service centers offer beginning, intermediate, and advanced classes. Classes usually focus on a particular type of computer or on a particular software application, such as WordPerfect (WordPerfect Corporation), a word processing program; and Excel (Microsoft), a spreadsheet program. Many classes are available to help you get started on the Internet. Enrollment fees are usually modest.

Question the suppliers of training as you would vendors of equipment and software. Ask if you can preview sessions or visit the location, and learn what you can about follow-up or ongoing support. Accessibility of the training site and the equipment might be concerns for you. If you need assistive devices to access their computer systems, you will probably need to bring your own to participate in the class. Be aware that the instructor will be teaching the class how to use a keyboard and a mouse and will probably know little about how to assist you with your adaptive devices.

Learning more about assistive technologies

Finding training in how to use assistive technologies is more complex. As we mentioned in the budgeting discussion, it is important in your planning to set money aside for training. When comparing prices, ask vendors if they provide training. This may explain why one vendor charges more money than a competitor. Factor in what it would take to get training elsewhere if it's not included. If a vendor doesn't offer training, they may be able to point you toward an individual or organization that has purchased the same device in your area. Many people who have mastered a device themselves are happy to share their expertise. Private tutors and consultants can help people learn how to use adaptive equipment.

Today only a few community colleges and other community-based programs offer classes using assistive technology. Some community col-

126

Computer
Resources
for People
with
Disabilities

leges—in California, for example—do have such courses, and provide accessible computer labs.

If your community does not offer these opportunities, ask for them. Talk to people who offer educational programs about what it would take to make the existing program accessible and how you can assist them in making it work. The ultimate goal should be not to set up separate learning environments, but to make existing ones accessible.

Professional development

Taking advantage of continuing education opportunities in your community can be one of the most beneficial moves you will make to learn new skills and to network with others in your community. Many universities and teachers' colleges offer courses in the use of technology for students with disabilities. In some cases, these courses are required for degree candidates in special education. University extension programs and community-based organizations also offer opportunities for teachers to learn about assistive technology and to receive continuing education units (CEUs) in the process.

Computer conferences are conducted around the country. In addition to opportunities to see and test new products, they often offer training sessions on strategies for using products, especially in classroom and clinical settings. (See Part III for a list of conferences.)

Pushing the Limits of Technology

Technology does not replace humans; it challenges them to do better. Its effectiveness depends solely on how it is used. In a classroom, technology is not the teacher. But, when used creatively by a teacher, it can transform a mediocre lesson into an exciting, attention-grabbing learning experience.

Innovations in education

When used in conjunction with cooperative learning strategies, technology can be a powerful tool to promote the inclusion of students with disabilities in regular education classrooms.

> *Mrs. Rodriguez's* sixth-grade social studies class was studying ancient Egypt. In her room were 11-year-olds of every description, some excited about exploring the wonders of the ancient world, and

others quite reluctant, because they had experienced failure so often. Mrs. Rodriguez, using the principles of cooperative learning, had organized her class into heterogeneous learning groups of four students each.

Each group worked as a unit in the school library, exploring one aspect of ancient Egypt using books and the multimedia information available on CD-ROM. Mrs. Rodriguez, working with a local technology resource center and another halfway across the country (via modem), had accumulated many scanned images—called clip art—with an Egyptian theme: pharaohs, a sphinx, pottery, and pyramids, all available in electronic form.

Fresh from their library experience, each group worked as a team to produce a presentation for the class using Story-Ware software (Don Johnston, Inc.). Groups took turns planning, typing, organizing synthesized-speech examples, and choosing clip-art illustrations and sound clips. Everyone, regardless of ability level, contributed, and everyone's imagination worked overtime. Finally, the day came for the groups to demonstrate their collaborative efforts. They projected the images on a large screen using a computer specially connected to an overhead projector projection plate and amplified the sound through a speaker. Every student will remember something about ancient Egypt because everyone contributed.

Children often discover unanticipated ways to use technology. We can learn a great deal from them.

Kendra is 11 years old and in a regular fifth-grade class. She has cerebral palsy and operates the computer using just one finger with the help of Sticky Keys and Mouse Keys. (For information on these programs, see Keyboard Modifications in Part II). She is very creative and loves to add graphics to her work. She also likes to paint and color with her friends. Using Kid Pix and Kid Pix Companion (Brøderbund), she has been able to paint and create for hours on end.

Kendra learned the names of the continents and their locations using these tools. Starting with a map of the world from Kid Art (Brøderbund), she listed the names of the continents around the perimeter of the screen. Using the Moving Truck tool, she selected the name of the continent and "drove" it to the proper location on the map. She colored the continents to distinguish them, then labeled them. She repeated this process until she had the names of all the continents down. Her peers had to use paper and pencils and

128

Computer
Resources
for People
with
Disabilities

only had a couple sheets of paper to practice on. Because she was using the computer, Kendra was able to play and learn until she had mastered the subject. She thoroughly enjoyed the independence and sense of accomplishment it gave her.

Stretching technology to work for you

We all are stretching technology to do what we need, regardless of what it was originally designed to do. In this field, you just can't settle for "because that's just the way it is." If the way it is doesn't work for you, there is often someone who can help figure out how to change it. Question things; don't take them for granted. You may not be the only person who has wanted to do what you want to do.

If you want your computer to do more than it is currently doing and you haven't found a way to make it work, check around. Refer to the manual. Ask other people you know who use the program, consult with members of your support team, call the vendor, or learn to get

Photo courtesy of EduQuest/IBM

Software programs such as Stories and More can help build reading compre-hension skills in interesting and moti-vating ways (IBM)

online and put your interest out, literally, into a world of resources. You just might discover that it can easily be made to do what you want.

Assuming that the program cannot do what you need, try combining it with another program. There are lots of little programs, some of them shareware, that may or may not have been designed to work with adaptive technology but that can increase the functionality of your system. For example, a program that writes macros (keyboard shortcuts) can decrease the time it takes to accomplish a complicated task. No matter what input device you are using, you can probably benefit from a program that allows you to do more than one thing with a single keystroke. (See Abbreviation Expansion and Macros, and Access Utilities in Part II.)

What would you like to see? Why do you want it? What will it help you accomplish? If you have an idea on how a product can be improved, consider talking to the people who designed it. Vendors are usually interested in users' insights. Those of us in the trenches often have ideas that designers are eager to hear.

Achieving Comfort

Once you are using your computer to fulfill your original goals, you will be surprised how comfortable you feel with your new tools. Let us say that you purchased your computer to help your child write reports for school. The largest percentage of your time at first was spent on getting familiar with the equipment. Later, you were focused on your tasks. Preparing the first report took a long time and caused quite a bit of tension; the second report was somewhat stressful; the third report was a lot easier; and by the time your child was working on the fourth report, you found yourself comfortable enough to experiment with some of the software's special features. Your original mission was accomplished. Now what?

Mollie is 11 years old. A combination of learning disabilities and fine-motor problems make learning and writing very difficult for her. Her mother explains that Mollie needs to "over-learn everything." When she was 6 years old, her parents purchased a few drill and practice programs for an older computer that had been given to them and used the early software programs to provide Mollie with the repetitious practice she needed to learn short and long vowel sounds and basic math facts. They found that the computer practice was much more enjoyable and effective than flashcards. As

130

Computer
Resources
for People
with
Disabilities

Mollie got older, her parents wanted to address her writing difficulties, so they purchased a more powerful computer. To learn about new software, her mother began volunteering at her local Alliance center, organizing the center's software collection.

Mollie now uses the computer as her primary writing tool at home. Her handwriting is poor—barely legible to Mollie herself—and writing takes her a long time, so she completes most of her written homework on the computer. For science homework she writes definitions and answers questions using a word processing program. This has the added advantage of providing her with a copy of the homework from which to study (she cannot study from notes written in her own hand). She writes her compositions on the computer, taking full advantage of the computer's ability to assist with spell checking, editing, and rewriting. Freed from the mechanics of writing, she is able to focus on thinking and expressing her thoughts. Her mother is also pleased that she is getting enrichment from playing such educational programs as Oregon Trail (MECC) and Where in the World Is Carmen Sandiego? (Brøderbund).

Mollie's story is a good example of a family getting involved with computers for a specific purpose and then moving on to other beneficial uses. We think you will find this part of your journey to be the most fun. Once you have acquired the right computer system for you, much of the pressure is off. You can pursue the fulfillment of your original goals and be free to experiment, improvise, and discover other uses of your system.

Trying new software for new uses

Your first new use will probably entail trying a different software program. Mollie progressed from relatively simple drill and practice programs to word processing and problem-solving programs for entertainment and education. Many adults begin with a word-processing program as a writing tool, then move on to a paint or draw program (they're so much fun, they're irresistible) or to a spreadsheet program for working with finances and budgets. As a parent, you may surprise yourself and find the next use of your child's computer system will be to make *your* work easier—perhaps to print labels for all those holiday greeting cards or to produce the PTA's annual directory (which you volunteered to do even though last year it took hours of tedious typing).

Adding options: the upgrade phenomenon

You may have noticed the upgrade phenomenon already. It is occurring on two levels: the technology is advancing, and so are you. You may have started out in awe of what technology could do, but now, as a more sophisticated user, you have higher expectations and want the technology to do more. Look at what has happened with copy machines. Not too long ago, copy machines were a marvel of modern science: no more retyping an entire page, no more carbons. After a while, we got tired of feeding papers one by one and of only printing on one side of the page; we wanted to use different sizes of paper and different colors of ink. The evolution of copy machines and their users pales in comparison to computer technology and its users. Whereas copy machines have one basic function, computers are tremendously versatile and every aspect is being constantly revised. Take it for granted that technology will improve. This is the good news: change means you will have new options that might be important to you. However, just because there are new products on the market doesn't mean you need them, but it does give you an opportunity to review your situation in light of new developments.

No matter which computer system and adaptations you purchase, within a couple of years you will probably want to add hardware or peripherals. Your first add-on might be an item you had originally considered but rejected in an effort to keep your costs down, such as a scanner or a modem. If you enjoy programs with music, you may decide to purchase a pair of external speakers to improve the quality of sound coming from your computer. You may choose to add a CD-ROM drive to take advantage of the exciting new programs being released in CD-ROM format.

Probably the most common addition to personal computer systems is more memory. As your interests in software expand, you will eventually find a program you feel you must have, but that requires more memory to operate than your computer has. Or, you might find that you are rapidly filling your hard disk and need a larger one or some other storage device.

We cannot foresee what the changes the next few years will bring, but you can be sure that the computers of 5 years from now will be able to do things we can't even imagine now. By then, as an experienced computer user, you will be eager to move on. Rest assured that deciding on your next computer will not take half as long as purchasing your first.

132

Computer
Resources
for People
with
Disabilities

Connecting to the world

One of the things we can foresee is that computers will be easier to use. Future generations of technology will be designed to seamlessly connect us to a universe of information and knowledgeable people. A response to a survey on how to improve special education included this comment: "Stop buying computers; children need to connect with human beings." Clearly the writer had not spent much time around children working with computers. Everyone needs to connect with other human beings, especially youngsters with disabilities. Technology has the power to bring people together by providing them with the ability to interact and communicate in new ways.

Andy and *Jonathan* are two boys in a school in Australia for children who are deaf. Through a commercial online service connected to the Internet, the boys posted a message asking for pen pals. *Joshua* and *Caleb* are brothers, ages 12 and 10, who have no disabilities and who live in Kentucky. Their father, an Internet user, saw the message and had them write Andy and Jonathan. Now the four boys exchange electronic pen-pal letters. They write about Nintendo games, basketball, school, their homes, their friends, and the weather, which is especially interesting because it's winter in Australia when it's summer in Kentucky. It was a month before Joshua and Caleb knew that Andy and Jonathan were completely deaf. The boys think it's great

*Computers can help to foster social interaction as children
enjoy the learning process*

that they can't tell anything about race, size, age, appearance, or disability by sending and reading email, but they can share the secrets of Nintendo and have a lot of fun getting to know each other. Andy and Jonathan hope to come to the United States one day, and Joshua and Caleb are finding someone to teach them sign language.

The new frontier of the world of telecommunications, sometimes called the information superhighway, allows you to use your phone to access databases of information stored on another computer and, in many cases, to transfer (or download) information to your own computer. The number of people using telecommunications is increasing at a phenomenal rate. How could someone with a disability take advantage of this technology? First of all, in the same ways that anybody would:

- Telecommuting in order to work from home

- Operating a home-based business

- Accessing vast databases of information beyond their geographic limits

- Tapping on-line educational programs

- Sending and receiving electronic mail to share interests with others

Some aspects of telecommunications are particularly well suited to people with disabilities because of the access they provide. You can bring information right into your home and use your computer and assistive technology to read or edit it. You can write a message with any sort of input device and take as much time as necessary. After you have composed the message, you can send it to one individual or to many by posting it to a bulletin board (an electronic information center). A person's functional limitations or disability are not apparent or relevant to the process.

Through telecommunications, you can take advantage of a wide range of services without leaving your home. You can get up-to-date information on the stock market, make airline reservations, and order clothes. You can access libraries that are otherwise inaccessible to you because of transportation and architectural barriers or difficulty with manipulating books or reading print. You can develop and maintain friendships via email. Says *Vanessa,*

For the first time in my life, I am totally independent. I am doing what every other teenager is doing—talking on the phone. The great

134

Computer
Resources
for People
with
Disabilities

thing is there's no one looking over my shoulder! Being online is exciting. I love to hear the voice of America Online say, "You've got mail!"

I talk to all kinds of people on the Internet. I talk to my uncle at Oracle. Now, I can write my feelings down and email them to my best friend, who just got online. This is important because she just started college and I don't see her as often as I would like, especially when I am used to seeing her every day and chatting with her every day. Email helps ease the pain.

There's a lot of stuff waiting to be explored online. I almost ordered flowers for my sister, but mom caught me in the act! Sometimes I use chat rooms to talk to people online. You can download all kinds of research. You can even download games.

Recently, I discovered how to use my modem to access the telephone relay service (TTY) for deaf and disabled people. I can call people who don't have email without the help of anyone. Here's how it works: I use my modem to dial the relay service. When I've made a connection, I type the number I want them to call. They read what I write on the computer to the person I'm calling. The agent writes back to me what the person says and I read it on my computer monitor. It is neat having "private" conversations. For the first time in my life I've had secrets.

How can you try telecommunications? You will need a computer, a modem, a phone line, and telecommunications software. (See Part III for a list of online services and bulletin boards, then call and get brochures.)

There are ways you can experiment with online services for free or nearly free to make sure they would be of value to you. Ask the services if they have demonstration packages or trial subscriptions. Find out if any of your friends are connected and willing to show you around. Your local library or school may have access to online services or the Internet, which connects thousands of universities, schools, businesses, and government offices across the nation and around the world and provides for the free flow of electronic mail and information.

Gaining access to commercial services using assistive technology might require some effort or customization, depending on the system you are using. For example, using a voice recognition system to access bulletin boards might be a problem because of telephone-line noise. If these problems arise for you, call an Alliance for Technology Access center to help work through them.

Many services have forums where you can exchange messages with people who have similar interests. You can develop friendships with people you may never physically meet. You may want to check out the areas that focus on people with disabilities. People share their experiences, frustrations, and triumphs. You will find letters from people who are experiencing life-changing adjustments and others who have gone down similar roads and are able to commiserate and guide.

A constantly growing number of online resources focus on issues of interest to people with disabilities, including discussions about access to technology. They appear in many different formats called World Wide Web sites, discussion lists, newsgroups, and bulletin boards. Through these routes you can find out virtually everything you'd like to know and keep updated on the issues. (For specific ideas on where to start, see Part III, Telecommunications Resources.)

Telecommunications is one of a thousand important uses to which technology can be put and holds a great deal of promise for us all. For example, the Alliance uses a telecommunications system to connect its centers on a daily basis to share information and expertise. Thousands of people seeking technology assistance each year benefit from the collective experience of one another and add to the knowledge of all.

There are a great many resources to explore in developing strategies for computer use at home, at school, and on the job. Part III contains references for books and periodicals that can be of use in this process.

The tools of technology are fabulously flexible. The possibilities are limited only by our imaginations. The challenge is to use our powers of creativity to maximize their potential now and in the years ahead, as our needs change and as technology transforms the ways in which we connect with our environment and the people in it.

Chapter 11

Sharing What You Learn

Interest in the field of assistive technology is exploding on every level. And the demand for knowledge about how to make it work in real life is likewise increasing. Throughout your search for technological solutions, you will encounter individuals who are at different points in their search and are as determined as you are. The potential of technology energizes people in a way that is both creative and contagious. Most people are only too happy to share what they have discovered and how it works for them.

You may want to find ways to share your knowledge and experience with people who are starting on the journey, answering their questions the way someone answered yours. You may be thinking, "I hardly know how to turn my computer on; how in the world could I help anyone?" But you will be surprised. You may be able to recommend a piece of software your child loves or a good place to purchase educational software.

Mara, the mother of a son with cerebral palsy and visual impairments, helped her son become involved with computers. Other parents said to her, "That's interesting, but my child can't use a regular keyboard." Although Mara's knowledge of assistive technology was limited, she found herself telling parent after parent that "you don't have to be able to use a keyboard; there are lots of other ways to use a computer." She succeeded in communicating to them that there are many possibilities.

Whatever small piece of the technology puzzle you have had experience with, someone else may be seeking the same piece, and you can help.

Phyllis considers herself a newcomer to the world of assistive technology. She does not yet realize that other people can learn from her experience of getting her state office of vocational rehabilitation to pay for her laptop computer.

Phyllis is in her mid-30s and a recovering alcoholic. Recently she discovered that the problems she had had all her life with reading, memorizing, and numbers were not due to a lack of intelligence but to learning disabilities. For the first 10 years of her adult life, she worked as a horse trainer, but couldn't move up in the world of horse training because she could not reliably read a stopwatch or racing forms. She finally decided she wanted to get away from the tough racetrack environment and find a job with security. She was fearful but enrolled in a community college.

At the same time, Phyllis was referred to the county office of vocational rehabilitation. She took their required tests and was told that she was not college material and that they would not provide support for her to attend college. However, when she finished her first semester with a 4.0 grade point average, the decision was reversed. While at the community college, Phyllis taught herself to type in the college's computer lab and began to complete assignments on a computer. She transferred to a 4-year college and continued to rely on the college computer lab for doing her written assignments.

When laptop computers became affordable, Phyllis saw a more efficient solution to her problems. She could carry a laptop to class and the library for note taking, and she could work on papers at home. She completed all the paperwork to apply for assistance from the vocational rehabilitation office, including a formal letter with a clear rationale for the laptop, several cost estimates, and a letter from one of her professors. The rehabilitation office approved the purchase. One of her fellow students, who also has learning disabilities, approached her and asked how the laptop helped her and how she acquired it. Before she had even mastered her computer, Phyllis found herself sharing her beginning experiences and advising others.

One of the exciting things about the field of assistive technology is how supportive people have been to each other. The name of the game is problem solving. Instead of "it can't be done," you are more likely to hear "there must be a way; how can we find it?" This commitment to finding solutions is coupled with a willingness to help. Everyone is new to some degree, and no one person knows everything, so most people are willing to share their experiences with others who are interested. The guiding belief is, "If I answer your question today, maybe someone will answer my question tomorrow."

Becoming a Leader

As you gain more experience and answer more and more questions about your computer system, you may decide to take an active role in a number of efforts: organizing an assistive technology user group, participating in a bulletin board on a telecommunications network, working with your PTA to promote creative computer use in your school district, lobbying political bodies to support technology integration in vocational or educational programs, or, like many of the writers of this book, organizing a technology access center in your area. These activities are natural extensions of informal networking and well within the realm of possibility. In fact, it has been grassroots efforts such as these that have resulted in assistive technology having the impact it has had on the lives of people with disabilities. It has been the initiative, creativity, and persistence of people like you who have turned possibilities into realities.

Chris is the mother of *Franklin,* who has physical disabilities as a result of anoxic brain damage from near-drowning. When Franklin was two and a half, Chris discovered that computers could do interesting things, and she sent away for a slew of brochures, hoping to find the right equipment for her son. When that approach did not work, she enrolled in a special education technology program at a local university. She bought Franklin his first computer when he was 4 years old. At Franklin's preschool, other parents and therapists asked Chris all kinds of questions about computers, and before long she started tutoring other parents in her dining room. Because of Franklin's needs, the aspects of technology she knew best were switches, scanning, and software to teach cause-and-effect and choice-making to young children. She was not comfortable answering other technical questions, such as which word-processing program is best for children with learning disabilities. But she enthusiastically answered questions in her area of experience.

Then Chris read an article in *Exceptional Parent* magazine about computer resource centers in other areas of the country that had joined together to form the Alliance for Technology Access, and she realized that a resource center was what her city needed—and what she needed to keep up with new developments in technology. She contacted the professor at the university who coordinated the special education technology program, her local office of The Arc, and fellow parents, and led a collaborative effort that resulted in the establishment of an Alliance for Technology Access Center. Now

Chris is Director of Education at the center and a self-described "technology junkie." In addition to her knowledge about computers and augmentative communication systems, she probably knows more about adapting video games than anyone.

People can become leaders in this field in many ways, bringing others together over a variety of issues and topics. Collaborating on the development of an Alliance for Technology Access center is just one of many avenues open to people. (For information on starting a center, see Part III.)

Sue helped establish an Alliance center, and in addition has shared her skills and enthusiasm for computers with children living in poverty in a New Jersey inner city.

Before Sue raised five children, she taught high school math and science and worked at AT&T, managing a group that helped set up office computers. At that time computers were large machines that required their own climate-controlled rooms. Several years later, when Sue was a full-time homemaker, microcomputers came on the market, and Sue bought an early Apple II+ computer "just to keep up." She volunteered at her children's school as a computer tutor, then got the PTA interested in organizing a Computers in Education program. The PTA purchased a few computers and some early educational software, and small groups of children started coming in for the simple computer classes Sue taught. The program grew to 12 computers, with every class participating. Eventually, the school hired a math teacher to take over the program and make computers an integral part of the curriculum.

Around this time, a pastor from a grassroots community corporation spoke at Sue's church, and in describing his organization's needs, mentioned that old computers had been donated to their school by local corporations but nobody knew what to do with them. Sue saw a new volunteer opportunity. She took her computer skills to the school, recruited a few volunteers, and now devotes two days a week to designing and running their Computers in Education program. With the program having demonstrated its viability, the community foundation has been able to procure funds for new equipment, and now all children enrolled at the school—those with and without disabilities—receive weekly instruction in computer use.

One person can accomplish astounding things, if she or he has a vision, a desire, and the willingness and perseverance to work toward trans-

140

Computer
Resources
for People
with
Disabilities

lating that vision into reality and sharing it with others. We all started with our own technology needs, but eventually we connected with others and became part of the community of people who believe in the vast potential of technology to change the lives of children and adults with disabilities. And, in helping others, we definitely help ourselves.

Chapter 12

Some Thoughts About the Future

John Scully, when serving as the CEO of Apple Computer, Inc., once remarked that "the best way to predict the future is to invent it." That way of thinking and that attitude speak to the real power of technology. This book will have accomplished its purpose if it convinced you that assistive technologies can empower you to invent your own future.

When you consider the bold language contained in recent pieces of legislation like the Americans with Disabilities Act and the Reauthorization of the Rehabilitation Act, it becomes clear that all across the nation a spirit of empowerment and high expectation is seizing people's hearts and imaginations. Every day, people using assistive technologies are eliminating barriers and expanding the concept of what is or isn't an accessible activity for an individual with disabilities. And who better to decide what is or isn't—what will or will not be—an accessible activity for an individual with a disability than that individual? In every sense of the word, *empowerment* is an attitude available to everyone with a disability. The law provides the legal rights and sanctions, but technology and imagination provide the real capacity and ability to choose, to act, and to invent your future.

Every achievement should give rise to new and expanded expectations. And in pursuing the tools to realize those expectations, let no one ever say "It can't be done." Instead, let the response be, "I don't know of that having been done before, but let's find out," or, better yet, "Let's see who and what we need to bring together to make it happen."

New Dimensions in Computer Technology

Two trends in technology, integration, and miniaturization, are resulting in portable, personalizable, versatile equipment. This means that Victor, the young man you may remember from Chapter 1, could have more functionality and far-better quality of speech in a computer he

142

Computer
Resources
for People
with
Disabilities

could transport to different environments. It also means he could use the same computer and system of access for word processing, creating spreadsheets, drawing, controlling his environment, and using the phone. He might also choose to access printed text by placing it in a scanner and letting optical character-recognition software decode and transfer it into a standard computer text file, which can then be read aloud by a computer with a speech synthesizer.

A whole new wave of miniature and very powerful technologies (personal digital assistants, or PDAs) are even more portable; have interfaces that can be personalized to individual abilities; and will soon have cellular, fax, message, satellite locator, and speech capabilities. An older person or someone with a cognitive disability, for example, could carry a PDA in a pocket and be reminded of everything from taking medication to showing up on time for a job interview or catching a bus. Such a system is functioning in the Chicago area, where a group is employing a personal computer to call and send messages to up to 50 people with traumatic brain injury as many times as needed during the day to help them stay on track. With the new generation of PDAs, capabilities will be even more extensive. For example, the locator capability could alert someone with Alzheimer's disease that they are more than a certain number of blocks from home and, if requested, give them printed or verbal instructions as to how to return.

These are just a few examples of what is available for us today. Try to imagine what is coming, what is in the works in labs around the country, or what will be developed in the next 5 years.

Much of what is being done focuses on what the government is calling *technology transfer*—finding new purposes for technologies originally developed for other reasons, often military. A great deal of technology originally developed for military purposes has had extremely important implications in the peace-time realm of assistive technologies. For example, pilots flying in multinational forces or within foreign territories already have a foreign language translation system that automatically translates what a pilot is saying into any one of several languages, and that translates whatever language other pilots or service people are using into the language of the first pilot. It's easy to imagine how this technology could be adapted to recognize the speech of individuals with disabilities in articulation, and to put an individual's speech into an articulated form in either his native language or any of several foreign languages. In another area, virtual realities are already being employed to train pilots in flying over territories thousands of miles away without ever leaving the safety of the training room. There is a vast educational potential in the ability to simulate realistic experiences for people who have not had the opportunity to access such experiences before.

Speech-recognition technology (the ability of the computer to understand the human voice) is taking quantum leaps and will be a mainstream tool that we will soon use for everything from word processing to environmental control. We will also have virtual reality (the ability to provide realistic, interactive, multisensory experiences) options for everything from educational experiences to vocational simulation to social decision-making simulations and recreational experiences.

143

Some
Thoughts
About
the
Future

Looking Toward the Future

What is available now is really the tip of the iceberg when compared to what is coming. And, while none of us can anticipate exactly what the next technology will be or how it might be used, we need to be aware of apparent and accelerating trends and to see these developments as more conclusive evidence that we should never limit our expectations or be completely content with today's solutions.

Tomorrow we will have fast, accurate, and reliable speech recognition systems that will allow any of us to talk to all computers. We will have vastly improved eye interface capabilities that will allow us to control many types of technology or indicate where we want our wheelchair to go with a glance. We will have the first practical applications of virtual reality to provide educational, vocational, and recreational experiences for a wide range of persons with disabilities, and they will be available in multisensory format, with each individual choosing how he or she wants to receive the information.

In the very near future, we should all be travelers on the global telecommunications highway, which will provide almost instantaneous access to electronic mail communications and to information in most libraries worldwide. We will each be able to customize the way we interact with that wealth of information. We will have interactive access to information, education, vocational, and recreational opportunities in whatever form we choose.

What we are describing is commonly being called the "information superhighway" or the "national information infrastructure." It will contain many elements we already recognize from our personal computers, telephone systems, and cable television—only the elements will be combined in new ways. The information superhighway presents unprecedented opportunities for all of us.

144

Computer
Resources
for People
with
Disabilities

The Right to Achieve Unrealistic Expectations

There has never been a better time for an individual with a disability to challenge all of the stereotypes and notions of "unrealistic" expectations existing in our culture. Not only do we have the right to envision and develop unrealistic expectations, but we have a right to achieve them. Numerous legislative mandates have affirmed the right of people with disabilities to access assistive technology and services to help support its use to increase independence and participation at home, school, work, recreation, and community environments. This includes off-the-shelf technologies, as well as technology that is customized or specifically developed for an individual's abilities and needs.

We have only scratched the surface of what we can do with the technology that exists right now, today. Technology will continue to develop at exponential rates, and people with disabilities have the right to access it and integrate it into all aspects of their lives, the right to realize their own expectations, and the right to develop new expectations. Technology is redefining human potential—and that means the potential of all of us, according to our individual hopes and dreams.

Your Action Is Required

There is much work to be done if we are to ensure that new technologies are being designed with access in mind. Perhaps you thought that buying this book was going to make your life easier, and hopefully it has in many respects. We hope it has also inspired you to take on a whole new set of challenges that may cancel out much of that easiness showing up in other areas. Access now—and access in the future—cannot occur without your diligent, active involvement in every area of your life. From education, employment, recreation, and communication, to living independently in the community, individuals and organizations who can make universal access a reality for all of us—one neighborhood at a time—and starting in *your* neighborhood.

Part II

The Technology Toolbox

Contents

Using the Technology Toolbox

Many people start their search for technology by asking questions—questions that often follow a similar pattern. The Technology Toolbox was created with a knowledge of these common questions, and it can help you develop your own route for navigating the technology solutions you will find. Rather than approaching the subject from a problem or disability perspective, the Technology Toolbox approaches it from the viewpoint of the significant task to be done and a person's ability to perform that task. This approach reflects our philosophy that it is not the person with the disability that has the problem, but the environment that is deficient for not appropriately accommodating the individual's needs.

The Technology Toolbox was designed to provide you with information and ideas so you can be a good consumer of technology and make well-informed decisions. We provide information but do not suggest that any one approach or tool is right for you. Only you can make that determination.

Charts

To use the charts, start by finding the **question** that most closely fits the key questions you are asking about the access you, your child, your student, or your client needs in order to use technology. If you have a number of issues to address, you will probably choose to employ more than one chart.

Next, locate the **ability** on the continuum, which runs from top to bottom, that most aptly describes your situation. When there are multiple choices in a column, each is keyed to a symbol (● ■ ▲◆☆○). In the next column, identify the **difficulty or difficulties** you feel you might encounter in attempting to use computer technology. Then read through the **approaches** to consider and the **tools** to explore that are marked with the same symbols in the next two columns.

For difficulties marked with ●, read the approaches marked with ● and the tools marked with ●. For difficulties marked with ■, read the approaches marked with ■ and the tools marked with ■. And so on.

Once you hit on a tool that bears further investigation, turn to the product description for that item to learn more (page numbers are in parentheses).

Product Descriptions

The product descriptions are intended to provide you with enough information to get a good feeling for the assistive technology product without going into complex technical details. You will get a sense of the range of available features and an understanding of why there may be a wide variation in cost—for example, because of differences in sound quality, speed, capacity, or user flexibility and friendliness.

Each product description lists related products that may also be useful. For more comprehensive information about specific assistive technology products, the following resources will be helpful. (See Part III for phone numbers and addresses.)

- Closing the Gap Annual Resource Directory

- Trace Resource Book: Assistive Technologies for Communication, Control and Computer Access, 1996–97 Edition.

- CO-NET, a CD-ROM containing the Cooperative Electronic Library on Disability. This CD, available from the Trace R&D Center, contains several databases on assistive technology products and vendors, service providers, and publications. It also contains copies of legislation and other relevant documents.

- ABLEDATA, a database containing information on the full range of assistive technology products. This database is included on the Trace CO-NET CD. You can also call the Trace R&D Center at (608) 263-1156 and they will search the database for specific information for you. Additionally, you can contact the National Rehabilitation Information Center (NARIC) at (800) 346-2742.

All the products in the Technology Toolbox meet the following criteria: they have been used successfully by people with disabilities; the manufacturer or the vendor generally offers customer support; and they run on either a Macintosh or an IBM-compatible system. The inclusion of a product is not an endorsement of its suitability for any one individual or situation. It is simply one product to consider in your search for solutions.

It is true that specific information on technology is often out of date before it is printed—an inevitability in a field that is changing so rapidly. Companies expand, reduce, and merge, often changing addresses, phone numbers, and sometimes even names. Although we can't include tomorrow's products, we have listed today's key vendors. Part III includes an alphabetical listing of all the vendors mentioned in the Technology Toolbox along with the most current information about them. Stay in touch with them; they will be putting new products on the market soon. In addition, more and more people around the country are specializing in keeping track of what is happening in the field. Find and befriend them. And happy exploring!

Ask Yourself…How Effectively Can I See the Computer Screen?

Ability	Difficulty	Approach	Tool
See the screen well	● Small text ▲ Small cursor ■ Screen glare	● Increase text size ▲ Increase cursor size ■ Reduce glare	● Software features: easy-to-read screens (158) ▲ Software features: optional cursors (162) ■ Monitor additions (228)
See the screen close up	● Monitor not close enough ■ Small monitor	● Modify position of monitor ■ Use large monitor ▲ Magnify screen	● ▲ Monitor additions (228) ■ Monitors ▲ Screen enlargement programs (226)
See large text and graphics	Small text and graphics	● Magnify screen ■ Large-print program ☆ Use speech output	● Screen enlargement programs (226) ● Monitor additions (228) ■ Software feature: easy-to-read screens (158) ☆ ■ Talking and large-print word processors (213) ☆ Screen readers (223) ☆ Speech synthesizers (220)
Use senses other than vision	Information is visual	◆ Use speech output ● Tactile output	◆ Screen readers (223) ◆ Speech synthesizers (220) ● Refreshable braille displays (218) ● Braille embossers, translators (216)

Ask Yourself... How Effectively Can I Use the Keyboard?

Ability	Difficulty	Approach	Tool
Use two hands	● Task is tiring ■ Typing goes slowly ☆ Keys too close together ▲ Keys too far apart	◆ Use physical supports ● Accelerate input ☆ Isolate keys ▲ Use small or programmable keyboard	◆ Arm and wrist supports (198) ■ Word prediction (202) ● ▲ Alternate keyboards (163) ● Abbreviation expansion and macros (200) ● Voice recognition (183) ☆ Keyboard additions (172)
Use one hand	◆ ● Must hit two keys at a time ■ ▲ Typing goes slowly ○ Keys too close together	◆ Latching keys ● ▲ Alternate keyboard layouts ■ Accelerate input ○ Isolate keys	◆ Access utilities (169) ● ▲ ■ Alternate keyboards (163) ■ Abbreviation expansion and macros (200) ■ Word prediction (202) ■ Voice recognition (183) ○ Keyboard additions (172)
Point	● ■ ☆ Limited use of hands ▲ Keys too close together ○ Typing goes slowly	● Larger keys ■ Point and type ○ Accelerate input ☆ Use on-screen keyboard with mouse alternative ▲ Isolate keys	○ ☆ ● Alternate keyboards (163) ☆ Trackballs (196) ■ Pointing and typing aids (190) ○ Voice recognition (183) ☆ Touch screens (192) ○ Abbreviation expansion and macros (200) ☆ Electronic pointing devices (188) ○ Word prediction (202) ▲ Keyboard additions (172)
One or more controllable movements	Physically accessing keyboard	◆ Use speech input ● Use switch input	◆ Voice recognition (183) ● Switches and switch software (175) ● Interface devices (179)

Ask Yourself...How Effectively Can I Use the Mouse?

Ability	Difficulty	Approach	Tool
Make hand movements	Relating the mouse to the screen	● Use direct selection ▲ Use mouse replacements	● ▲ Touch screens (192) ▲ Joysticks (194) ▲ Alternate keyboards (163)
Make some hand movements	◆ Fine motor dexterity ■ Gross motor dexterity	◆ Use gross movements ■ Use fine movements	◆ Alternate keyboards (163) ■ Trackballs (196) ■ Joysticks (194) ■ Access utilities (169)
Use other controllable movements	Manipulating mouse	☆ Use mouse replacements	☆ Pointing and typing aids (190) ☆ Electronic pointing devices (188) ☆ Switches and switch software (175) ☆ Interface devices (179) ☆ Joysticks (194)

TECHNOLOGY TOOLBOX

Ask Yourself...How Effectively Can I Interact with Information?

★ Ability	🔒 Difficulty	🔑 Approach	🔧 Tool
Interact with auditory support	Written instructions, directions, or prompts	● Use programs with verbal instructions, directions, and prompts	● Speech synthesizers (220) ● Software features: auditory cues (160) ● Talking and large print word processors (213)
Interact with written support	Verbal instructions, directions, or prompts	◆ Use programs with written instructions, directions, and prompts	◆ Software features: visual cues (161) ◆ Operating system
Understand information	▲ ● Maintaining attention ■ Inaccessible format	● Use motivating and interesting approaches ▲ Simplify methods of input ■ Create accessible format	▲ Talking and large-print word processors (213) ● Speech synthesizers (220) ▲ Joysticks (194) ▲ Touch screens (192) ● Software features: interactive ▲ Software features: easy-to-read screens, instructional choices (158, 159) ▲ Alternate keyboards (163) ■ Optical character recognition, scanners (186)
Interact with limited information	Excessive or overwhelming information	◆ Limit information presented ● Use graphics ■ Provide fewer keys	◆ Software features: instructional choices (159) ● Software features: graphics (159) ■ Alternate keyboards (163)
Interact with some of the environment	Understanding cause and effect	▲ Train in cause/effect skills	▲ Switches and switch software (175) ▲ Touch screens (192) ▲ Alternate keyboards (163)

Ask Yourself...How Effectively Can I Read (Comprehend)?

★ Ability	🔒 Difficulty	🔑 Approach	🔧 Tool
Read at a lower than expected level	Reading at expected level	● Have computer speak text ■ Isolate text into manageable chunks ☆ Transfer print materials to computer ◆ Train in reading comprehension	● Speech synthesizers (220) ● Talking and large-print word processors (213) ■ Software features: easy-to-read screens (158) ☆ Optical character recognition and scanners (186) ◆ Reading comprehension programs (204)
Comprehend single sentences	Too many words at a time	● Have computer speak text ■ Isolate text into manageable chunks ☆ Transfer print materials to computer ▲ Train in reading comprehension ◆ Support reading with graphics	● Speech synthesizers (220) ● Talking and large-print word processors (213) ■ Software features: easy-to-read screens (158) ☆ Optical character recognition and scanners (186) ▲ Reading comprehension programs (204) ◆ Software features: graphics (159)
Comprehend single words	Decoding	■ Practice letter recognition ☆ Practice letter-sound recognition	■ Reading comprehension programs (204) ☆ Alternate keyboards (163) ☆ Speech synthesizers (220)
Comprehend the meaning of symbols	Understanding words	◆ Use graphic symbols ● Have computer speak text	◆ Reading comprehension programs (204) ◆ Software features: graphics (159) ◆ Alternate keyboards (163) ● Speech synthesizers (220) ● Talking and large-print word processors (213) ● Software features: auditory cues (160)

TECHNOLOGY TOOLBOX

Ask Yourself...How Effectively Can I Write (Compose)?

★ Ability	🔒 Difficulty	🔑 Approach	🔧 Tool
Write at a lower than expected level	◆ Organizational skills ■ Writing ideas	◆ Train in Composition	◆ ■ Writing composition programs (207)
Compose single sentences	◆ Vocabulary ● Grammar/syntax ▲ Spelling ■ Writing ideas	◆ Support vocabulary ● Support grammar ▲ Support spelling ■ Train in composition	◆ Electronic reference tools (209) ◆ ● ▲ Word prediction (202) ◆ ● ▲ Software features: built-in utilities (161) ■ Writing composition programs (207)
Combine words and phrases	Communicating meaning	● Train in composition ■ Enter whole words and phrases	● Writing composition programs (207) ■ Alternate keyboards (163)
Use alternative to writing	Communicating meaning	◆ Use graphics with voice output ● Speak sentences to computer	◆ Software features: custom programs, graphics (162, 159) ◆ Alternate keyboards (163) ◆ Speech synthesizers (220) ● Voice recognition (183)

Ask Yourself . . . How Effectively Can I Handle Computer Equipment?

★ Ability	🔒 Difficulty	🔑 Approach	🔧 Tool
Can understand how to handle equipment	● ■ ◆ Physical manipulation ▲ ○ Reading print materials and manuals	● Create access to disks ■ Create access to system ◆ Create access to printer ▲ Request accessible format ○ Create accessible format	● Hard disk drives ■ Environmental control units (237) ◆ Printers ○ Braille embossers, translators (216) ▲ Software features: friendly documentation (160) ○ Screen readers (223) ○ Speech synthesizers (220) ○ Reading machines (241) ○ Optical character recognition and scanners (186)
Can physically handle equipment	Comprehending task	◆ Simplify entry to programs and files ● Simplify disk operation ■ Simplify on/off	◆ Operating system ● Hard disk drives ■ Menu management programs (211)

TECHNOLOGY TOOLBOX

Software Features

The following features, incorporated into many software programs, may be helpful to someone who needs support to access a computer. You may want to keep these features in mind when you explore and compare software.

☑ Easy-to-Read Screens

Screens that are easy to read and understand can make a critical difference for many users. Clear, uncluttered screens may reduce distraction. Features to consider are simple and legible text, and menu items that are represented with both graphics and text, with options for large characters. It is important for some users that the style, font, or spacing of text can be altered. Many programs allow for these types of adjustments.

If voice-synthesis software will be used, programs that place text in one column, rather than in multiple columns, can be read more easily. Multiple columns or boxes of text are very difficult for screen-reading software to interpret. Similarly, asterisks or other non-alphabetical characters used for decoration make it more difficult to use a screen reader. (The user would hear "asterisk, asterisk, asterisk" or "dash, dash, dash.")

☑ Consistency

Consistent placement of menus and objects on the screen makes using a program much more intuitive and predictable. A consistent layout provides easier navigation for users of screen enlargement programs, because they know where to look for things. Consistency supports the use of devices that employ "markers," which identify fixed locations on the screen where particular menus or objects are found. These locations are "marked," and the cursor jumps to the mark when a switch or key is pressed. Also important for consistency are objects and menus that respond dependably throughout the program.

☑ Intuitive Characteristics

An intuitive program makes users feel that they already know how to navigate its features. Clear and obvious options, presented as they are needed, can make a user feel comfortable right from the beginning.

Some programs alter the material presented based on the progress of the user. An example of this is an educational drill or game that automatically advances to the next level of difficulty after a certain number of correct answers. Another example is a grammar-checking program that reacts to particular aspects of word usage, such as frequency and word length, by giving feedback to the user. An intuitive program will let the user make a choice and make the consequences clear and simple.

☑ Logical Labels

Programs generally present the user with a series of choices, either in a list or a menu. These choices should be labeled with logical, understandable names that give the user a reasonable sense of what will happen when a specific choice is made. This is particularly important when the user is dependent on auditory cues, such as someone using a screen-reader program.

☑ Instructional Choices

Instructional software programs generally allow parents or teachers to control content and lesson presentation. The difficulty level, vocabulary, sound, timing, speed, and amount of graphics and text presented can often be adjusted. Some programs of this type keep track of the student's record or progress. Some instructional programs allow parents or teachers to personalize content, such as spelling lists, vocabulary lists, and math problems.

☑ Graphics

Graphics can be used to encourage interaction or to convey information in interesting and motivating ways. Graphics or icons may be used as

160

Computer
Resources
for People
with
Disabilities

alternatives to words or commands, providing access to nonreaders. Some programs use cues that involve color (for example, "find the red sock") and therefore require a color monitor for optimal use. Other programs allow you to import or scan in graphics, such as a picture of your dog, to add personal content. Graphics can play a role in supporting reading.

☑ Friendly Documentation

Easy-to-understand software manuals can be important. Many include easy-to-follow diagrams and illustrations of what should be on the screen. Some manuals are available in large print, in braille, on audiocassette, on computer disk, or in a print layout that is easy to use with a scanner or reading machine. Remember that well-written software is often intuitive and the documentation is needed only for occasional reference.

☑ On-Screen Instructions

Some programs provide on-screen instructions—in the form of help lines, help balloons, or help windows—and instructional prompts to guide the user through the program. It is best if the user has control over how long these instructions remain on the screen.

☑ Auditory Cues

The form of prompts and instructions—verbal, written, or animated—is often critical to making a program accessible and, for some people, easier to understand. Some programs are written to offer verbal prompts or instructions that use synthetic (robotic) speech and might require a speech synthesizer. Others use digitized recorded speech, sounds, or music and might require a sound card. At times both sound and visual indicators are used simultaneously and are noticeable even when one's full attention is not on the screen. Some programs use auditory prompts or signals to get the user's attention, which can be helpful for users whose attention can wander quickly from the computer program.

☑ Visual Cues

Some programs use visual prompts at different times during program operation to assist the user in understanding the task. When visual cues accompany auditory cues, more complete access to the program is provided. This can be important to people who do not benefit from auditory cues.

Prompted writing is a feature that allows a facilitator to guide the writer in creating sentences or stories by providing step-by-step written instructions that appear in a box on the screen. These directions usually don't print out as part of the written assignment, and are invisible to the person who reads the final product.

Note: If a screen-enlargement program is being used, it might be that these prompts or windows are not visible to a user who is focused on another part of the screen.

☑ Built-in Access Methods

Some programs have built-in alternative access methods and allow you to select the option you want. You can choose to have the program accept input from alternative devices—such as a single switch, alternate keyboard, joystick, touch screen, or game controller—in lieu of the standard keyboard and mouse. Some programs change the presentation of the program to match the requirements of the device. For example, if "single switch" were selected, the program might change from a point-and-click selection method to one that scans the available choices.

☑ Built-in Utilities

Many conventional software programs, such as word processors, spreadsheets, and databases come with utilities as part of their package. These utilities may include spell checkers, dictionaries with options for user dictionaries, a thesaurus, macros, abbreviation expansion capabilities, and grammar tips. Some programs also come with text-to-speech options in the menu. Having these utilities built into the software program eliminates the need to run multiple programs simultaneously. This helps to reduce system conflicts and makes it easier to navigate between features.

☑ Alternatives to a Mouse

Some programs are designed to be used primarily with a mouse or joystick. Some software packages allow the user to navigate and operate the program through the keyboard and avoid the use of a mouse. This is accomplished by using the arrow (or cursor) keys, and by making menu choices by pressing a specific combination of keys (keyboard equivalents) that activate the desired function. Accessing items in tool palettes—commonly found in draw programs and paint programs—can also be done through the keyboard. Be aware that some programs provide a way to operate only certain parts of the program by keyboard and require a mouse to do the rest. Some programs are designed to be used primarily with a mouse or joystick.

☑ Optional Cursors

A cursor is the pointer or marker—typically a small flashing square, two cross-hairs, an I-beam, or an arrow—that indicates where you are on the screen. Cursors take a variety of forms. A number of software programs allow the user to adjust what the cursor looks like. The options might include a larger arrow, a thicker I-beam, a hand, a pointed finger, a pencil, or thick cross-hairs.

☑ Creation of Custom Programs

Authoring programs, such as HyperCard (Claris Corporation) for the Macintosh, and LinkWay (IBM Corporation) for IBM and IBM-compatible computers, allows users to build their own tutorials, drill and practice software, communication boards, instructional aids, informational resources, and other styles of software. A wide range of users—from students to business professionals—can create programs of their own using authoring software. Most authoring programs allow you to work with graphics, text, sounds, and often video. The more customized and sophisticated you want your program to be, the more knowledge you will need of the program language and tools.

Product Descriptions: Alternate Input

Alternate Keyboards

Alternate keyboards offer a variety of ways to provide input to a computer through various options in size, layout, and complexity.

Programmable keyboards are versatile and often can be programmed so letters, numbers, words, or phrases can be entered by pressing custom keys. They can be larger in size than a standard keyboard, allowing for a larger target area. Smaller keys can also be set up so less range of motion is required. Overlays are used to define the customized keyboard layout.

Miniature keyboards are designed with keys spaced close together to allow someone with a small range of motion to access all the keys. They are typically lightweight and small in size.

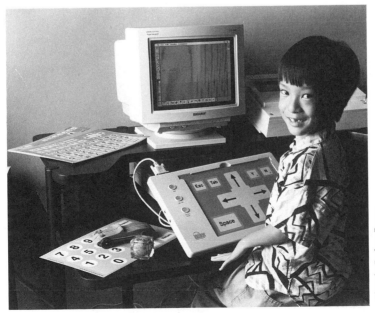

Photo by Barbara Brown

Alternate keyboards, such as IntelliKeys, can be customized to match the needs of any software program (IntelliTools)

164

Computer
Resources
for People
with
Disabilities

Chording keyboards generally have a limited number of keys. Text is entered by pressing combinations of keys. The keys are sometimes programmable so certain combinations will enter custom words or phrases.

On-screen keyboards are software images of a standard or modified keyboard placed on the computer screen by software. The keys are selected by a mouse, touch screen, trackball, joystick, switch, or electronic pointing device.

 Use this tool to...

Simplify the method of entering information

Create keyboards using pictures instead of words or letters

Create keyboards using tactile materials instead of words or letters

Type with words and phrases instead of letters

Access communication boards

Communicate meaning through graphics, photographs, or objects

Practice letter-sound recognition

Learn the meaning of words through graphics, photographs, or objects

Limit the number of keys to the specific ones required to do the task

Enter information using a switch with an on-screen keyboard

Replace the mouse

Enter information by head movement with an electronic pointing device and an on-screen keyboard

Enter information using a mouse or mouse alternative with an on-screen keyboard

Provide easy-to-use, motivating activities

 Potential users...

Interact with limited information and benefit from structured choices

Use two hands but the task is tiring

Use two hands but the keys are too far apart

Use one hand but type slowly

*ScreenDoors will replace your physical keyboard with one
that is on-screen (Madenta Communications, Inc.)*

Combine words and phrases rather than letters to communicate meaning

Use alternate methods of writing, through symbols and speech

Have limited fine motor skills

Point, but the task is designed for full use of hands

Need to operate a computer without the use of their hands

Comprehend single words but require help with decoding

Communicate through language-based symbols or graphics

Comprehend the meaning of graphic symbols rather than letters

Have limited gross motor skills

See keys that have higher visual contrast

Have visual impairments that limit the ability to discriminate keys

Features to consider

Some can be customized for different key sizes and arrangements

Some need software that translates the keyboard functions to the computer

Some have an internal computer interface, others require an external one

166

Computer
Resources
for People
with
Disabilities

Some allow the standard keyboard and the alternate keyboard to be used at the same time

Some require less pressure to activate a key

Some on-screen keyboards come with dictionaries or word prediction programs

Some replace mouse and keyboard

Some replace keyboard only

Some can customize the color contrast between the keys and the background

Some can be used to create a series of keyboard layouts by making overlays

 Cost

Programmable Keyboards

Range: $250–1,700
Common: $300–500

Miniature Keyboards

Range: $400–800
Common: 450

Chording Keyboards

Range: $250–650
Common: $300

On-Screen Keyboards

Range: $100–1200
Common: $350–800

 Common vendors

Programmable Keyboards

Don Johnston, Inc.

Dunamis, Inc.

EKEG Electronics Company, Ltd.

Exceptional Computing, Inc.

Hach Associates

Handykey Corporation

IntelliTools

Sunburst Communications

TASH International, Inc.

Zygo Industries, Inc.

Miniature Keyboards

EKEG Electronics Company

In Touch Systems

TASH International, Inc.

Chording Keyboards

Infogrip, Inc.

TASH International, Inc.

Photo courtesy of TASH International, Inc.

*Small-size keys, such as on this mini keyboard, ensure that
a small range of motion allows full access to the keyboard
(TASH International, Inc.)*

168

Computer
Resources
for People
with
Disabilities

On-Screen Keyboards

Don Johnston, Inc.

Gus Communications

Innovation Management Group, Inc.

Madenta Communications

Mayer-Johnson Company

McIntyre Computer Systems Division

Prentke Romich Company

R. J. Cooper and Associates

Words+, Inc.

World Communications

Additional information

The layout and key size of the standard keyboard is not always the best choice for access. Alternate keyboards provide different means of accessing a computer. Some alternate keyboards can be modified and the layouts customized for individual use. Paper or plastic overlays fit on top of the keyboard and are used to designate where to press on the keyboard for a desired keystroke or customized response. The areas to be pressed can be defined by letters, numbers, punctuation, words, pictures, tactile materials, or objects. Many innovative teaching strategies can be implemented using an alternate keyboard.

Chording keyboards often come with a tutorial for learning chord combinations and a quick reference chart of chord combinations. The hand size the device accommodates may be limited (for example, some are sized for an adult male hand only). The number of keys varies among devices (12 finger and 6 thumb, 10 finger and 4 thumb, etc.). Software may allow reconfiguration of the chords. Additional software utilities—such as abbreviation expansion programs—can be used with a chording keyboard to increase typing speed by reducing keystrokes. Braille note-takers are another chording device.

On-screen keyboards may have built-in scanning options to be used with a single switch.

Related products

Arm and Wrist Supports

Joysticks

Keyboard Additions

Electronic Pointing Devices

Pointing and Typing Aids

Speech Synthesizers

Talking and Large-Print Word Processors

Touch Screens

Trackballs

Switches and Switch Software

Access Utilities

Access utilities are software programs that modify various aspects of the standard keyboard to simplify operation of the keyboard, replace the mouse, substitute visual cues for sound signals, or add sound cues to keystrokes.

 Use this tool to...

Increase speed when using a pointing aid or typing device

Change the layout of the keyboard

Limit the entering of unwanted keys

Provide other indicators (visual or auditory) when some key functions are on or off

Eliminate the need to press more than one key at a time

 Potential users...

Use one finger and a pointing aid, and need to increase speed or reduce the number of keystrokes required

170

———

Computer
Resources
for People
with
Disabilities

Have better gross motor dexterity than fine motor dexterity

Use one hand but the task requires pressing two keys at a time

Strike keys by mistake because of tremors

Require visual notification of computer alert sounds

 Features to consider

Some allow access to menus through function keys or combinations of key strokes

Some eliminate the need to press two keys at a time

Some can adjust the key repeat rate

Some can adjust the time required to hold a key down before it is entered

Some prevent the keyboard from accepting two quick presses of the same key (repeat defeat)

Some let the user replace the mouse and use the number pad on the keyboard to control cursor movements

Some indicate if keys such as Num Lock, Scroll Lock, and Caps Lock are on or off

Some replace computer sounds with visual indicators

Some allow the user to redefine the keyboard to create other layouts

 Cost

Range: free–$1,200
Common: $150

 Common vendors

Apple Computer, Inc.

Gus Communications

IBM Special Needs Systems

IntelliTools

Kinetic Designs, Inc.

The Matias Corporation

Microsoft Corporation

Microsystems Software, Inc.

Now Software, Inc.

Words+, Inc.

World Communications

 Additional information

Macintosh: The system software for Macintosh computers comes with an application program called Easy Access that has many modification features. The Control Panel also offers a variety of keyboard adjustments, depending on the version of the system software that you are using. Check your Macintosh user's manual for more information.

IBM and IBM-compatible: Basic keyboard modification programs are available for both MS-DOS (AccessDOS) and Windows (Access Pack for Windows). AccessDOS is available free from IBM by calling (800) 426-7282 and ordering Part #83G7828. Access Pack for Windows 3.0 and 3.1 is available from Microsoft and can be ordered by calling (800) 426-9400. AccessDOS and Access Pack for Windows 3.0 and 3.1 can also be ordered directly from the Trace Center by calling (608) 262-6966 (voice) and (608) 263-5408 (TTY).

Windows 95 offers a number of accessibility options that are built into the software itself. For more information about these features and Access Pack you can visit the "Accessibility Support" page at Microsoft's world wide web site (http://www.microsoft.com/windows/enable/default.htm).

AccessDOS can be downloaded from the Trace Center web site (http://www.trace.wisc.edu/comp_access/dos). Access Pack for Windows can also be downloaded from Trace (http://www.trace.wisc.edu/comp_access/win), as well as other online bulletin boards and services.

 Related products

Abbreviation Expansion and Macro Programs

Keyboard Additions

Joysticks

172

Computer
Resources
for People
with
Disabilities

Pointing and Typing Aids

Trackballs

Word Prediction

Keyboard Additions

A variety of accessories have been designed to make keyboards more accessible.

Keyguards are hard plastic covers with holes for each key. Using a keyguard, someone with an unsteady finger or with a pointing device can avoid striking unwanted keys.

Moisture guards are thin sheets of plastic that protect keyboards from spills and drooling.

Alternate labels add visual clarity or tactile information to the keys.

 Use this tool to...

Keyguards

Increase accuracy

Maintain correct placement of hand while typing

Moisture Guards

Protect from spills and other moisture

Alternate Labels

Provide cues for frequently used keys

Increase color contrast on the tops of the keys

 Potential users...

Need more separation between the keys

Benefit from visual or tactile enhancement of the keyboard

Benefit from guarding keys from accidental pressing

Photo courtesy of IBM, Inc.

A keyguard helps to isolate keys, making each target easier to find (IBM, Inc.)

 Features to consider

Keyguards must match the specific keyboard layout

Moisture guards must match the specific keyboard layout

Some labels add color to specific keys

Some labels add tactile cues to the keys

Some labels enlarge the name or include the function of specific keys

 Cost

Keyguards

Range: $50–150
Common: $80

Moisture Guards

Range: $25
Common: $25

Alternate Labels

Range: $5–20
Common: $10

174

Computer
Resources
for People
with
Disabilities

 Common vendors

Keyguards

Don Johnston, Inc.

IBM Special Needs Systems

IntelliTools

Prentke Romich Company

REACH Inc.

TASH International, Inc.

Tech-Able

Toys for Special Children, Inc.

Words+, Inc.

Moisture Guards

Moisture guards are commonly available. Vendors include:

Don Johnston, Inc.

Global Computer Supplies

Hooleon Corporation

International Datawares, Inc.

Span-America Medical Systems, Inc.

Labels

Carolyn's Products for Enhanced Living

Data Cal Corporation

Hooleon Corporation

 Additional information

Keyguards are available for many of the alternate keyboards. Many sta-
tionery stores carry printed labels that can be put on keys to enlarge letters and numbers or to increase the color contrast.

Related products

Access Utilites

Alternate Keyboards

Arm and Wrist Supports

Monitor Additions

Pointing and Typing Aids

Talking and Large-Print Word Processors

Switches and Switch Software

Switches offer ways to provide input to a computer when a more direct access method, like a standard keyboard or mouse, is not possible. Switches come in various sizes, shapes, colors, methods of activation, and placement options. An interface device and software must be used to connect the switch to the computer and interpret the operation of the switch.

Some software programs have been developed specifically for use with a switch and can employ on-screen scanning. With on-screen scanning the computer highlights (either by sound, visual cue, or both) options available to a user about what action they want the computer to take. Using these specialized products, when a visual or auditory prompt indicates a desired keyboard or mouse function, the user activates the switch and the desired function occurs.

Other programs have built-in options to allow switch use. Many standard software programs can be accessed through a switch with the use of additional software and devices.

Use this tool to...

Enter text or data when using the keyboard is not feasible

Interact with the computer by selecting choices as they are highlighted

Set up a series of responses using multiple switches

Train in cause-and-effect

Facilitate choice-making

176

Computer
Resources
for People
with
Disabilities

Photo courtesy of TASH International, Inc.

*Single switches come in a wide range of sizes and
shapes, and allow you to do anything on the computer
that anyone else can do with one touch of the switch
(TASH International, Inc.)*

 Potential users...

Need to operate a computer without enough dexterity to accurately
activate all keys needed

Need to operate a computer with one or two movements

Benefit from structured interaction with the environment

 Features to consider

Most can be mounted and activated by any part of the body

Some are sensitive to light touch

Some are activated by pressure (the pressure required may vary from
switch to switch)

Some are activated by sound

Some are activated by interrupting a light beam

Some can be fastened to any part of the body

Some are activated by pulling

Some are activated by squeezing

Some are activated when bent

Some are available in different sizes and colors

Some are activated by the blink of an eye

 Cost

Range: $30–400
Common: $40–65

 Common vendors

Switches

Ability Research

AbleNet, Inc.

Adaptivation

Adaptive Devices Group

Brown & Company, Inc.

Creative Switch Industries

Don Johnston, Inc.

DU-IT Control Systems Group, Inc.

Exceptional Computing, Inc.

Hach Associates

Innocomp

KY Enterprises/Custom Computer Solutions

Luminaud, Inc.

Med Labs Inc.

ORCCA Technology

Prentke Romich Company

TASH International, Inc.

Toys for Special Children, Inc.

Zygo Industries, Inc.

178

Computer
Resources
for People
with
Disabilities

Switch Software

Academic Software, Inc.

Colorado Easter Seal Society, Inc.

Computers to Help People, Inc.

Consultants for Communication Technology

Don Johnston, Inc.

Edmark Corporation

Gus Communications

Institute on Applied Technology

IntelliTools

KidTECH

Laureate Learning Systems, Inc.

Madenta Communications

MarbleSoft

Mayer-Johnson Company

Microsystems Software, Inc.

NanoPac, Inc.

Prentke Romich Company

R. J. Cooper and Associates

Simtech Publications

Switch In Time

Switch Kids

Synergy

Technology for Language and Learning

UCLA Intervention Program for Young Handicapped Children (UCLA/LAUSD)

Visuaide 2000, Inc.

Words+, Inc.

World Communications

Additional information

Switches can operate environmental controls, radios, appliances, battery-operated toys, and augmentative and alternative communication devices, and can control powered mobility. A switch and switch interface will operate programs designed for single-switch input. Some programs that require a single input (mouse click, space bar, return key, etc.) may also work with a switch interface. For access to the entire keyboard and most commercial programs, additional software and hardware is required.

Switches can be custom made. *Utilizing Switch Interfaces with Children Who Are Severely Physically Challenged* contains useful information on this topic (see Part III, Books, for reference).

 Related products

Interface Devices

Joysticks

Interface Devices

Interface devices provide access to the alpha/numeric keyboard, the keyboard functions, and sometimes the mouse controls by enabling the use of single switches, alternate keyboards, or other input devices.

Switch interfaces are used to connect the switch to the computer and are used with software written for single switch use.

Multiple-switch interfaces are used to connect a series of switches to the computer. Each switch can be defined as a character, word, phrase, or action.

Multiple-input interfaces are used to connect switches, alternate keyboards, and other input devices to the computer. Software is often included that interprets the information from these devices to the computer. These devices can allow the user to operate software with a switch even though it was not originally written for switch use.

When switches are used, the choices of letters, numbers, or pictures are displayed and sequentially highlighted on the screen. When the high-

180

Computer
Resources
for People
with
Disabilities

Photo courtesy of WesTest Corporation

Darci Too, an interface device, lets you control a wide range of computers using switches, joysticks, video-game controllers, and expanded keyboards (WesTest Engineering Corporation)

light indicates the desired choice, the user activates the switch, which enters the choice into the computer. This selection process is called *scanning.*

 Use this tool to...

Enter text or data when the keyboard is not feasible

Design customized keyboards to simplify activities

Make communication boards that can be accessed by a switch or alternate keyboard.

Set up a series of responses or keyboard functions, one for each switch, using multiple switches

Enter text by sending Morse code through one or two switches

Use standard software programs by a switch-and-scanning method

Connect a switch, and use software with built-in scanning options

 Potential users...

Need to operate a computer without the use of their hands

Use switches, alternate keyboards, or directional joysticks to operate a computer

Need to operate a computer with one or two movements

Features to consider

Most have control of the rate at which the selections are highlighted when using scanning

Some keyboard interfaces operate with any software program

Most can work while the standard keyboard and mouse remain active

Some can use pictures or graphics, instead of text, to indicate choices

Some show the highlighted choices on the computer screen

Some show the highlighted choices through a built-in display on the interface device

Some can replace the mouse

Some allow a variety of methods for selecting the choice (for example, the choice is made when switch is pressed versus when it is released)

Some can interpret Morse code

Some can work with a speech synthesizer for auditory prompts to indicate choices

Some have built-in word prediction capabilities

 Cost

Switch Interfaces

Range: $75–500
Common: $125

Multiple-Switch Interfaces

Range: $75–150
Common: $100

Multiple-Input Interfaces

Range: $400–1,000
Common: $500–800

182

Computer
Resources
for People
with
Disabilities

Common vendors

Switch Interfaces

AbleNet, Inc.

Adaptive Devices Group

BEST

Brown & Company, Inc.

Consultants for Communication Technology

Don Johnston, Inc.

Gus Communications

Hach Associates

R. J. Cooper and Associates

Multiple-Switch Interfaces

AbleNet, Inc.

Don Johnston, Inc.

Multiple-Input Interfaces

Don Johnston, Inc.

TASH International, Inc.

WesTest Engineering Corporation

Words+, Inc.

Additional information

Some software programs have built-in scanning. All that is needed is a simple switch interface to connect the switch to the computer.

Some standard software programs can be operated by a switch. This requires an interface device that connects the switch to the computer and has software that creates the choices and interprets the switch activation.

Morse code can be used to enter text into the computer by using switches. One, two, or three switches may be used depending on the needs of the user. This requires an interface device that connects the switch to the computer and has software that interprets the code.

IBM and IBM-compatible: Carefully select software for the on-screen display to make sure it is compatible with other programs and your operating system, especially if you are using Windows. Hardware solutions have the advantage of being independent of software compatibility problems, but may require the user to visually attend both to the computer screen and to a separate scanning device.

 Related products

Abbreviation Expansion and Macros

Alternate Keyboards

Joysticks

Speech Synthesizers

Switches and Switch Software

Word Prediction

Voice Recognition

A voice-recognition system allows the user to input data and/or control computer functions by voice.

 Use this tool to...

Input text or data by voice

Navigate among files, applications, and menus by voice

Execute standard commands by voice

Learn to write by speaking ideas and meanings into a word processor

 Potential users...

Make one or more controllable movements but have physical difficulty using the keyboard

Use dictation to avoid repetitive-stress syndrome

184

Computer
Resources
for People
with
Disabilities

*With voice-recognition systems you can be
a computer user by talking instead of typing (IBM Corporation)*

Use dictation as the method of typing instead of a keyboard

 Features to consider

Most must be trained to respond to a particular voice

Most require the user's speech to be consistent

Most will require the user to pause slightly between words

Most allow the user to navigate the computer (control the cursor, execute commands)

Some are full dictation systems

Some have very limited vocabularies

Some have larger vocabularies and provide a wider range of navigation or dictation capabilities

Some have vocabularies (journalism, medical, engineering) specific to a vocational field

Some dictation systems can recognize phrases that the user uses fre-quently

Some can recognize a wide range of voices and do not require training

Some computers have voice navigation built into the system.

 Cost

Navigation Products

Range: $300–400
Common: $350

Dictation Products

Range: $600–$13,000
Common: $1,000

 Common vendors

Apple Computer, Inc.

Articulate Systems, Inc.

Dragon Systems

IBM Special Needs Systems

Kurzweil Applied Intelligence

Microsoft Corporation

NanoPac, Inc.

Voice Communications

 Additional information

Navigation programs recognize commands such as "Open file" but are not specifically designed to dictate text; this requires a dictation pro-gram. There are products available that do both.

Macintosh: Apple Plain Talk, a navigation program, is an extension of System 7.1. To do dictation, you need a product that will enable both dictation and navigation.

IBM and IBM-compatible: With Windows, a program specifically designed to allow navigation in that environment is required. Several

186

Computer
Resources
for People
with
Disabilities

voice-recognition products require the appropriate IBM M-Audio Capture (M-ACPA), an expansion slot for the M-ACPA card, and an AT or Micro Channel bus.

 Related products

Environmental Controls

Optical Character Recognition and Scanners

Optical Character Recognition and Scanners

Optical-character-recognition (OCR) software works with a scanner to convert images from a printed page into a standard computer file.

A scanner is a device that converts an image from a printed page to a computer file. Optical-character-recognition (OCR) software makes the resulting computer file capable of being edited. Pictures and photographs do not require OCR software to be manipulated.

 Use this tool to...

Transfer a printed worksheet to the computer so it can be accessed by assistive devices

Transfer printed documents so they can be read aloud by a speech synthesizer, printed in large text, or embossed in braille

Transfer printed materials to the computer to change text size, style, and layout

Scan family photographs to include in stories or create personal overlays for alternate keyboards

 Potential users...

Physically can handle the equipment but cannot read printed manuals or documents

May read at a lower level than their potential

Need materials in an accessible format to complete an activity

Features to consider

All OCR programs translate text from print form to a text file on the computer, which can be edited

Most OCR programs adjust for scanning single or multiple pages

Most OCR programs have light adjustment

Most OCR programs can be set for a specific adjustment for page orientation (portrait or landscape)

Some OCR programs can be set to scan a whole page or selected portions of a page

All scanners have utility programs that allow the scanner to communicate with the computer and save the scanned image as a graphic file on the computer

Most scanners store images in shades of gray (called gray-scale images)

Some scanners are capable of detecting colors

Hand-held scanners can scan small portions of text at a time

Flat-bed scanners can scan full-size pieces of paper at a time

Some scanners require the installation of an interface board to the computer

 Cost

OCR Programs

Range: $300–700
Common: $600

Scanners

Range: $300–2,000
Common: $1,500

 Common vendors

Optical Character Recognition and Scanners are commonly available

188

Computer
Resources
for People
with
Disabilities

 Additional information

OCR software is invaluable in converting materials from print to electronic formats. The OCR software translates the images into text by comparing the scanned-in materials against a table of letters, numbers, and symbols, and makes a best guess as to what each character is. The resulting file can then be altered like any file.

Scanners come in two varieties: flatbed and hand-held. Flatbed scanners look very much like desktop copiers. Hand-held scanners are easily held in the hand. Flatbed scanners are great for scanning full-sized images and multiple pages at high resolutions (the amount of detail that a scanner can perceive), but cost quite a bit more than the hand-held variety. Scanners (and accompanying software) are available to run on both Macintosh and IBM platforms. Most scanner software does not distinguish between pictures and text. To the scanner everything is just an image. To edit text that has been scanned, the user must also have OCR software.

Copyright laws must be respected when scanning printed material.

 Related products

Reading Machines

Screen Readers

Electronic Pointing Devices

Electronic pointing devices allow the user to operate the cursor on the screen using ultrasound or an infrared beam.

 Use this tool to...

Enter text or data into a computer when a mouse and keyboard are not feasible

Operate a draw program or a computer-aided design program

 Potential users...

Need to operate a computer without the use of their hands

Have good head control

 Features to consider

Some require activating a switch to make a selection

Some allow the user to pause or dwell on a key to select it

All work with an on-screen keyboard

Some allow the user to control the cursor by head motions

Some have wires connecting them to the computer; others operate remotely

 Cost

Range: $1,000–2,000
Common: $1,000

 Common vendors

Ability Research

Innocomp

The HeadMaster provides full mouse control for people who are unable to use their hands but have good head control (Prentke Romich Company)

190

Computer
Resources
for People
with
Disabilities

Madenta Communications

Origin Instruments Corporation

Prentke Romich Company

Words+, Inc.

 Additional information

Once the cursor has been placed in the desired location, the user can make a selection by dwelling in that location or using one of a variety of switches. The pointer will work with any on-screen keyboard compatible with the computer system.

 Related products

Alternate Keyboards

Switches and Switch Software

Pointing and Typing Aids

A pointing or typing aid is typically a wand or stick used to strike keys on the keyboard. They are most commonly worn on the head, held in the mouth, strapped to the chin, or held in the hand.

 Use this tool to...

Enter text or data using a standard or alternate keyboard

Operate a trackball, touch screen, or alternate keyboard

 Potential users...

Need to operate a computer without the use of their hands

Need to point with a single digit

 Features to consider

All can be used with keyguards

All can be used with standard, alternate, or modified keyboards

Most are adjustable in length and fit

Some have an adjustable headstrap to be worn on the head or across the chin

Some have a bite plate to be held in the mouth

Some are used with a splint on the hand or arm

 Cost

Range: $25–600
Common: $60

 Common vendors

Adlib, Inc.

Crestwood Company

Extensions for Independence

Photo courtesy of Madenta

*Bill Miller shows how Tracker can be used to help him in
his career as a graphic designer*

192

Computer
Resources
for People
with
Disabilities

Fred Sammons, Inc.

Maddak, Inc.

North Coast Medical, Inc.

 Related products

Alternate Keyboards

Access Utilities

Touch Screens

Trackballs

Touch Screens

A touch screen is a device placed on the computer monitor (or built into it) that allows direct selection or activation of the computer by a touch of the screen.

Use this tool to...

Build cause-and-effect skills

Motivate computer use

Enter text or data using an on-screen keyboard

Make a direct selection by pointing at the screen

Potential users...

Need a more direct method of moving the cursor on the screen

Interact well with information but need a simpler method of input

Interact well with information but require interesting and motivating approaches

Interact with environment with a closer connection between cause and effect

Features to consider

All allow direct selection of items on the screen by touching a monitor

All take the place of the mouse

Some are integrated into the monitor

Some are detachable from the monitor

Some require software specifically written to work with the touch screen

Some can be used with an on-screen keyboard

 Cost

Range: $200–5,000
Common: $350–2,000

 Common vendors

Edmark Corporation

Gus Communications

Information Strategies Incorporated

Keytec

Microtouch Systems, Inc.

Troll Touch

 Additional information

Touch sensitive screens may be used to move a cursor, imitate a mouse, or make selections. The touch screen may be used as one large single switch with some switch software. Some users point and type on an on-screen keyboard using a touch screen to provide a direct cognitive connection between the keys and the screen. The mouse and keyboard may still be used while the touch screen is active.

Touch screens are effective with young children, or people whose skills are at a lower functional level, when the software has simple point-and-click options.

194

———

Computer
Resources
for People
with
Disabilities

Macintosh: The detachable screen plugs into the Apple Desktop Bus (ADB) port on the back of the computer. It functions transparently as a mouse replacement with all software programs.

IBM and IBM-compatible: The detachable screen plugs into the serial port. Other types of screens may be built directly into the monitor. Most IBM versions require special drivers (utility programs) that are supplied with the touch screen. The screen will only work with those programs that involve the use of a mouse.

 Related products

Alternate Keyboards

Pointing and Typing Aids

Speech Synthesizers

Switches and Switch Software

Joysticks

A joystick may be used as an alternate input device. Joysticks that can be plugged into the computer's mouse port can control the cursor on the screen. Other joysticks plug into game ports and depend on software that is designed to accept joystick control. There are three types of control offered by joysticks: digital, glide, and direct. Digital control allows movement in a limited number of directions such as up, down, left, and right. Glide and direct-control allow movements in all directions (360 degrees). Direct-control joysticks have the added ability to respond to the distance and speed with which the user moves the stick.

 Use this tool to...

Motivate computer use

Operate a communication system or environmental control unit

Activate the computer with different parts of the body

Enter text or data using an on-screen keyboard

Practice mobility skills for operating a power wheelchair

Potential users...

Have use of hands but the task requires relating the mouse movement to the screen

Need to operate a computer without the use of their hands

Interact well with information but need a simpler method of input

Interact well with information but require interesting and motivating approaches

Practice use of a joystick for wheelchair control

 Features to consider

Some are equipped with up to three control buttons that can be programmed to perform various functions

Some require more force to operate than others

Some are designed to be operated with the chin or head

Some work only with software written specifically for use with joysticks

Some have switch adaptation

 Cost

Range: $60–500
Common: $70

 Common vendors

Joysticks are commonly available. Vendors include:

Advanced Gravis Computer Technology, Ltd.

KY Enterprises

McIntyre Computer Systems Division

Penny and Giles Computer Products Ltd.

Prentke Romich Company

R. J. Cooper and Associates

TASH International, Inc.

196

Computer
Resources
for People
with
Disabilities

 Additional information

Joysticks come in many sizes and shapes. Available options include the capacity for audio feedback, mounting hardware, and cables allowing use with different computers. Some interface devices accept joysticks as an input method.

Macintosh: Joysticks can plug directly into the mouse port and control the cursor on the computer screen in all programs.

IBM and IBM-compatibles: The joystick plugs into the game port and does not have direct control of the cursor unless using software designed for joystick control. Many computers come with a built-in game port or can have a game port card installed.

 Related products

Interface Devices

On-Screen Keyboards

Switches and Switch Software

Trackballs

Trackballs

A trackball looks like an upside-down mouse, with a movable ball on top of a stationary base. The ball can be rotated with a pointing device or hand.

 Use this tool to...

Enter text or data with an on-screen keyboard

Perform mouse functions using fewer hand movements or a pointing aid

 Potential users...

Have fine motor skills but not gross motor skills

Use a pointing aid to manipulate the cursor

Control a single finger well

 Features to consider

Some have buttons that lock in the down position for easy dragging

Some have buttons that are programmable to perform computer operations

Some have adjustable cursor speed and sensitivity

Some are designed for maximum comfort of the user

 Cost

Range: $60–170
Common: $75–130

 Common vendors

Trackballs are commonly available. Vendors include:

Costar Corporation

Fellowes

Kare Pillows, Inc./Ergo Kare

Kensington Microware Ltd.

Logitech, Inc.

Microsoft Corporation

Mouse Systems

Penny and Giles Computer Products Ltd.

 Additional information

A trackball is a mouse alternative used to control cursor movements and actions on a computer screen. The cursor is activated when buttons on the device are pressed, similar to a standard mouse. Trackballs are common features in laptop computer systems. The drag and click-lock feature enables the user to operate a trackball with a single digit.

198

Computer
Resources
for People
with
Disabilities

 Related products

Joysticks

Alternate Keyboards

Touch Screens

Arm and Wrist Supports

Arm supports are devices that stabilize and support arms and wrists while the user is typing or using a mouse or trackball. Wrist rests support the wrist while using a keyboard.

 Use this tool to...

Provide physical support while typing or using a mouse or trackball

 Potential users...

Need support to avoid fatigue or pain

Benefit from having arms stabilized

 Features to consider

Most provide support at the arm or wrist

Some attach to the table in front of the computer

Some have cuffs to support the forearm

Some have adjustable heights

Some swivel in two or more directions

Some mount on the chair instead of the table

Some wrist supports are built into the keyboard

Cost

Arm Supports:

Range: $100–600
Common: $100

Wrist Supports:

Range: $10-20
Common: $15

 Common vendors

Wrist rests are commonly available. Vendors include:

Adaptability

Air Technologies Corporation

ErgoFlex Systems

Kare Pillows Inc./Ergo Kare

KLAI Enterprises

Less Gauss, Inc.

SaundersErgo Source

 Additional information

One or both arms can be supported in a variety of ways, depending on individual preference. Before the release of commercial products, people used foam wedges, foam bars, and other supports.

 Related products

Alternate Keyboards

Keyboard Additions

Monitor Additions

Product Descriptions: Processing Aids

Abbreviation Expansion and Macro Programs

Abbreviation expansion programs allow the user to assign a series of letters, words, or sentences to one or more keystrokes. When the assigned keys (the abbreviations) are entered, the program will automatically insert the expanded text.

Macros allow users to "record" a long series of commands and assign them to a function key or combination of keys. Once a macro is recorded, the user can execute the complicated task exactly as recorded simply by typing the assigned key(s). For example, with one or two keys, you could open a word processor, enlarge the text, and enter your name or address. You might create another macro to save and print your document in one keystroke.

Use this tool to...

Store words, phrases, or groups of words to be entered later by typing one or more keystrokes

Automate a series of events such as locating a word processor, starting it up, setting the text to a large size, entering the date at the top, and setting the margins

Create a simple communication tool by storing phrases that can be entered by a keystroke into a word processor and read aloud by a speech synthesizer

Store phrases that can be entered by a communication device

 Potential users...

Benefit from using fewer keystrokes

Need to increase speed

Need to perform repetitive tasks on the computer accurately and efficiently

201

Product
Descriptions:
Processing
Aids

PROCESSING AIDS

 Features to consider

Many can be used with most software programs

Some can be found as a part of other programs, such as word processors and word prediction programs

Some come with pre-stored abbreviations for specific fields of study

Some can record mouse movements

Some can use multiple characters as the abbreviation

Some can use only single characters as the abbreviation

Some require two or more keys to be typed simultaneously

 Cost

Range: $40–500
Common: $80–150

 Common vendors

Affinity Micro Systems

CE Software, Inc.

Gus Communications

Productivity Software International, Inc.

TASH International, Inc.

 Additional information

Many abbreviation expansion features are combined with word prediction programs. See Word Prediction Programs for vendors to call. Some word processors and standard packages come with built-in macro features.

 Related products

Access Utilities

Word Prediction Programs

202

———

Computer
Resources
for People
with
Disabilities

Word Prediction Programs

Word prediction programs enable the user to select a desired word from an on-screen list or prediction window. This list, generated by the computer, predicts words from the first one or two letters typed by the user. The word may then be selected from the list and inserted into the text.

 Use this tool to...

Increase written productivity and accuracy

Increase vocabulary skill through word prompting

Reduce fatigue by eliminating unnecessary keystrokes

 Potential users...

Produce written work but need help with spelling

Benefit from word prompts to build vocabulary skills

Need to increase speed or reduce keystrokes

Features to consider

All have prediction windows that appear on the screen

Most can be used with common word-processing programs

Some allow users to add their own words

Some can customize text size and position of the word list on the screen

Some predict words based on rules of grammar

Some make predictions based on the user's pattern of word usage

Some automatically capitalize the first word in a sentence

Some provide choices that are visually highlighted in order to be selected with a scanning process

Some are packaged with abbreviation and expansion features

Begin typing a word and Telepathic, a word prediction program, will help you quickly finish it by offering you a list of intelligent word choices (Madenta Communications, Inc.)

 ## Cost

Range: $100–1,200
Common: $300–500

 ## Common vendors

Don Johnston, Inc.

Gus Communications

Innovative Designs

Madenta Communications

Microsystems Software, Inc.

OMS Development

Prentke Romich Company

Words+, Inc.

World Communications

Related products

Abbreviation Expansion and Macro Programs

Access Utilities

204

Computer
Resources
for People
with
Disabilities

Reading Comprehension Programs

Reading comprehension programs are software programs that focus on establishing or improving reading skills.

 Use this tool to...

Improve reading level and comprehension skills

Practice letter-sound recognition

Combine graphics with words to increase understanding of words

Develop decoding skills

Provide letter sequence practice for word building

Provide word sequence practice for sentence building

Improve word recognition

Improve reading comprehension

Increase vocabulary

 Potential users...

Read lower than their potential level

Comprehend single sentences

Comprehend single words

Comprehend the meaning of symbols

Features to consider

Some allow you to adjust the vocabulary level

Some have speech output

Some have placement tests

Some do student record keeping

Some have supplementary materials

Many provide graphics

Some provide animation and sound

Some highlight text as it is read aloud

 Cost

Range: $25–2,000
Common: $50–100

 Common vendors

A/V Concepts Corporation

Advanced Ideas, Inc.

Compu-Teach

Continental Press, Inc.

Creative Learning, Inc.

Davidson & Associates, Inc.

Discis Knowledge Research, Inc.

Don Johnston, Inc.

Edmark Corporation

Educational Activities, Inc.

Educational Press

Great Wave Software

Hartley Courseware, Inc.

Houghton Mifflin School Division

IBM Special Needs Systems

K-12 MicroMedia Publishing

Laureate Learning Systems, Inc.

Learning Company

Lexia Learning System, Inc.

Looking Glass Learning Products, Inc.

MarbleSoft

205

Product
Descriptions:
Processing
Aids

PROCESSING AIDS

206

Computer
Resources
for People
with
Disabilities

MECC

Millenium Software

Milliken Publishing Company

Mindplay

Optimum Resources, Inc.

Scholastic Software

Skills Bank Corporation

Society for Visual Education, Inc.

Stone and Associates

Sunburst Communications

Taylor Associates Communications

Teacher Support Software

Tom Snyder Productions

William K. Bradford Publishing Company

 Additional information

The software may start at the level of letter recognition and move sequentially to the level of passage comprehension, or it may focus on passage comprehension only.

Macintosh: Many reading programs are available as Apple II software and can be used on a Macintosh system (Macintosh LC series and Color Classic), which come with a special expansion slot that will accept an Apple IIE emulation card. The card has a port to attach a 5.25 disk drive to the system.

Many reading comprehension programs now come in CD-ROM versions which allow for greater voice output, graphics, and animation. The size of the text, the complexity of the graphics and text on the screen, and the level of voice output vary greatly from program to program. Most CD-ROM versions require at least a two-speed CD player.

 Related products

Optical Character Recognition and Scanners

Speech Synthesizers

Talking and Large-Print Word Processors

207

Product
Descriptions:
Processing
Aids

Writing Composition Programs

Writing composition programs provide a structured environment which enhances an individual's ability to produce written material.

 Use this tool to...

Train in brainstorming, mapping, freewriting, journal writing, and classification

Develop outlines and main ideas, write first drafts, and learn how to proofread

Learn sentence completion, story completion, and proper sequencing

Facilitate communication using graphics and speech output

 Potential users...

Write at a lower than potential level

Compose simple single sentences but require writing ideas

Combine words and phrases but need help to communicate meaning

Use an alternative to traditional writing methods

 Features to consider

Most have activities at various levels to develop writing skills

Some have prewriting activities

Some have writing development activities

Some have graphics to use in place of written words

Some have instructional choice options

Some have voice output

Some have text prompts on-screen to use as guides

208

—

Computer
Resources
for People
with
Disabilities

 Cost

Range: $40–250
Common: $50

 Common vendors

ACS Technologies

Blissymbolics Communication International

Communication Skill Builders

Creative Learning, Inc.

Davidson & Associates, Inc.

Don Johnston, Inc.

Humanities Software

IBM Special Needs Systems

Information Services, Inc.

Inspiration Software

Laureate Learning Systems, Inc.

Learning Company

MECC

Microsoft Corporation

Mindplay

PEAL Software

Psychological Corporation

Scholastic Software

Skills Bank Corporation

Stone and Associates

Teacher Support Software

Tom Snyder Productions

Toucan Press

William K. Bradford Publishing Company

 Additional information

As there is a vast number of programs for Macintosh and IBM and IBM-compatible computers, it is possible to match programs to individual user needs at different skill levels. Most products are standard educational programs.

IBM and IBM-compatible: Programs using voice output will need to be matched with speech synthesizers that support the particular program.

 Related products

Abbreviation Expansion and Macro Programs

Electronic Reference Tools

Software Features: Built-in Utilities

Talking and Large-Print Word Processors

Voice Recognition

Electronic Reference Tools

Electronic reference tools provide the user with a way to access traditional print materials and resources via the computer. Such references include dictionaries, thesauruses, atlases, almanacs, encyclopedias, and professional journals.

 Use this tool to...

Access traditionally print-based materials via computer

Transfer information, definitions, images, or statistics into a word-processing program

Electronically search for a specific name, date, word, or topic

Interact with multisensory reference materials

210

Computer
Resources
for People
with
Disabilities

Electronic reference tools, such as this World Atlas, can make the world more accessible than ever

 Potential users...

Need access to reference materials in formats other than print

Interact well with information but require interesting and motivating approaches

Need clear, direct access to information

 Features to consider

Many are available on CD-ROM disks and hold huge volumes of information

Some are available through the Internet

Some are accompanied by photos, music, sounds, and video clips, animation timelines, or tables

Most allow searches in a variety of ways

Most allow the user to use standard computer operations such as copy, paste, and print

 Cost

Range: $40-2,000
Common: $100

Common vendors

Electronic reference tools are commonly available. Vendors include:

Arkenstone, Inc.

Franklin Electronic Publishers, Inc.

Society for Visual Education, Inc.

Special Needs Project

 Related products

Software Features: Built-in utilities

Menu Management Programs

Menu management programs allow users to interact with a simplified and customized computer environment.

 Use this tool to...

Operate programs and utilities independently at home or school

Set up access to different sets of files for groups of students in a classroom

Provide access to menus for a nonreader

Personalize access to programs and utilities

Protect files by limiting access by young children

 Potential users...

Benefit from a simplified access route to computer programs

Interact well with a structured environment

 Features to consider

Most allow menu selection by mouse or keyboard

Some provide easy access to selected programs from predesigned menus

212

Computer
Resources
for People
with
Disabilities

Some can hide and secure menu items and files not in use

Some use icons to identify available applications

Some allow menu selection by number

Some can be set up to scan for use with a switch

Some bypass MS-DOS commands

Some have password protection for files

Some include various utilities such as a calculator, calendar, and time-and-date display

Some allow saving setups for different users

Some allow the user to designate where files should be saved

 Cost

Range: $45–65
Common: $55

 Common vendors

Menu management programs are commonly available. Vendors include:

Apple Computer, Inc.

Edmark Corporation

Microsoft Corporation

Reasonable Solutions

Software Excitement

Symantec

 Related products

Abbreviation Expansion and Macro Programs

Talking and Large-Print Word Processors

A talking word processor is a software program that uses a speech synthesizer to provide auditory feedback of what has been typed. Large-print word processors allow the user to view everything in large text without added screen enlargement.

 Use this tool to...

Talking Word Processors

Have text spoken out loud by chosen parameters (letter, word, sentence, selected text)

Practice letter-name recognition

Combine graphics with speech

Provide a motivating and interesting element to the task

Provide confirmation of a key stroke without looking at the screen

Create a simple communication board using an alternative keyboard

Large-Print Word Processors

Use large-text options without losing full view of the program

 Potential users...

Need alternatives or supplements to printed text

Need large text

Read at lower than potential level

Are assisted by auditory input

214

Computer
Resources
for People
with
Disabilities

Comprehend the meaning of symbols but not words

Interact well with auditory support

Need text specifically formatted to be readable

 Features to consider

All speak selected text aloud

Some have large-text options

Some have cursor options

Some have color text and background options

Talking Word Processors

Most allow letter, word, or sentence to be read

Some have speech-editing capability to correct the pronunciation of words by the computer

Some have voice options, including male, female, child, and adult

Large-Print Word Processors

Some come with built-in spell checkers

Most may be used with a word prediction program

 Cost

Range: free-$1700
Common: $100

Common vendors

Talking Word Processors

Bytes of Learning

Center for Applied Special Technology (CAST)

Davidson and Associates, Inc.

Don Johnston, Inc.

Hartley Courseware, Inc.

IBM Special Needs Systems

IntelliTools

Jostens Home Learning

Teacher Support Software

Large-Print Word Processors

Don Johnston, Inc.

EduQuest

Gus Communications

Hartley Courseware, Inc.

Hexagon Systems

Institute on Applied Technology

IntelliTools

Kidsview Software

SkiSoft Publishing Corporation

Sunburst Communications

Teacher Support Software

 Additional information

A talking word processor does not generally have all the capabilities of a screen reader. Some programs can be both large-print and talking word processors.

Macintosh: No special sound cards or synthesizers are needed to use talking word processors with Macintosh computers. You do need software specifically designed for speech output.

IBM and IBM-compatible: You will probably need to have a sound card or a speech synthesizer to use a talking word processor on these computers. Check the programs to see what synthesizers are compatible.

Related products

Screen Readers

Speech Synthesizers

215

Product
Descriptions:
Alternate
Output

ALTERNATE OUTPUT

216

Computer
Resources
for People
with
Disabilities

Braille Embossers and Translators

A braille printer transfers computer-generated text into embossed braille output. Translation programs create a braille version of the original file for the computer.

 Use this tool to...

Print computer-generated documents

Produce braille print materials including books, handouts, signs, restaurant menus, and maps

 Potential users...

Require braille instead of standard print

 Features to consider

All emboss braille

Most need translation software to create Grade 2 braille

Some are equipped with speech feedback menu options

A braille printer such as Braillo can print out text files in braille format (American Thermoform)

Some have liquid crystal displays to indicate page count

Some will print graphics

Some emboss on two sides of a page

Some will do braille and standard ink print on same page

 Cost

Embossers

Range: $1,700–40,000
Common: $3,000–4,500

Translators

Range: $200–1,000
Common: $400

 Common vendors

Embossers

American Thermoform Corporation

Beyond Sight, Inc.

Blazie Engineering, Inc.

Enabling Technologies Company

Index Braille Printer Company

Reading Technologies

TeleSensory

Translators

Duxbury Systems, Inc.

GW Micro

HumanWare, Inc.

MicroTalk

Raised Dot Computing, Inc.

218

Computer
Resources
for People
with
Disabilities

 Additional information

Braille embossers are available in two categories: those designed for individual use, and those designed for high-volume production of large amounts of embossed materials.

 Related products

Refreshable Braille Displays

Reading Machines

Screen Readers

Refreshable Braille Displays

Refreshable braille displays provide tactile output of information presented on the computer screen. Unlike conventional braille, which is permanently embossed onto paper, refreshable braille displays are mechanical in nature and lift small, rounded plastic or metal pins as needed to form braille characters. Refreshable braille displays contain 20, 40, or 80 braille cells. After the line is read, the user can "refresh" the display to read the next line.

 Use this tool to...

Display commands, prompts, and entered text in braille

Allow the user to get precise information about text attributes, screen formatting, and spelling on the computer display

Provide computer access to persons who are visually impaired, where speech output might not be practical or desired

 Potential users...

Require braille output from the computer

 Features to consider

All units can display text from the computer screen

Some models can show an 80-column screen on a single braille line

*Alva, a refreshable braille display, provides tactile feedback from the
computer for braille users, including those with hearing impairments
(HumanWare, Inc.)*

Some units can indicate text attributes, such as upper case, highlighted
text, and boldface

Some devices have a touch cursor, which enables the user to move the
computer cursor to a particular character with the touch of a button
located directly above it

Some have controls for reviewing screen contents with the braille display conveniently located on the front panel

Some models include software that provides braille access to Microsoft
Windows

 Cost

Range: $3,500–15,000
Common: $4,500–8,000

 Common vendors

American Thermoform Corporation

220

Computer
Resources
for People
with
Disabilities

HumanWare, Inc.

TeleSensory

 Additional information

No refreshable braille access is currently available for Macintosh computers

Some manufacturers of screen-review programs provide facilities for using refreshable braille displays for screen access

Some devices connect to a parallel port, others connect to a serial port on IBM-compatible computers

 Related products

Screen Readers

Braille Embossers and Translators

Speech Synthesizers

With appropriate software, a speech synthesizer can receive information going to the screen in the form of letters, numbers, and punctuation marks, then "speak" it out loud.

Use this tool to...

Have computer text spoken out loud

Practice letter-sound recognition

Provide a motivating and interesting element to a task

Provide confirmation of a key stroke without looking at the screen

Hear auditory prompts and feedback from a screen-reading program or talking word processor

Listen to text from manuals and documents transferred to the computer using an optical character recognition program and a scanner

Potential users...

Read lower than their potential level but benefit from text spoken aloud

Comprehend single words but require decoding skills

Comprehend the meaning of symbols but need to hear words

Require manuals and documents read aloud

Need auditory support when screen text is too small

Need auditory feedback to navigate the screen and select commands

Need materials in an accessible format to complete activities

Benefit from auditory feedback

Understand information but need to maintain attention to the task

Use auditory feedback when information on the screen is not usable

 Features to consider

Most work together with software that can convert text to speech

Most have a robotic voice

Most have adjustable volume

Most are equipped with an external jack for speakers or headphones

Some have settings for pitch or speaking voices (for example, male or female)

Some can define special pronunciation rules and add words to the synthesizer's dictionary

 Cost

Range: $100–1,200
Common : $125–750

 Common vendors

American Printing House for the Blind, Inc.

Aicom Corporation

222

Computer
Resources
for People
with
Disabilities

Artic Technologies

Audapter Personal Data Systems, Inc.

Beyond Sight, Inc.

Compusult Limited

Consultants for Communication Technology

Digital Equipment Corporation

Echo Speech Corporation

Gus Communications

GW Micro

HumanWare, Inc.

Institute on Applied Technology

MicroTalk

Raised Dot Computing, Inc.

Reading Technologies

TeleSensory

Additional information

To read text characters, speech synthesizers use special memory chips or software in which is stored the thousands of rules the synthesizer uses to translate written text into speech. The translated text is known as *synthesized speech,* as opposed to *digitized speech,* which is recorded sound. A synthesizer is either an external device that plugs into the computer (an external synthesizer) or a card that is put into a slot in the computer (an internal synthesizer).

Macintosh: In Macintosh computer systems, speech synthesis is built in but still requires a screen-reading program or talking word processor

IBM and IBM-compatible: In MS-DOS computers, a separate speech synthesizer or speech card is required for text-to-speech capability. A software program, usually referred to as a *screen reader,* that supports that specific speech synthesizer must be used.

Related products

Optical Character Recognition and Scanners

Screen Readers

Reading Machines

Talking and Large Print Word Processors

Screen Readers

A screen reader is a software program that works in conjunction with a speech synthesizer to provide verbalization of everything on the screen including menus, text, and punctuation.

 Use this tool to...

Provide access to print materials and manuals after they have been scanned into a computer

Provide auditory prompts, menus, and commands

Provide confirmation of keystrokes without looking at the screen

Make a computer accessible to someone with limited or no vision

 Potential users...

Need auditory feedback to read text on the screen

Understand how to handle equipment but need print materials and manuals to be read aloud

Need auditory feedback to navigate the screen and select commands

 Features to consider

All can read units of text such as characters, words, lines, and paragraphs

Some are designed to work with MS-DOS and other text-based operating systems

*A screen reader reads printed material for people who have
visual impairments*

Some are designed to work with the graphic user interfaces of Windows
and Macintosh operating systems

Some read selected portions of the screen either automatically or
through commands from the keyboard

Some control the rate, pitch, and volume of speech output

Some are compatible with a variety of internal and external speech synthesizers

Some use an external keypad or a touch tablet instead of or in addition
to the regular keyboard to control screen-reading functions

Some employ artificial intelligence to make decisions about what the
user wants spoken after making changes

Some include the speech synthesizer as part of the package

Cost

Range: $75–2,100
Common: $450–600

 Common vendors

American Printing House for the Blind, Inc.

Artic Technologies

Berkeley Systems, Inc.

Beyond Sight, Inc.

Biolink Research and Development, Ltd.

GW Micro

Henter-Joyce, Inc.

HumanWare, Inc.

IBM Special Needs Systems

MicroTalk

OMS Development

Raised Dot Computing, Inc.

Reading Technologies

Syntha-Voice Computers, Inc.

TeleSensory

Additional information

Macintosh: A screen reader designed for the Macintosh can use the built-in speech hardware to access Macintosh applications. It does not require an additional speech synthesizer.

IBM and IBM-compatible: Speech synthesizers are available in internal and external versions. Internal versions require a suitable expansion slot to be available in the computer; external versions require a free serial or parallel port compatible with the synthesizer. Check for compatibility of screen readers when using MS-DOS or Windows operating systems.

226

Computer
Resources
for People
with
Disabilities

 Related products

Optical Character Recognition and Scanners

Reading Machines

Speech Synthesizers

Talking and Large-Print Word Processors

Screen Enlargement Programs

An enlargement program focuses on a single portion of the screen at a time and enlarges it.

 Use this tool to...

Magnify the text and graphics on the screen

 Potential users...

Need large text

 Features to consider

All magnify text by at least 200 percent

Most have variable magnification levels (much higher than 200 percent)

Most have a cursor that tracks the area being magnified

Some magnify graphics

Some have split-screen viewing of magnified and unmagnified windows

 Cost

Range: free–$600
Common: $500

Common vendors

Ai Squared

Apple Computer, Inc.

Artic Technologies

Berkeley Systems, Inc.

Beyond Sight, Inc.

GW Micro

Hexagon Products

HumanWare, Inc.

Microsystems Software, Inc.

Optelec USA, Inc.

Reading Technologies

Syntha-Voice Computers

TeleSensory

Visionware Software, Inc.

Additional information

Screen magnifiers work best with software programs that do not use a large portion of the screen at one time. Programs with graphic images that stretch from one side of the screen to the other (or from the top to the bottom), such as games, will not work well with screen magnifiers, because the "zoom" window leaves out too much of the image. Programs with graphics that rapidly jump to different parts of the screen will also be difficult to use with screen-enlargement software. Instead, large-print word processors may be easier to use.

Macintosh: CloseView, a screen-magnifying utility, is included in the Macintosh System Software.

IBM and IBM-compatible: Compatibility issues involve the type of monitor, the version of operating system, and the software programs to be used with the screen enlargement program.

228

———

Computer
Resources
for People
with
Disabilities

 Related products

Monitor Additions

Speech Synthesizers

Talking and Large-Print Word Processors

Monitor Additions

A monitor addition or add-on is any device that enhances or alters the use of a standard computer monitor.

Exterior screen-magnifiers fit over the screen of a computer monitor and magnify what is on the screen.

Anti-glare filters are clear screens that fit on a computer monitor and reduce glare and improve contrast. They also reduce ultraviolet rays and other energy emissions.

Monitor mounts come in a variety of styles and degrees of flexibility and allow adjustment of the monitor position.

Use this tool to...

Screen Magnifiers

Magnify the monitor screen to increase image of graphics or text

Anti-Glare Filters

Reduce glare from overhead lights and large windows to improve contrast and clarity

Reduce screen flicker

Increase the contrast of the monitor

Monitor Mounts

Modify the position of the monitor to increase visibility

Accommodate many users of different heights or those in a prone or other nonstandard position

Potential users…

Need magnification to see the screen

Benefit from decreased glare

Need increased clarity

Use a monitor mount to bring the screen closer

Need a monitor mount to operate the computer from a nonstandard position

 Features to consider

All monitor mounts have a specific weight capacity

Some anti-glare filters have protection to reduce ELF and VLF electromagnetic energy

Some anti-glare filters block damaging UV and UVB rays to protect eyes from burning

Some screen magnifiers are made to reduce distortion caused by the magnification

Some screen magnifiers include an anti-glare polarizing filter and/or mounting hood to reduce room reflections and soften the light from the screen

Some monitor mounts can move 360 degrees, tilt, or swivel

Some monitor mounts can be part of the table, or can clamp to a table, bolt down, or attach to a wall or ceiling

 Cost

Anti-Glare Filters

Range: $10–200
Common: $50

Exterior-Screen Magnifiers

Range: $80–250
Common: $80

230

Computer
Resources
for People
with
Disabilities

Monitor Mounts

Range: $50–800
Common: $50

 Common vendors

Anti-Glare Filters

Anti-glare filters are commonly available. Vendors include:

Kensington Microware Ltd.

Power Plus The Accessories People

Magnifiers

AbleTech Connection

Florida New Concepts

Innoventions

Less Gauss

Monitor Mounts

American Marketing Executives

Cables to Go

Hunt Manufacturing

 Additional information

The products must fit the specific monitor used

 Related products

Screen Enlargement Programs

Assistive Communication Products

Some individuals choose to use electronic devices to augment or replace their voice. How we choose to communicate is an important and personal decision that involves both access issues and personal preference. Some preliminary information is provided here to introduce you to this field. We recommend that individuals who are interested in assistive communication products bring together a team to explore the range of products and uses carefully.

Computer-based Systems These communication devices use specific software integrated into a standard computer. Some software allows the display on the computer screen to change in response to the communicator's input. Computer-based systems are useful for communication as well as typical computer applications such as word processing, telecommunications, and environmental control.

Stand-alone or Dedicated Communication Devices These devices use either digitized or synthesized speech, and are for the sole purpose of replacing or augmenting speech to communicate. Digitized communication devices use recorded speech for the messages which will be heard by the communicators. Synthesized communication devices use text translated into electronic speech. They are usually programmable and come in a wide variety of sizes, shapes, and means of access.

 Use These Tools To:

Communicate using a desk-top or lap-top computer

Communicate using small, portable, dedicated devices

Communicate using short messages, phrases, and sentences

Represent symbols, pictures, and objects through recorded messages

Change content of messages on a dynamic basis

232

———

Computer
Resources
for People
with
Disabilities

Create speech which may be age, gender, and language specific to an individual

Clarify when verbal communication is unclear

Present long messages, reports, or stories

 Potential Users:

People who require a method of communicating other than speech.

People who require support to communicate verbally

People who benefit from using symbols, pictures, and/or words when communicating

 Features to Consider:

Some units can be connected to a computer and used to replace the mouse and keyboard

Some units are dedicated solely to communication

Some units are easily customized by the user

Some units use software with language-based symbol systems to create communication layouts

Some units can be accessed through a variety of input devices including touch screens, switches, and alternate keyboards

Many units offer display options including color, black-and-white, and back-lit screens

Some screens are very difficult to see outdoors in daylight

Many units vary in the quality of speech, depending on the type of synthesizer used

Some units support both digitized speech and synthesized speech

Some can integrate a variety of functions into one unit, such as operating environmental controls and computer programs

Some units can plug into a printer; some have built-in printers

Some units vary in the number and size of messages that can be stored

Many units are portable

Some units have the ability to store banks of phrases or messages for easy retrieval

 Cost:

Computer-based Systems

Range: $1,800–8,000
Common: $3,000

Standalone or Dedicated Communication Devices

Range: $45–8,000
Common: $1,000

 Common Vendors:

AbleNet, Inc.

Adaptivation

Crestwood Company

Don Johnston, Inc.

Franklin Electronic Publishers, Inc.

The Great Talking Box Company

Gus Communications

Infra-Link, Inc.

Luminaud, Inc.

Mayer-Johnson Co.

Microsystems Software, Inc.

Phonic Ear, Inc.

Prentke Romich Company

Sentient Systems Technology, Inc.

Shea Products

TASH International, Inc.

Words+, Inc.

234

Computer
Resources
for People
with
Disabilities

World Communications

Zygo Industries, Inc.

 Additional Information:

When a consumer chooses a device, he or she is making a very important personal decision. In moving through the selection process, it is very important to have a strong team in place that includes the individual, the family, educators, and specialists. Devices vary in the training required and the level of independent cognitive skills needed. A trial period with several devices may help eliminate costly mistakes.

"Guide to Augmentative Communication Products, 1996 Edition," is a chart comparing 91 communication devices and products. It has been designed for consumers, family members, and professionals alike. You can get an order form and more information by writing:

Applied Science and Engineering Laboratories
University of Delaware/A. I. DuPont Institute   (302) 651-6830, voice
1600 Rockland Road   (302) 651-6895, fax
Wilmington DE 19803   email: rerc-aac@asel.udel.edu

 Other Related Products:

environmental control units

switches

alternate keyboards

touch screens

speech synthesizers

Closed-Circuit Televisions

Closed-circuit televisions (CCTV) scan the printed page with a special television camera and display the image enlarged on a monitor.

Use this tool to...

Read print materials with the aid of magnification

Write notes, letters, and other handwritten documents with the aid of magnification

Potential users...

Require large text

Benefit from greater contrast

Benefit from white text on a black background

Benefit from being able to select their own text and background color combinations

 Features to consider

All provide magnification of print materials

Most magnify in adjustable increments

Most are capable of reverse polarity, i.e., a white image on a black background or a black image on a white background

Most have black-and-white screens

Some have color screens with selectable colors or full-color options

Some are hand-held and portable

Photo courtesy of HumanWare, Inc.

*A CCTV can enlarge a variety of materials,
including maps and other print resources
(HumanWare, Inc.)*

236

———

Computer
Resources
for People
with
Disabilities

Some have the capability to show an image on a computer screen and on the CCTV screen at the same time

Some magnify output from a computer, typewriter, microfiche reader, chalkboard, or even a microscope

Some have motorized reading tables

 Cost

Range: $1,400–3,400
Average: $2,400

 Common vendors

Beyond Sight, Inc.

Carolyn's Products for Enhanced Living

HumanWare, Inc.

LS&S Group

Okay Vision-Aide Corp.

Optelec U.S.A., Inc.

Seeing Technologies, International

TeleSensory

 Additional information

Text can be magnified up to 60 times on some units. The user normally moves, or "tracks," the item to be read under a fixed camera, either manually with a standard reading table or automatically with an optional motorized table. With some portable units a hand-held camera is moved across the printed page.

 Related products

Screen Enlargement Programs

Monitor Additions

Environmental Control Units

An environmental control unit (ECU) is used to control, from a remote location, electric appliances, telephones, and other items that plug into an outlet.

 Use this tool to...

Turn on a computer system independently

Turn on lamps, fans, stereos, intercoms, and other household devices

Activate an emergency call button wired to a remote location in the building

Adjust a hospital bed independently

Activate a security system

 Potential users...

Need an alternate way to handle common devices and appliances

 Features to consider

All control appliances plugged into an outlet

Photo courtesy of Madenta

Darryl Park uses voice commands to help him control his home through PROXI

238

Computer
Resources
for People
with
Disabilities

Some can control telephones

Some can control televisions, VCRs, stereo systems, and other devices with infrared remote control

Some can be controlled by a single switch or voice

 Cost

Range: $250–6,500
Common: basic functions $450; advanced functions $3,000

 Common vendors

AbleNet, Inc.

ACS Technologies

Consultants for Communication Technology

DU-IT Control Systems Group, Inc.

Gus Communications

Infra-Link, Inc.

KY Enterprises/Custom Computer Solutions

LC Technologies, Inc.

Madenta Communications

Med Labs Inc.

Microsystems Software

Prentke Romich Company

TASH International, Inc.

Teledyne Brown Engineering/Imperium Products Division

Toys for Special Children, Inc.

VME Technologies, Inc.

Words+, Inc.

X-10 (USA) Inc.

Zygo Industries, Inc.

Additional information

An ECU can be purchased as a software package, to be used on a personal computer, or as a stand-alone device. ECU software is available for both Macintosh and IBM and IBM-compatible computers.

To use these devices with a single switch, you will need an additional interface.

 Related products

Interface Devices

Switches and Switch Software

Voice Recognition

Notetakers

Notetakers are very small, portable units that employ either a braille keyboard or a standard keyboard to allow the user to enter information. Text is stored in files that can be read and edited using the built-in speech synthesizer or braille display. Files may also be sent to a printer or braille embosser, or transferred to a computer.

 Use this tool to...

Take notes in class, meetings, or conferences

Access electronic information services by connecting to a phone line

Instruct in writing and reading braille

 Potential users...

Read and write in braille

Need a way to take notes and be able to transfer them to a computer

 Features to consider

Most allow information to be entered in braille

240

Computer
Resources
for People
with
Disabilities

Most have text-editing capability

Most have built-in speech synthesizers

Most can accommodate headphones to permit private listening

Some can turn auditory feedback on or off

Some include a clock and calendar

Some include an appointment book, which can sound a tone to remind the user of scheduled appointments

Most can print using conventional printers or braille embossers

Some have refreshable braille displays

Some can produce 8-dot braille

 Cost

Range: $1,000–3,400
Common: $1,300

 Common vendors

American Printing House for the Blind, Inc.

Blazie Engineering, Inc.

HumanWare, Inc.

Intelligent Peripheral Devices

TeleSensory

TFI Engineering

 Additional Information

Generally, notetakers are limited in functionality when compared to a laptop or desktop computer because of their processor design and limited memory and storage capacity. However, they do have the advantage of long battery life and portability.

 Related products

Screen Readers

Speech Synthesizers

Reading Machines

A reading machine transforms printed material into an electronic data format that is read aloud by a speech synthesizer. A standard computer can be modified to become a reading machine by adding a scanner and reading system software. A stand-alone reading machine incorporates a scanner, speech synthesizer, and other electronics in a single unit.

 Use this tool to...

Read books, mail, business documents, and faxed information

Improve reading comprehension by listening to materials being read as they are displayed on the computer screen.

 Potential users...

Need print materials read aloud

 Features to consider

All have speech output

All have some type of scanner

Some have a document feeder for the scanner

Most determine page orientation automatically

Most recognize many type styles

Most can handle multicolumn pages

Most recognize a variety of print qualities

Some are compact for greater portability

Some are specially designed to more easily accommodate books

Some support braille or large-print output

SPECIALIZED PRODUCTS

242

Computer
Resources
for People
with
Disabilities

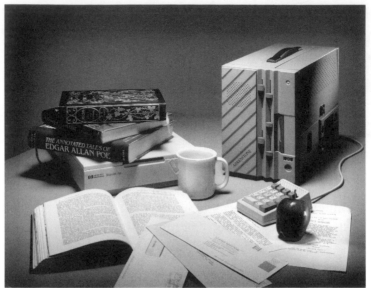

*With an Open Book, a reading machine, any printed material can
be converted to an electronic format, allowing you to read books,
magazines and even junk mail (Arkenstone, Inc.)*

Some read faxed images

Some control scanning and reading functions with a computer keyboard, a separate keypad, or a joystick

 Cost

To Upgrade an Existing Computer

Range: $1,600–4,400
Common: $1,800–3,000

Stand-Alone Machines

Range: $4,700–6,000
Common: $5,000

 Common vendors

Arkenstone, Inc.

TeleSensory

Schamex Research

Xerox Imaging Systems, Inc.

243

Computer
Resources
for People
with
Disabilities

 Additional information

Macintosh: Although there are no reading system software programs specifically for Macintosh computers and specifically for blind users, commercial OCR systems can be used with a scanner and a screen reader to give people with visual disabilities access to printed material.

IBM and IBM-compatible: The scanning hardware and reading system software for these computers have specific system requirements—such as bus architecture, processor type, and memory size—that must be taken into consideration. A reading machine is a unique combination of access products. If you are modifying a standard computer to also be used as a reading machine, you will need to be certain that all the hardware and software components are compatible.

Related products

Notetakers

OCR and Scanners

Screen Readers

Speech Synthesizers

TTYs and TTY Modems

The TTY is a portable device used to communicate by transmitting text over telephone lines. It has a typewriter-like keyboard and a readable display.

Standard modems will not allow you to use a computer to communicate with someone using a TTY. TTY modems are specially designed for that purpose.

Use This Tool To:

Call other TTY users

Call a relay system which will read your message to a standard phone user

Connect with automated services such as a bank

Potential Users:

Require text to communicate by telephone

Communicate with someone else using a TTY for telephone communication

 Features to Consider:

All TTYs have keyboards to type a message

All TTYs have a display that shows the message as it is entered or received

Some TTYs have built-in printers

Some TTYs offer options for the display such as color, text size, and direction of scrolling

Some TTYs are compatible with braille devices

All TTY modems require telecommunication software for communication

Some TTYs and TTY modems allow storage of messages

Some TTYs and TTY modems can be answered automatically

Some TTY modems can automatically adjust to receive from a TTY or another computer

 Cost:

TTYs

Range: $200-6,000
Common: $350

TTY Modems

Range: $300-350
Common: $330

 Common Vendors:

TTYs

AT&T Accessible Communication Products

HARC Mercantile, LTD

Harris Communications, Inc.

Hear More Inc.

HITEC Group International

IBM Special Needs Systems

Phone TTY, Inc.

Prime Performance Technologies, Inc.

SSK Technology, Inc.

TeleSensory

Ultratec

TTY Modems

Hear More Products

Prime TTY, Inc.

Prime Performances

 Additional Information:

Telecommunications Devices for the Deaf (TDD) and Text Telephones are other terms referring to TTYs.

TTY modems are a new technology and the issues are complex. There is no software to convert your standard modem into a TTY modem. A special modem that supports TTY encoding, known as v.18 standard, is required. Eventually, all modems may be equipped with this standard, making communication with TTYs universal.

Other Related Products:

There are no related products at the time of this printing.

Part III

Helpful Resources and References

Helpful Resources and References

This section contains a series of starter resources to point you in appropriate directions. The lists in Part III include key references and resources. In some cases the value of a given resource will be to lead you to other resources. By following up on some of the national references listed here you should be able to identify resources and contacts in your own community which, of course, is the main goal. The references and resources are organized into eight sections:

Alliance for Technology Access Resource Centers

The Alliance for Technology Access is a growing organization with new members joining regularly. If you are interested in starting an Alliance for Technology Access center in your community, please contact us for guidelines and an application.

Many ATA centers currently maintain sites on the World Wide Web, and the number is increasing rapidly. Check the ATA website for the most current ATA center web addresses.

Alliance for Technology Access
2175 East Francisco Boulevard, Suite L   (415) 455-4575
San Rafael CA 94901
email: atafta@aol.com
website: http://marin.org/npo/ata/

ALABAMA
Birmingham Alliance for Technology Access Center
Birmingham Independent Living Center   (205) 251-2223, voice/TTY
206 13th Street South
Birmingham AL 35253-1317
email: dkessle@ix.netcom.com

Technology Assistance for Special Consumers
P.O. Box 443   (205) 532-5996, voice/TTY
Huntsville AL 35804
email: tascal@aol.com

ALASKA
Alaska Services for Enabling Technology
P.O. Box 6485   (907) 747-7615
207 Moller Drive
Sitka AK 99835
email: asetseak@aol.com

250

Computer
Resources
for People
with
Disabilities

ARIZONA

Technology Access Center of Tucson, Inc.
P.O. Box 13178   (520) 745-5588 ext. 412
4710 East 29th Street
Tucson AZ 85732-3178
email: tactaz@aol.com

ARKANSAS

Technology Resource Center
c/o Arkansas Easter Seal Society   (501) 227-3602
3920 Woodland Heights Road   (501) 227-3686, TTY
Little Rock AR 72212-2495
email: aess@cei.net

CALIFORNIA

Center for Accessible Technology
2547 8th Street, 12-A   (510) 841-3224, voice/TTY
Berkeley CA 94710-2572   (510) 841-5621, BBS
website: http://www.el.net/CAT
email: cforat@aol.com

Computer Access Center
5901 Green Valley Circle, Suite #320   (310) 338-1597
Culver City CA 90230   (310) 338-9318, TTY
email: cacofsmca@aol.com

Sacramento Center for Assistive Technology
650 Howe Avenue, Suite 300   (916) 927-7228, voice/TTY
Sacramento CA 95825
email: scatca@aol.com

SACC* Assistive Technology
S.V. Hospital, Rehab Unit North   (805) 582-1881
P.O. Box 1325
Simi Valley CA 93062
email: dssacca@aol.com

Special Technology Center
590 Castro Street   (415) 961-6789, voice/TTY
Mountain View CA 94041
e-mail: stcca@aol.com

Team of Advocates for Special Kids
100 W. Cerritos Avenue (714) 533-8275
Anaheim CA 92805-6546
email: taskca@aol.com

251

Alliiance for
Technology
Access
Resources
Centers

FLORIDA
Center for Independence, Technology and Education (CITE)
215 E. New Hampshire Street (407) 898-2483
Orlando FL 32804
email: comcite@aol.com

GEORGIA
Tech-Able, Inc.
1112A Brett Drive (770) 922-6768
Conyers GA 30207
email: techable@onramp.net
website: http://www.onramp.net/tech-able

HAWAII
Aloha Special Technology Access Center
710 Green Street (808) 523-5547
Honolulu HI 96813
email: stachi@aol.com

ILLINOIS
Northern Illinois Center for Adaptive Technology (NICAT)
3615 Louisiana Road (815) 229-2163
Rockford IL 61108-6195 (815) 229-2881, TTY
email: ilcat@aol.com

TAAD Center (Technical Aids & Assistance for Persons with Disabilities)
1950 West Roosevelt Road (800) 346-2939, in state
Chicago IL 60608 (312) 421-3373
email: taad@interaccess.com

INDIANA
Assistive Technology Training and Information Center (ATTIC)
P.O. Box 2441 (800) 96-ATTIC (962-8842), voice/TTY
3354 Pine Hill Drive (812) 886-0575, voice/TTY
Vincennes IN 47591
email: inattic1@aol.com

252

Computer
Resources
for People
with
Disabilities

KANSAS

Technology Resource Solutions for People, OCCK, Inc.
P.O. Box 1160   (913) 827-9383, voice/TTY
1710 West Schilling Road
Salina KS 67402-1160
email: trspks@midusa.net

KENTUCKY

Bluegrass Technology Center
169 N. Limestone Street   (606) 255-9951, voice/TTY
Lexington KY 40507
e-mail: bluegrass@uky.campus.mci.net
website: http://www.kde.state.ky.us/assistive/Assistive_Technology.html

Enabling Technologies of Kentuckiana (enTECH)
301 York Street   (800) 890-1840
Louisville KY 40203-2205   (800) 327-5287, in state
email: entech@iglou.com   (502) 574-1637, voice/TTY
website: http://www.kde.state.ky.us/assistive/Assistive_Technology.html

SpeciaLink
36 West 5th Street   (606) 491-2464, voice/TTY
Covington KY 41011
(greater Cincinnati area)
email: speclink@iglou.com
website: http://www.kde.state.ky.us/assistive/Assistive_Technology.html

MARYLAND

Learning Independence Through Computers, Inc. (LINC)
28 E. Ostend Street   (410) 659-5462
Baltimore MD 21230   (410) 659-5472, TTY
email: lincmd@aol.com
website: http://www.linc.org

MASSACHUSETTS

Massachusetts Special Technology Access Center (MASTAC)
12 Mudge Way 1–6   (617) 275-2446, voice/TTY
Bedford MA 01730-2138
email: mastacma@aol.com

MICHIGAN
Living & Learning Resource Centre
PIAM
1023 S. U.S. 27, Suite B31
St. Johns, MI 48879
email: llrcmi@aol.com

(800) 833-1996, in state
(517) 487-0883, voice/TTY

MINNESOTA
PACER Computer Resource Center
4826 Chicago Avenue South
Minneapolis MN 55417-1055
email: pacercrc@aol.com
website: http://freenet.msp.us/ip/family/pacer/

(612) 827-2966, voice/TTY

MISSOURI
Technology Access Center
12110 Clayton Road
St Louis MO 63131-2599
email: mostltac@aol.com

(314) 569-8404
(314) 569-8446, TTY

MONTANA
Parents, Let's Unite for Kids (PLUK)
MSU-B
1500 North 30th Street
Billings MT 59101-0298
email: plukmt@aol.com

(800) 222-7585, in state
(406) 657-2055, voice/TTY

NEW JERSEY
Computer Center for People with disAbilities
c/o Family Resource Associates, Inc.
35 Haddon Avenue
Shrewsbury NJ 07702
email: ccdanj@aol.com

(908) 747-5310

The Center for Enabling Technology
622 Route 10 West, Suite 22B
Whippany NJ 07981
email: cetnj@aol.com

(201) 428-1455

ATA CENTERS

254

Computer
Resources
for People
with
Disabilities

NEW YORK
Techspress
Resource Center for Independent Living   (315) 797-4642
P.O. Box 210   (315) 797-5837, TTY
401-409 Columbia Street
Utica NY 13501
email: txprsny@aol.com
website: http://www.cybervillage.com

NORTH CAROLINA
Carolina Computer Access Center
Metro School   (704) 342-3004
700 East Second Street
Charlotte NC 28202-2826
email: ccacnc@aol.com
website: http://www.charweb.org/health/ccac

OHIO
Technology Resource Center
301 Valley Street   (513) 222-5222
Dayton OH 45404-1840
email: trcdoh@aol.com

RHODE ISLAND
TechACCESS Center of Rhode Island
300 Richmond Street   (800) 916-TECH (916-8234), in state
Providence RI 02903-4222   (401) 273-1990, voice/TTY
email: accessri@aol.com   (401) 831-1131, fax

TENNESSEE
East Tennessee Technology Access Center
3525 Emory Road, NW   (423) 947-2191, voice/TTY
Powell TN 37849
email: etstactn@aol.com

Technology Access Center of Middle Tennessee
2222 Metrocenter Boulevard, Suite 126   (800) 368-4651
Nashville TN 37228   (615) 248-6733, voice/TTY
email: tactn@aol.com

West Tennessee Special Technology Access Resource Center (STAR)
P.O. Box 3683   (901) 668-3888
60 Lynoak Cove   (901) 668-1666, fax
Jackson TN 38305
email: startn@aol.com

UTAH

The Computer Center for Citizens with Disabilities
c/o Utah Center for Assistive Technology   (801) 485-9152, voice/TTY
2056 South 1100 East
Salt Lake City UT 84106
email: cccdut@aol.com

VIRGIN ISLANDS

Virgin Islands Resource Center for the Disabled, Inc.
PO Box 308427   (809) 777-2253, voice/TTY
St. Thomas USVI 00803-8427   (809) 774-9330, fax
email: wayneram@aol.com

VIRGINIA

Tidewater Center for Technology Access
Special Education Annex   (804) 474-8650, voice/TTY
960 Windsor Oaks Boulevard
Virginia Beach VA 23462
email: tcta@aol.com

WEST VIRGINIA

Eastern Panhandle Technology Access Center, Inc.
P.O. Box 987   (304) 725-6473
Charlestown WV 25414

State Tech Act Programs

The Technology-Related Assistance for Individuals with Disabilities Act provides funding to states to assist them in developing easily accessible, consumer-responsive systems of access to assistive technology, technology services, and information. State programs vary widely. Contact your state's Tech Act Project for more information. If you are unable to reach your state's project, call the RESNA Technical Assistance Project at (703) 524-6686, extension 313 for assistance.

256

—

Computer
Resources
for People
with
Disabilities

ALABAMA

Alabama Statewide Technology Access and Response Project (STAR) System for Alabamians with Disabilities

P.O. Box 20752   (800) STAR656 (782-7656), in state
2125 East South Blvd.   (334) 613-3480
Montgomery AL 36120-0752   (334) 613-3485, fax

ALASKA

Assistive Technologies of Alaska

701 E. Tudor Road, Suite 280   (800) 770-0138, voice/TTY
Anchorage AK 99503-7445   (907) 563-0146, fax
email: atadvr@corcom.com

AMERICAN SAMOA

American Samoa Assistive Technology Project

Division of Vocational Rehabilitation   (684) 699-1529
Department of Human Resources   (684) 233-7874, TTY
Pago Pago, American Samoa 96799   (684) 699-1376, fax

ARIZONA

Arizona Technology Access Program (AZTAP)

2600 N. Wyatt Drive, 2nd Floor   (520) 324-3170
Tucson AZ 85712   (520) 324-3177, TTY
email: demetras@ccit.arizona.edu   (520) 324-3176, fax

ARKANSAS

Arkansas Increasing Capabilities Access Network

2201 Brookwood, Suite 117   (800) 828-2799, in state, voice/TTY
Little Rock AR 72202   (501) 666-8868, voice/TTY
email: 102503.3602@compuserve.com   (501) 666-5319, fax

CALIFORNIA

California Assistive Technology System

California Department of Rehabilitation   (916) 324-3062, voice/TTY
830 K Street Mall
Sacramento CA 95814

COLORADO
Colorado Assistive Technology Project
Rocky Mountain Resource and Training Institute   (303) 534-1027
1391 N. Speer Boulevard, Suite 350   (303) 534-1063, TTY
Denver CO 80204   (303) 534-1075, fax
email: rmrti@essex.uchsc.edu

COMMONWEALTH OF THE NORTHERN MARIANA ISLANDS
Assistive Technology Project
Developmental Disabilities Planning Office   (670) 322-3015
Office of the Governor   (670) 322-4168, fax
P.O. Box 2565
Faipan MP 96950
email: dd.council@faipan.com

CONNECTICUT
Connecticut Assistive Technology Project
Bureau of Rehabilitation Services   (203) 298-2042
10 Griffin Road N.   (203) 298-2018, TTY
Windsor CT 06095   (203) 298-9590, fax
email: cttap@aol.com

DELAWARE
Delaware Assistive Technology Initiative Applied Science and Engineering Laboratories
University of Delaware, A.I. duPont Institute   (302) 651-6790
1600 Rockland Road, Room 154   (302) 651-6794, TTY
P.O. Box 269   (302) 651-6793, fax
Wilmington DE 19899-0269
email: dati@asel.udel.edu

DISTRICT OF COLUMBIA
DC Partnership for Assistive Technology
801 Pennsylvania Avenue, SE   (202) 546-9164
Suite 210   (202) 546-9168, TTY
Washington DC 20003   (202) 546-9169, fax
email: jodywild@dcpat.org

258

Computer
Resources
for People
with
Disabilities

FLORIDA
Florida Alliance for Assistive Service and Technology
2002-A Old St. Augustine Road   (904) 487-3278, voice/TTY
Tallahassee FL 32399-0696   (904) 921-7214, fax
email: faast@freenet.scri.fsu.edu

GEORGIA
Georgia Tools for Life
Division of Rehabilitation Services   (800) 726-9119
2 Peachtree Street, NW, Suite 23-411   (404) 894-4960
Atlanta GA 30303-3142   (404) 657-3085, TTY
email: 102476.1737@compuserve.com   (404) 657-3086, fax

GUAM
Guam System for Assistive Technology
University Affiliated Program—Developmental Disabilities
House #12 Dean's Circle   (671) 734-9309
University of Guam   (761) 734-5709, fax
UOG Station
Mangilao Guam 96923
email: sspencer@uog.edu

HAWAII
Hawaii Assistive Technology Training and Service Project
677 Ala Moana Blvd., Suite 403   (808) 532-7110, voice/TTY
Honolulu HI 96813   (808) 532-7120, fax
email: bfl@pixi.com

IDAHO
Idaho Assistive Technology Project   (208) 885-3630
129 W. Third Street   (208) 885-3559, voice/TTY
Moscow ID 83843   (208) 885-3628, fax

ILLINOIS
Illinois Assistive Technology Project
528 S. Fifth Street, Suite 100   (800) 852-5110, in state, voice/TTY
Springfield IL 62701   (217) 522-7985
email: iatp@cencom.net   (217) 522-8067, fax

INDIANA

Indiana Attain (Accessing Technology Through Awareness in Indiana) Project

402 W. Washington Street, Room W453   (800) 545-7763, voice/TTY
P.O. Box 7083   (317) 232-6478, fax
Indianapolis IN 46207-7083
email: cris_fulford@inspeced.ccmail.compuserve.com

IOWA

Iowa Program for Assistive Technology

Iowa University Affiliated Program   (800) 331-3027, voice/TTY
University Hospital School   (319) 356-8284, fax
Iowa City IA 52242-1011
email: james_hardy@uiowa.edu

KANSAS

Assistive Technology for Kansans Project

2601 Gabriel   (800) KAN DO IT (526-3648)
P.O. Box 738   (316) 421-8367
Parsons KS 67357   (316) 421-0954, fax/TTY
email: ssimmons@parsons.lsi.ukans.edu

KENTUCKY

Kentucky Assistive Technology Services Network

P.O. Box 757   (800) 327-5287, in state, voice/TTY
Frankfort KY 40602-0757   (502) 564-2733, voice/TTY
    (502) 564-2951, fax

LOUISIANA

Louisiana Assistance Technology Access Network

P.O. Box 14115   (504) 925-9500
Baton Rouge LA 70898-4115   (504) 925-9560, fax
email: jmnesbit@aol.com
latanstate@aol.com

260

Computer
Resources
for People
with
Disabilities

MAINE
Maine Consumer Information and Technology Training Exchange (Maine CITE)

Maine CITE Coordinating Center   (207) 621-3195, voice/TTY
Education Network of Maine   (207) 621-3193, fax
46 University Drive
Augusta ME 04330
email: kpowers@maine.caps.maine.edu

MARYLAND
Maryland Technology Assistance Program
Governor's Office for Individuals with Disabilities

300 W. Lexington Street, Box 10   (800) TECH-TAP (832-4827)
Baltimore MD 21201   (410) 333-4975, voice/TTY
email: mdtap@clark.net   (410) 333-6674, fax

MASSACHUSETTS
Massachusetts Assistive Technology Partnership

MATP Center   (800) 848-8867, in state, voice/TTY
Children's Hospital   (617) 355-7153
1295 Boylston, Suite 310   (617) 355-7301, TTY
Boston MA 02115   (617) 355-6345, fax
email: brewer_ju@a1.tch.harvard.edu

MICHIGAN
Michigan Tech 2000

Michigan Rehabilitation Services/TECH 2000   (517) 335-6874
P.O. Box 30010   (517) 373-4035, TTY
Lansing MI 48909-7510   (517) 373-0565, fax
email: mbarnes@msu.edu

MINNESOTA
Minnesota Star Program

300 Centennial Bldg   (800) 331-3027, voice/TTY
658 Cedar Street.   (612) 296-9962, TTY
St. Paul MN 55155   (612) 282-6671, fax
email: mnstars@gteens.com

MISSISSIPPI
Mississippi Project Start

P.O. Box 1000   (800) 852-8328, in state, voice/TTY
Jackson MS 39205-1000   (601) 987-4872
email: mspjtstr@gteens.com   (601) 364-2349, fax

MISSOURI
Missouri Assistive Technology Project
4731 South Cochise, Suite 114   (800) 647-8557, in state, voice/TTY
Independence MO 64055-6975   (816) 373-5193
email: matpmo@qni.com   (816) 373-9314, fax

MONTANA
MonTECH
MUARID, The University of Montana   (406) 243-5676
634 Eddy Avenue   (800) 732-0323, TTY
Missoula MT 59812   (406) 243-4730, fax
email: leech@selway.umt.edu

NEBRASKA
Nebraska Assistive Technology Project
301 Centennial Mall South   (800) 742-7594, in state
P.O. Box 94987   (402) 471-3647, voice/TTY
Lincoln NE 68509-4987   (402) 471-0117, fax
email: mschultz@nde4.nde.state.ne.us

NEVADA
Nevada Assistive Technology Collaborative Rehabilitation Division
Office of Community-Based Services   (702) 687-4452
711 S. Stewart Street   (702) 687-3388, TTY
Carson City NV 89710   (702) 687-3292, fax
email: nvreach@gteens.com

NEW HAMPSHIRE
New Hampshire Technology Partnership Project
Institute on Disability/UAP
#14, Ten Ferry Street   (603) 224-0630, voice/TTY
The Concord Center   (603) 226-0389, fax
Concord NH 03301
email: mjpawlek@christa.unh.edu

NEW JERSEY
New Jersey Technology Assistive Resource Program
135 E. State Street, CN 398   (609) 292-7498
Trenton NJ 08625   (609) 292-8347, fax
email: njdvr@gteens.com

262

Computer
Resources
for People
with
Disabilities

NEW MEXICO
New Mexico Technology Assistance Program
435 St. Michael's Drive, Bldg. D   (800) 866-ABLE (866-2253), voice/TTY
Santa Fe NM 87503   (505) 827-3746, fax
email: nmdvrtap@aol.com

NEW YORK
New York State Triad Project
Office of Advocate for Persons with Disabilities   (518) 474-2825
One Empire State Plaza, Suite 1001   (800) 522-4369, in state, voice/TTY
Albany NY 12223-1150   (518) 473-4231, TTY
email: d.buck@oapwd.state.ny.us   (518) 473-6005, fax

NORTH CAROLINA
North Carolina Assistive Technology Project
Department of Human Resources   (800) 852-0042
Division of Vocational Rehabilitation Services   (919) 850-2787, voice/TTY
1110 Navaho Drive, Suite 101   (919) 850-2792, fax
Raleigh NC 27609
email: atp@med.unc.edu

NORTH DAKOTA
North Dakota Interagency Program for Assistive Technology (IPAT)
P.O. Box 743   (701) 265-4807, voice/TTY
Cavalier ND 58220   (701) 265-3150, fax
email: lee@pioneer.state.nd.us

OHIO
Ohio Technology Related Information Network
1224 Kinnear Road   (614) 292-2426
Columbus OH 43212   (614) 292-5866, fax
email: dhuntt@mailcar.orl.osc.edu

OKLAHOMA
Able Tech
Oklahoma State University   (800) 257-1705, voice/TTY
Wellness Center   (405) 744-9748
1514 W. Hall of Fame   (405) 744-7670, fax
Stillwater OK 74078-0618
email: mljwell@okway.okstate.edu

OREGON

Oregon Technology Access For Life Needs Project
1257 Ferry Street, SE
Salem OR 97310

(503) 361-1201, voice/TTY
(503) 378-3599, fax

PENNSYLVANIA

Pennsylvania's Initiative on Assistive Technology
Institute on Disability/UAP
Ritter Annex 433
Philadelphia PA 19122
email: piat@astro.ocis.temple.edu

(800) 204-PIAT (204-7428)
(800) 750-PIAT (750-7428), TTY
(215) 204-9371, fax

PUERTO RICO

Puerto Rico Assistive Technology Project
University of Puerto Rico
Medical Sciences Campus
College of Related Health Professionals
Department of Communication Disorders
P.O. Box 365067
San Juan, Puerto Rico 00936
email: pratp@rcmad.upr.clu.edu

(800) 496-6035, from U.S. mainland
(800) 981-6033, in P.R.
(809) 754-8034, TTY

RHODE ISLAND

Rhode Island Assistive Technology Access Project
Office of Rehabilitation Services
40 Fountain Street
Providence RI 02903-1898

(800) 752-8038 ext. 2608, in state
(401) 421-7005
(401) 421-7016, fax

SOUTH CAROLINA

South Carolina Assistive Technology Program
Vocational Rehabilitation Dept.
P.O. Box 15
1410-C Boston Avenue
West Columbia SC 29171-0015
email: scatp@scsn.net

(803) 822-5404, voice/TTY
(803) 822-4301, fax

SOUTH DAKOTA

Dakota Link
1925 Plaza Blvd.
Rapid City SD 57702
email: jplloyd@sdtie.sdserv.org

(800) 645-0673, voice/TTY
(605) 394-1876, voice/TTY
(605) 394-5315, fax

264

Computer
Resources
for People
with
Disabilities

TENNESSEE

Tennessee Technology Access Project
710 James Robertson Parkway   (800) 732-5059, in state
Gateway Plaza, 11th Floor   (615) 532-6530
Nashville TN 37243-0675   (615) 532-6612, TTY
email: akoshakj@mail.state.tn.us   (615) 532-9940, fax

TEXAS

Texas Assistive Technology Program
The University of Texas at Austin, UAP of Texas   (800) 828-7839
Dept. of Special Education, EDB 306   (512) 471-7621
Austin TX 78712   (512) 471-1844, TTY
email: bbryant@mail.utexas.edu   (512) 471-7549, fax

UTAH

Utah Assistive Technology Program: Center for Persons with
Disabilities   (800) 333-UTAH (333-8824), voice/TTY
UMC 6855   (801) 797-2096, TTY
Logan UT 84322   (801) 797-2355, fax
email: mmenlove@cc.usu.edu

VERMONT

Vermont Assistive Technology Project
103 S. Main Street, Weeks I   (802) 241-2620, voice/TTY
Waterbury VT 05671-2305   (802) 241-3052, fax
email: chrisp@dad.state.vt.us

VIRGIN ISLANDS

Virgin Islands Assistive Technology Project
University of the Virgin Islands/UAP   (809) 693-1323
#2 John Brewers Bay   (809) 693-1325, fax
St. Thomas VI 00801

VIRGINIA

Virginia Assistive Technology System
8004 Franklin Farms Drive   (804) 662-9993
P.O. Box K300   (804) 662-9990, voice/TTY
Richmond VA 23288-0300   (804) 662-9478, fax
email: vatskhk@aol.com

WASHINGTON
Washington Assistive Technology Alliance
DSHS/DVR
P.O. Box 45340
Olympia WA 98504-5340
email: dhooks@dshs.wa.gov

(206) 438-8051
(206) 438-8644, TTY
(206) 438-8007, fax

WEST VIRGINIA
West Virginia Assistive Technology System
Division of Rehabilitation Services
P.O. Box 50890, State Capitol
Charleston WV 25305-0890

(304) 766-4698
(304) 293-4692, TTY
(304) 293-7294, fax

WISCONSIN
WISTECH
Division of Vocational Rehabilitation
P.O. Box 7852
2917 International Lane
Madison WI 53707-7852
email: trampf@aol.com

(800) 426-STEP (426-7837), in state
(608) 243-5601, TTY
(608) 243-5681, fax

WYOMING
Wyoming's New Options in Technology
Division of Vocational Rehabilitation
1100 Herschler Building.
Cheyenne WY 82002
email: wy813h@wydsprod.state.wy.us

(307) 777-4386, voice/TTY
(307) 777-7450, voice/TTY
(307) 777-5939, fax

Americans with Disabilities Act

ADA technology resources

There are many agencies and organizations that provide support for the implementation of the Americans with Disabilities Act. The following agencies and organizations can provide you with information and referrals.

American Printing House for the Blind
P.O. Box 6085
Louisville KY 40206

(800) 223-1839
(502) 895-2405

266

Computer
Resources
for People
with
Disabilities

Job Accommodation Network (JAN)
West Virginia University   (800) 526-7234, voice/TTY
P.O. Box 6080   (800) 526-2262, Canada
Morgantown WV 26506-6080
A service of the President's Committee on Employment of People with
Disabilities

Office of the Americans with Disabilities Act
Civil Rights Division   (800) 514-0301
U.S. Dept. of Justice   (202) 514-0301
P.O. Box 66118   (800) 514-0383, TTY
Washington DC 20035-6118   (202) 514-0380, TTY

Equal Employment Opportunity Commission
1801 L Street NW   (800) 669-EEOC (669-3362)
Washington DC 20507   (800) 800-3002, TTY

ADA technical assistance programs

The National Institute on Disability and Rehabilitation Research
(NIDRR) sponsors 10 federally funded agencies, one in each region of
the country, to provide information and technical assistance. Call (800)
949-4232 and your call will be directed to the assistance center for your
region.

Region I: CT, ME, MA, NH, RI, VT
145 Newberry Street
Portland ME 04101   (800) 949-4232, voice/TTY

Region II: NJ, NY, PR
United Cerebral Palsy Association of New Jersey
354 South Broad Street
Trenton NJ 08608   (800) 949-4232, voice/TTY

Region III: DE, DC, MD, PA, VA, WV
Endependence Center of Northern Virginia
2111 Wilson Blvd., #400
Arlington, VA 22201   (800) 949-4232, voice/TTY

Region IV: AL, FL, GA, KY, MS, NC, SC, TN
SE Disability & Business Technical Assistance Center
1776 Peachtree Street, Suite 310 North
Atlanta GA 30309   (800) 949-4232, voice/TTY

Region V: IL, IN, MI, MN, OH, WI
Great Lakes Disability & Business Technical Assistance Center
University of Illinois at Chicago
Affiliated Program in Developmental Disabilities
1640 West Roosevelt Road
Chicago IL 60608   (800) 949-4232, voice/TTY

Region VI: AR, LA, NM, OK, TX
Independent Living Research Utilization
The Institute for Rehabilitation and Research
2323 South Shepherd Blvd., Suite 1000
Houston, TX 77019   (800) 949-4232, voice/TTY

Region VII: IA, KS, NB, MO
University of Missouri at Columbia
4816 Santana Drive
Columbia MO 65203   (800) 949-4232, voice/TTY

Region VIII: CO, MT, ND, SD, UT, WY
Meeting the Challenge, Inc.
3630 Sinton Road, Suite 103
Colorado Springs CO 80907-5072   (800) 949-4232, voice/TTY

Region IX: AZ, CA, HI, NV, PB
Berkeley Planning Associates
440 Grand Avenue, Suite 500
Oakland CA 94610   (800) 949-4232, voice/TTY

Region X: AK, ID, OR, WA
Washington State Governor's Committee
P.O. Box 9046
Olympia WA 98507-9046   (800) 949-4232, voice/TTY

General
Disability Rights Education Defense Fund
2212 6th Street
Berkeley CA 94710
Technical Assistance Information Line: (800) 949-4232, voice/TTY
(Spanish translation available)

AMERICANS WITH DISABILITIES ACT

268

Computer
Resources
for People
with
Disabilities

Organizations

There are thousands of organizations focused on people with disabilities. The ones listed here represent some of the many organizations that have an interest in technology and can provide technology-related services, information, or referrals.

Activating Children Through Technology (ACTT)
Macomb Projects   (309) 298-1634
1 University Circle 27 Horrabin Hall   (309) 298-2305, fax
Western Illinois University
Macomb IL 61455
email: terry_carley@ccmail.wiv.edu
website: http://www.ecn.edu/users/mimacp/wiv/index.html

Alexander Graham Bell Association for the Deaf
3417 Volta Place, NW   (202) 337-5220, voice/TTY
Washington, DC 20007-2778

Alliance for Public Technology
901 15th Street NW, Suite 230   (202) 408-1403, voice/TTY
Washington, DC 20005   (202) 408-1134, fax
email: apt@apt.org
website: http://apt.org/apt/

American Association of People with Disabilities
4401-A Connecticut Avenue NW, Suite 223   (202)363-8970
Washington DC 20008

American Foundation for the Blind
National Technology Center   (800) 232-5463
11 Penn Plaza, Suite 300   (212) 502-7642
New York NY 10001   (212) 502-7773, fax
email: techctr@afb.org

American Occupational Therapy Association (AOTA)
P.O. Box 31220   (301) 652-2682
4720 Montgomery Lane   (800) 377-8555, TTY
Bethesda MD 20824-1220   (301) 652-7711, fax

American Printing House for the Blind
1839 Frankfort Avenue   (800) 223-1839
P.O. Box 6085   (502) 895-2405
Louisville KY 40206-0085   (502) 899-2274, fax

American Speech-Language-Hearing Association (ASHA)

10801 Rockville Pike	(800) 638-8255, voice/TTY (consumers)
Rockville MD 20852	(301) 897-5700, voice/TTY (members)
	(301) 571-0457, fax

The Arc (formerly Association for Retarded Citizens)

500 E. Border Street, Suite 300	(800) 433-5255
Arlington TX 76010	(817) 261-6003, voice
email: thearc@metronet.com	(817) 277-0553, TTY
website: http://thearc.org/welcome.html	(817) 277-3491, fax

Autism Society of America

	(800) 3-AUTISM (328-8476)
7910 Woodmont Avenue, Suite 650	(301) 657-0869
Bethesda MD 20814-3015	(301) 657-0869, fax

Center for Applied Special Technology (CAST)

39 Cross Street	(508) 531-8555
Peabody MA 01960	(508) 538-3110, TTY
email: cast@cast.org	(508) 531-0192, fax

Center for Information Technology Accomodation

GSA 18th and F Street NW, Room #1234	(202) 501-4906
MC:MWA	(202) 501-6269, fax
Washington DC 20405	

Center for Rehabilitation Technology

490 10th Street	(800) 726-9119
Atlanta GA 30332-0156	(404) 894-9320, fax
email: robert.todd@arch.gatech.edu	

The Center for Technology and Learning Disabilities

Frostig Center	(818) 791-1255
971 No. Altadena Drive	(818) 798-1801, fax
Pasadena CA 91107	

Computer Learning Foundation

2431 Park Boulevard	(415) 327-3349
Palo Alto CA 94306	(415) 327-3347, fax

The Council for Exceptional Children

1920 Association Drive	(800) 845-6232, voice/TTY
Reston VA 22091-1589	(703) 264-9494, fax

The Disability Resources, Affiliates and Groups Network (DRAGNET)

Computer Recyclers	(612) 378-9796
840 12th Avenue, Northwest	(612) 278-9794, fax
Minneapolis MN 55413-1537	

270

Computer
Resources
for People
with
Disabilities

Independent Living Centers
For a directory contact: (713) 520-0232
ILRU   (713) 520-5136, TTY
2323 South Shepherd, Suite 1000   (713) 520-5785, fax
Houston TX 77019
email: ilru@tsbbs02.tnet.com
website: http://www.bcm.tmc.edu/ilru/

Infinitec
155 N. Wacker Drive   (312) 368-0380
Chicago IL 60606   (312) 368-0179, TTY
                                                        (312) 368-0018, fax

International Braille and Technology Center for the Blind
National Federation for the Blind   (410) 659-9314
1800 Johnson Street, Suite 300   (410) 685-5653, fax
Baltimore MD 21230-4998
website: http://www.nfb.org

International Society for Augmentative and Alternative Communication (ISAAC)
P.O. Box 1762   (905) 737-9308
Station R   (905) 737-3624, fax
Toronto ON M4G 4A3
Canada
email: liz_baer@mail.cepp.org

International Society for Technical Education
480 Charnelton Street   (800) 336-5191
Eugene OR 97401-2626   (541) 302-3778, fax
email: cust_svc@ccmail.uoregon.edu

Job Accommodation Network
WVU P.O. Box 6080   (800) 526-7234
Morgantown, WV 26506   (304) 293-5407

Learning Disabilities Association of America
4156 Library Road   (412) 341-1515
Pittsburgh PA 15234   (412) 344-0224, fax

National Association of Protection and Advocacy Systems, Inc.
900 Second Street, NE, Suite 211   (202) 408-9514
Washington DC 20002   (202) 408-9520, TTY/fax
email: hn4537@handsnet.org

National Center for Learning Disabilities
381 Park Avenue S, Suite 1420   (212) 545-7510, voice only
New York NY 10016   (212) 545-9665, fax

National Center for Youth with Disabilities
University of Minnesota
Box 721   (612) 626-2825
420 Delaware Street SE   (612) 624-2134, fax
Minneapolis MN 55455-0392
email: ncyd@gold.tc.umn.edu

National Center to Improve Practice
Education Development Center   (617) 969-7100
EDC 55 Chapel Street
Newton MA 02158

National Easter Seal Society   (800) 221-6827
230 West Monroe Street, Suite 1800   (312) 726-6200
Chicago IL 60606-4802   (312) 726-4258, TTY
email: nessinfo@seals.com   (312) 726-1494, fax
website: http://www.seals.com

National Information Center for Children and Youth with Disabilities (NICHCY)
P.O. Box 1492   (800) 695-0285, voice/TTY
Washington DC 20013-1492
email: nichey@aed.org

National Information Center on Deafness
Gallaudet University   (202) 651-5051
800 Florida Avenue NE   (202) 651-5052, TTY
Washington DC 20002-3695   (202) 651-5054, fax
website: http://www.gallaudet.edu/~NICD

National Lekotek Center   (800) 366-PLAY (366-7529)
2100 Ridge Avenue   (847) 328-0001, voice/TTY
Evanston, IL 60201-2796   (847) 328-5514, fax
email: lekotek@interaccess.com

National Rehabilitation Information Center (NARIC)
8455 Colesville Road, Suite 935   (800) 346-2742
Silver Springs MD 20910   (301) 587-1967, fax

National Technical Institute for the Deaf
Rochester Institute of Technology   (716) 475-2411
52 Lomb Memorial Drive   (716) 475-2810, TTY
Rochester NY 14623-5604   (716) 475-6500, fax

272

Computer
Resources
for People
with
Disabilities

The Orton Dyslexia Society

Chester Bldg. Suite 382
8600 La Salle Road
Baltimore MD 21286-2044
email: ods@pie.org
website: http://pie.org/ODS

(800) 331-0688
(410) 296-0232
(410) 321-5069, fax

Parent Training and Information Centers

To find the PTI in your state, contact:
Federation for Children with Special Needs
Technical Assistance for Parent Programs (TAPP)
95 Berkeley Street, Suite 104
Boston MA 02116

(617) 482-2915, voice/TTY
(617) 695-2939, fax

Recording for the Blind and Dyslexic

20 Roszel Road
Princeton NJ 08540
email: info@rfbd.org
website: http://www.rfbd.org

(800) 221-4792, Customer Service
(609) 452-0606
(609) 987-8116, fax

RESNA

1700 N. Moore Street, Suite 1540
Arlington VA 22209-1903

(703) 524-6686
(703) 524-6639, TTY
(703) 524-6630, fax

Sensory Access Foundation

385 Sherman Avenue, Suite 2
Palo Alto CA 94306

(415) 329-0430
(415) 323-1062, fax

TASH (Association for Persons with Severe Handicaps)

29 West Susquehanna, Suite 210
Baltimore MD 21204

(410) 828-8274
(410) 828-1306, TTY
(410) 828-6706, fax

Technology and Media (TAM)

Council for Exceptional Children
1920 Association Drive
Reston VA 22091-1589
email: yvetteh@cec.sped.org

(703) 620-3660
(703) 264-9446, TTY
(703) 264-9494, fax

Telecommunications for the Deaf Incorporated (TDI)

8719 Colesville Road, Suite 300
Silver Spring MD 20910
email: tdioffices@aol.com

(301) 589-3786
(301) 589-3006, TTY
(301) 589-3797, fax

Trace Research and Development Center

Waisman Center

(608) 262-6966

University of Wisconsin-Madison
1500 Highland Avenue
Madison WI 53705
email: info@trace.wisc.edu
website: http://www.trace.wisc.edu

(608) 263-5408, TTY
(608) 262-8848, fax

United Cerebral Palsy Associations
1660 L Street NW, Suite 700
Washington DC 20036
email:ucpaine@aol.com

(800) USA-5UCP (872-5827)
(800) 872-5827, voice/TTY
(202) 776-0406
(202) 776-0414, fax

United States Society for Augmentative and Alternative
Communication
(USSAAC)
P.O. Box 5271
Evanston IL 60204-5271

(847) 869-2122
(847) 869-2161, fax

University Affiliated Programs
American Association of University Affiliated Programs for Persons
with Developmental Disabilities
8630 Fenton Street, Suite 410
Silver Spring MD 20910

(301) 588-8252
(301) 588-3319, TTY
(301) 588-2842, fax

National Conferences

The conferences listed here are key annual events that address technology and people with disabilities. This list is not exhaustive. There are literally hundreds of conferences each year that relate to this field. You can find out about numerous state, regional, and local conferences by contacting your community technology resources and the Tech Act project in your state.

Abilities Expo
Expocon Management Associates, Inc.
363 Reef Road
P.O. Box 915
Fairfield CT 06430-0915

(203) 256-4700
(203) 256-4730, fax

Alliance for Public Technology
901 15th Street, NW, Suite 230
P.O. Box 28578
Washington DC 20038-8578

(202) 408-1403

274

Computer
Resources
for People
with
Disabilities

American Speech-Language-Hearing Association (ASHA)
10801 Rockville Pike   (800) 638-8255
Rockville MD 20852   (301) 897-5700
                                                    (301) 571-0457, fax

American Occupational Therapy Association (AOTA)
4720 Montgomery, P.O. Box 31220   (301) 948-9626
1383 Piccard Drive   (301) 652-2682, TTY/fax
Bethesda MD 20824

**Association for Education and Rehabilitation of the Blind and
Visually Impaired**
206 N. Washington Street, Suite 320   (703) 548-1884
Alexandria VA 22314   (703) 683-2926, fax

Closing the Gap
P.O. Box 68   (612) 248-3294
Henderson MN 56044   (612) 248-3810, fax

ConnSENSE for Software Education
249 Glenbrook Road U-64   (203) 486-0171
Storrs CT 06269-2064   (860) 486-0210, fax

Educational Computer Conferences
19 Calvert Court   (800) 255-2218
Piedmont CA 94611

Florida Adaptive Technology Impact Conference
Florida Instructional Center for the Visually Handicapped
5002 N. Lois Avenue   (813) 872-5281
Tampa FL 33614   (813) 872-5284, fax
email: fitterl@mail.firn.edu

International Conference on Computers for Handicapped Persons
c/o Austrian Computer Society   (43) 1 512 02 35
Wollzeile 1-3
A-1010 Vienna
Austria

**International Society for Augmentative and Alternative
Communication (ISAAC)**
P.O. Box 1762   (905) 737-9308
Station R
Toronto, ON M4G 4A3
Canada

Learning Disabilities Association of America
4156 Library Road (412) 341-1515
Pittsburgh PA 15234 (412) 344-0224, fax

National Symposium on Information Technology
Center for Developmental Disabilities (803) 935-5231
Midland Center, Educational Building (803) 935-5250, fax
8301 Farrow
Columbia SC 29203

President's Committee on Employment of People with Disabilities
1331 F Street NW, Suite 300 (202) 376-6200
Washington DC 20004 (202) 376-6219, fax

RESNA
1700 N. Moore Street, Suite 1540 (703) 524-6686
Arlington VA 22209-1903 (703) 524-6630, fax
email: natloffice@resna.org

Symposium on Augmentative Communication and Adaptive Technology
601 Childrens Lane (804) 668-9143
Norfolk VA 23507 (804) 668-7389, fax

Technology and Media (TAM)
Council for Exceptional Children (703) 620-3660
1920 Association Drive (703) 264-5494, fax
Reston VA 22091-1589
website: http://www.cec.sped.org

Technology and Persons with Disabilities Annual Conference
California State University, Northridge (CSUN)
Center on Disabilities (818) 885-2578, voice/TTY
18111 Nordoff Street (818) 885-4929, fax
Northridge CA 91330-8340
email: ltm@csun.edu

Publications

The newsletters, magazines, and books listed here represent a wide range of subjects related to technology and are geared to a wide range of audiences. Most of the Alliance for Technology Access centers, the Tech Act projects, and many of the other organizations cited in this

276

Computer
Resources
for People
with
Disabilities

book produce newsletters. Contact them directly for information about their various publications.

The roster of publications dealing with assistive technology changes weekly—new ones appear and older ones disappear. If you are having trouble locating any of the books listed here, or any other book related to the field, The Special Needs Project (a mail-order book company specializing in books on disability) can help you. They have an extensive catalog of books and can be reached at (800) 333-6867.

Newsletters and magazines

The Advance
650 Park Avenue West   (610) 265-7812
King of Prussia PA 19406   (610) 265-8249, fax
email: advance@merion.com

Alternatively Speaking
Michael Williams   (408) 649-3050
Augmentative Communication, Inc.   (408) 646-5428, fax
1 Surf Way, #237
Monterey CA 93940
email: sarablack@aol.com

Assistive Technology (RESNA)
Contact: Terry Reamer   (703) 524-6686
RESNA   (703) 524-6630, fax
1700 N. Moore Street
Arlington VA 22209-1903

Assistive Technology News
John M. Williams, Publisher   (703) 255-7104
19 Crescent Court   (703) 406-7831, voice/TTY
Sterling VA 20164   (703) 406-3728, fax

Augmentative and Alternative Communication
International Society for Augmentative and Alternative
Communication (ISAAC)   (905) 737-9308
P.O. Box 1762   (905) 737-0624, fax
Station R
Toronto ON
Canada M4G 4A3
email: liz_baer@mail.cepp.org

Augmentative and Alternative Communication Journal
Decker Publishing   (905) 522-7017
4 Hughson Street South, LCD1   (905) 522-7839, fax
Hamilton Ontario
Canada L8N 3K7

Augmentative Communication News
Augmentative Communication, Inc.   (408) 649-3050
1 Surf Way, #237   (408) 646-5428, fax
Monterey CA 93940
email:sarablack@aol.com

CATALYST
Western Center for Microcomputers in Special Education, Inc.
1259 El Camino Real, Suite 275   (415) 855-8064
Menlo Park CA 94025
email: catalystwc@aol.com

Closing the Gap Annual Resource Directory
Closing the Gap Newsletter   (507) 248-3294
P.O. Box 68   (507) 248-3810, fax
Henderson MN 56044
email: ctgap@aol.com

Communication Independence for the Neurologically Impaired, Inc.
CINI Resource Guide   (516) 874-8354
250 Mercer Street, Suite B1608   (516) 878-8412, fax
New York NY 10012
email: 73523.151@compuserve.com

Communication Outlook
Artificial Language Lab   (517) 353-0870
Michigan State University
405 Computer Center
East Lansing MI 48823
email: john@all.cps.msu.edu
website: http://www.msu.edu/user/eulenberg

Communicating Together
ISAAC   (519) 766-1757
Suite 215, 3-304 Stone Road West   (519) 763-6682, fax
Guelph Ontario N1G 4W4
Canada
email: plindsay@oise.on.ca
smcnaughton@oise.on.ca

278

Computer
Resources
for People
with
Disabilities

Compuplay News (formerly Innotek News)
National Lekotek Center   (847) 328-0001
2100 Ridge Avenue   (847) 328-5514, fax
Evanston IL 60201-2796

Connections
National Center for Youth with Disabilities   (612) 626-2825
University of Minnesota   (612) 626-2134, fax
Box 721
420 Delaware Street SE
Minneapolis MN 55455-0392
email: ncyd@gold.tc.umn.edu

CONNSense Bulletin
249 Glenbrook Road U-64   (860) 486-0172
Storrs CT 06269-2064   (860) 486-5037, fax

Counterpoint
National Association for Directors of Special Education   (215) 341-7874
LRP Publications—Education Department   (215) 784-9639, fax
747 Dresher Road, Suite 500
Horsham PA 19044

Directions
DREAMMS for Kids, Inc.   (813) 781-7711
2763 Tasha Drive
Clearwater FL 34621
email: dreamms@aol.com

Direct Link
C-Cad at Infomart   (214) 746-4217
1950 Stemmons Freeway, Suite 4041   (214) 746-4203, fax
Dallas TX 75207

Directory of National Information Sources on Disabilities
National Rehabilitation Information Center (NARIC)(800) 227-0216
8455 Colesville Road, Suite 935   (301) 588-9284, voice/TTY
Silver Spring MD 20910-3319   (301) 495-5626, TTY
                                                          (301) 587-1967, fax

Disability Resources Monthly
Disability Resources Inc.   (516) 585-0290, voice/fax
Four Glatter Lane
Centereach NY 11720-1032
email: jklauber@suffolk.lib.ny.us

Electronic Learning
Scholastic Inc.   (212) 505-4900
555 Broadway   (212) 260-8587, fax
New York NY 10012

Exceptional Parent Magazine
P.O. Box 3000   (800) 562-1973
Denville NJ 07834   (201) 627-5872, fax

Exceptional Parent Magazine
Annual Technology Issue
P.O. Box 3000, Department EP   (800) 372-7368
Denville NJ 07834   (201) 489-1240, fax

Family PC
P.O. Box 400451   (800) 413-9749
Des Moines IA 50347-0451

Financing Assistive Technology
Steve Mendelsohn, Editor   (415) 864-2220,voice/fax
Smiling Interface
PO Box 2792 Church Street Station
New York NY 10008-2792
email: mendelsohn@delphi.com

Guide to Catalogs: For People with Disabilities, Their Families,
and Their Friends
Evan Kemp Associates   (202) 296-1488
9151 Hampton Overlook   (202) 301-324-0121, fax
Capitol Heights MD 20743

Home Automation Newsletter
Home Tech Project   (800) 886-3050
Seaside Education Associates
284 North Avenue
Weston MA 02193

Information Technology and Disabilities
Tom McNulty, Editor-in-Chief   (212) 995-4583
Bobst Library, New York University   (212) 998-4980, TTY
70 Washington Square South
New York NY 10012
email: mcnulty@is.nyu.edu
website: http://www.isc.rit.edu/~easi/easijrnl/easijrnl.html

280

Computer
Resources
for People
with
Disabilities

Issues and Updates
Newsletter of the California Deaf and Disabled Telecommunications
Program (510) 874-1410
1939 Harrison Street, Suite 520 (510) 874-1411, TTY
Oakland CA 94612
email: sha@ix.netcom.com

Journal of Special Education Technology
Council for Exceptional Children (703) 620-3660
1920 Association Drive (703) 264-9494, fax
Reston VA 22091-1589

Journal of Visual Impairment and Blindness
American Foundation for the Blind (800) 232-5463
11 Penn Plaza (212) 620-2000
New York NY 10011 (212) 502-7771, fax
email: asbinfo@asb.org

Learning and Leading with Technology
International Society for Technical Education (800) 336-5191
480 Charnelton Street (541) 302-3778, fax
Eugene OR 97401-2626
email: cust_svc@ccmail.voregon.edu

Mainstream
P.O. Box 370598 (619) 234-3138
San Diego CA 92137-0598 (619) 234-3155, fax
email: subscribe@mainstream-mag.com
website: http//www.mainstream-mag.com

The Mouth
61 Brighton Street (716) 244-6599
Rochester NY 14607 (716) 244-9798, fax

New Mobility
Miramar Communications, Inc. (800) 543-4116
23815 Stuart Ranch Road (310) 317-4522
P.O. Box 8987 (310) 317-9644, fax
Malibu CA 90265

One Step Ahead
"Newsletter by People with Disabilities for People with Disabilities, Their Families, and Their Friends"   (800) 386-5367, voice/TTY
Robert Funk, Editor   (301) 324-0121, fax
Evan Kemp Publications
P.O. Box 65766
Washington DC 20035
email: info@eka.com

Poor Richard's LD Reader
Poor Richard's Publishing   (860) 567-4307
P.O. Box 1075
Litchfield CT 06759
email: rwanderman@aol.com
website: http://www.tiac.net/users/poorrich/

Public Domain Software Catalogue
Colorado Easter Seal Society   (303) 233-1666
5755 West Alameda Avenue   (303) 233-1028, fax
Lakewood CO 80226-3500

TAM Newsletter
Technology and Media   (703) 620-3660
Editor: Susan Simmons   (703) 264-9494, fax
Council for Exceptional Children
1920 Association Drive
Reston VA 22091-1589

TeamRehab
P.O. Box 16778   (310) 317-4522
North Hollywood CA 91615-6778

Technology and Disability
Elsevier Science   (212) 633-3750
655 Avenue of the Americas   (212) 633-3764, fax
New York NY 10010
email:usinfo-f@elsevier.com

Technology and Learning
P.O. Box 49727   (800) 543-4383
Dayton OH 45449-0727

Books

Adaptive PCs for Disabilities—With CD-ROM. J. Lazarro. Reading, MA: Addison-Wesley, 1996.

282

———

Computer
Resources
for People
with
Disabilities

Assistive Technology and the IEP. Katherine Kelker, et al. Arlington, VA: RESNA Press, 1992.

Assistive Technology: A Resource for School, Work and Community. K. Filippo, K. Inge, J. Barcus. Baltimore: Paul H. Brookes Publishing, 1995.

Assistive Technology for Persons with Disabilities: The Role of Occupational Therapy. William C. Mann & Joseph P. Lane. Rockville, MD: American Occupational Therapy Association, 1995. Second Edition.

Assistive Technology: Principles and Practice. A. Cook and S. Hussey. St. Louis, MO: Addison-Wesley, 1995.

Assistive Technology Sourcebook. Alexandra Enders & Marian Hall. Arlington, VA: RESNA Press, 1990.

A Switch to Turn Kids On. Macomb Projects, Project ACTT. Macomb, IL: Western Illinois University, 1994.

Augmentative and Alternative Communication: Management of Severe Communication Disorders in Children and Adults. David Beukelman and Pat Mirenda. Baltimore: Paul H. Brookes Publishing, 1992.

Augmentative and Alternative Communication Systems for Persons with Moderate and Severe Disabilities. Diane Baumgart, Jeanne Johnson, and Edwin Helmstetter. Baltimore: Paul H. Brookes Publishing, 1990.

Birth to Five: Early Childhood Special Education. Frank Bowe, Ph.D. Hempstead, NY: Hofstra University, 1995.

Breaking Barriers: How Children and Adults Can Access the World through Simple Technology. Jackie Levin and Lynn Scherfenberg. Minneapolis: AbleNet 1986.

Can't Wait to Communicate! Fun Activities That Shape Nonverbal Communication. Robbie Wise. Bisbee, AZ: Imaginart, 1989.

Catalog of Special Education Public Domain Software. East Rockaway, NY: Technology for Language and Learning, 1992.

The CD-ROM Advantage. Boston: National Braille Press, 1995.

Communication Skills in Children with Down Syndrome: A Guide for Parents. Libby Kumin. Rockville, MD: Woodbine House, 1993.

Communication Unbound: How Facilitated Communication Is Challenging Traditional Views of Autism and Ability/Disability. Douglas Biklen. New York: Teachers College Press, 1993.

The Complete Directory for People with Disabilities 1995/1996. L. Mackenzie. Lakeville, CT: Grey House, 1995.

Computers and the Americans with Disabilities Act: A Manager's Guide. J. McCormick. New York: Windcrest/McGraw-Hill, 1994.

Computer Bits—Computer Access for Persons with Spinal Cord Injury. S. O'Leary. Santa Barbara, CA: Special Needs Project. Publication date Fall 1996.

The Computer Museum Guide to the Best Software for Kids. C. Miranker and A. Elliot. New York: Harper, 1995.

The Computer User's Survival Guide—Staying Healthy in a High-Tech World. J. Stigliani. Sebastopol, CA: O'Reilly and Associates, 1995.

Directory of Computer and High Technology Grants. Richard Eckstein. Loxahatchee, FL: Research Grant Guides, 1996. Third Edition.

Directory of Grants for Organizations Serving People with Disabilities, Revised Edition. Richard Eckstein. Loxahatchee, FL: Research Grant Guides, 1995. Ninth Edition.

Engineering the Preschool Environment for Interactive Symbolic Communication—An Emphasis on the Developmental Period, 18 Months to Five Years. Carol Goossens, Sharon Crain, and Pamela Elder. Birmingham, AL: Southeast Augmentative Communication Conference Publications, 1992.

Evaluating, Selecting and Using Appropriate Assistive Technology. Jan Galvin and Marcia Scherer, Ph.D. Frederick, MD: Aspen Publishers. Publication date Fall 1996.

Facilitated Communication Training. Rosemary Crossley. New York: Teachers College Press, 1994.

Financial Aid for the Disabled and Their Families 1996-98. Gail Schlachter and R. David Weber. San Carlos, CA: Reference Service Press, 1996.

Fun for Everyone. Jackie Levin & Kathy Enselein. Minneapolis: AbleNet, 1989.

Funding for Assistive Technology and Related Services: An Annotated Bibliography. Alexandra Enders. Missoula, MT: University of Montana, Rural Institute on Disabilities, 1993.

Funding for Persons with Visual Impairments: Large Print Edition. Gail Ann Schlacter and David Weber. San Carlos, CA: Reference Service Press, 1996.

Funding for Persons with Visual Impairments: PLUS Edition (on disk). Gail Ann Schlacter and Davis Weber. San Carlos, CA.: Reference Service Press, 1996.

284

Computer
Resources
for People
with
Disabilities

The Handbook of Assistive Technology. Gregory Church and Sharon Glennen. San Diego: Singular Publishing Group, Inc., 1992.

High/Scope Buyers' Guide to Children's Software. C. Hohman, B. Carmody, and C. McCabe-Branz. Ypsilanti, MI: High/Scope Press, 1995.

High Tech and Small Folks: Learning and Growing with Technology. Alice Wershing and Lois Symington. Lenoir City, TN: Little Tennessee Valley Educational Cooperative, 1995.

Implementing Augmentative and Alternative Communication: Strategies for Learners with Severe Disabilities. Joe Reichle, Jennifer York, and Jeff Sigafoos. Baltimore: Paul Brookes Publishing, 1991.

Learning Difficulties and Computers: Access to the Curriculum. David Hawkridge & Tom Vincent. Bristol, PA: Taylor & Francis, 1992.

Living in a State of Stuck: How Technology Affects Persons with Disabilities. Marcia Scherer. Cambridge, MA: Brookline Books, 1993.

Mindstorms: Children, Computers and Powerful Ideas. Seymour Papert. Scranton, PA: HarperCollins, 1980.

More Homemade Battery Devices for Severely Handicapped Children, with Suggested Activities. Linda Burkhart. Eldersburg, MD: Linda Burkhart, 1985.

The New Language of Toys—Teaching Communication Skills to Special Needs Children. S. Schwartz and J. Heller-Miller. Bethesda, MD: Woodbine House, 1996. Second Edition.

On-Line Access to Disability Related Information. Marka Hayes. Arlington, VA: RESNA Press, 1992.

Quick Tech Activities for Literacy. Peggi McNairn and Cindy Shioleno. Wauconda, IL: Don Johnston, Inc., 1993.

Reflections from a Unicorn. R. Creech. Greenville, NC: RC Publishing Co., 1992.

Selection and Use of Simple Technology: In Home, School, Work and Community Settings. Jackie Levin and Lynn Scherfenberg. Minneapolis: AbleNet, 1987.

Silent Words. Margaret Eastham & David Eastham. Ottawa: Oliver-Pate, 1992.

Special Education Technology: Classroom Applications. Rena Lewis. Pacific Grove, CA: Brooks/Cole Publishing, 1993.

Spinal Network 2nd Edition. Sam Maddox. Boulder, CO: Spinal Network, 1993.

Study on the Financing of Assistive Technology Devices and Services for Individuals with Disabilities: A Report to the President and the Congress of the United States. United Cerebral Palsy Association. Washington, DC: National Council on Disability, 1993.

Summary of Existing Legislation Affecting People with Disabilities. Washington, DC: U.S. Department of Education, Office of Special Education and Rehabilitative Services, 1992.

Tax Options and Strategies for People with Disabilities. Steven Mendelsohn. New York: Demos Vermande Publications, Inc., 1996. Second Edition.

Technology for Inclusion: Meeting the Special Needs of All Students. Mary Male. Boston: Allyn & Bacon, 1994. Second Edition.

Total Augmentative Communication in the Early Childhood Classroom. Linda Burkhart. Eldersburg, MD: Linda Burkhart, 1993.

TRACE Cooperative Electronic Library, CO-NET, CD-ROM. Spring/Summer 1996. Madison, WI: Trace Research & Development Center, University of Wisconsin, 1996. Ninth Edition.

Trace Resource Book: Assistive Technologies for Communication, Control and Computer Access. Madison, WI: Trace Research & Development Center, 1996. 1996-97 Edition.

Using Computers and Speech Synthesis to Facilitate Communicative Interaction with Young and/or Severely Handicapped Children. Linda Burkhart. Eldersburg, MD: Linda Burkhart. 1987.

Utilizing Switch Interfaces with Children Who Are Severely Physically Challenged. Carol Gossens and Sharon Sapp Crain. Pro-Ed. 8700 Shoak Creek Blvd., Austin, TX: 1992.

Telecommunications Resources

Telecommunication services of specific interest to people with disabilities are increasing in number all the time. Many of the key commercial services offer resources for people with disabilities. Many organizations serving people with disabilities have developed their own electronic bulletin board systems. The number of World Wide Web sites and other internet resources focused on disability is extensive and expanding. The lists change often, and online addresses change often. As with every aspect of this field, the telecommunications scene changes rapidly, so the services and systems listed here are included to give you a sense of the scope of the field and where to begin exploring.

286

Computer
Resources
for People
with
Disabilities

Commercial services with resources for people with disabilities

America Online

AOL has a disABILITIES forum with a broad range of information, databases, chat rooms, software libraries, and presentations. You can get information on many topics of interest to people with disabilities, including ADA, job accomodations, and social security, to name a few. There is information about organizations you might want to know about, and opportunities for interactive sessions with others. A basic membership costs $9.95 a month (includes 5 hours of online time), and you need to have special graphic-interface software to log on. AOL will provide you with a disk and 10 free hours if you call customer service at (800) 827-6364.

CompuServe

CompuServe has a forum called Disabilities+ Forum. A wide range of topics are addressed, including information about mental health, learning disabilities, vision and hearing impairments, rights and legislation, and education and employment. There are areas ("rooms") for real-time chats, as well as libraries and discussion groups. A basic membership costs $9.95 per month (includes 5 hours of online time) and the first 10 hours are free. You can call (800) 848-8199 for more information. You can purchase the CompuServe graphic interface (CIM) which makes the system easier to understand and navigate, but CIM does not work for those who need voice input or output. You can connect to CompuServe using other communications software (such as Microphone on the Macintosh or MTEZ on the IBM); CompuServe will then be text-based by default.

Dimenet

Dimenet (Disabled Individuals' Movement for Equality Network) is an online service that provides access for communications and information-sharing among individuals involved in the disability rights and independent living movements. The network is comprehensive and consumer controlled. Because it was designed with access in mind, it is easy to navigate. The online phone numbers to reach Dimenet are: (508) 880-5412 in Taunton, Massachusetts, (513) 341-5205 in Dayton, Ohio, and (918) 582-3622 in Tulsa, Oklahoma. Once you are connected, the first thing you do is type "dime" in lower case letters and press <ENTER>. To create an account, type "new" and press <ENTER>. If you have questions or problems or would like to obtain a user manual, call (513) 237-8360 for voice assistance. Once you have signed on to Dimenet, you can "TELNET" from other systems by entering "Dimenet.org."

SeniorNet on America Online

SeniorNet is an organization dedicated to building a community of computer-using seniors. It has over 7,000 members and 55 learning centers. For more information, contact SeniorNet at (415) 750-5030 or write to them at 399 Arguello Blvd., San Francisco CA 94118. Email: seniornet@aol.com

GEnieNet

GEnie is text-based and requires no special software. The monthly rate varies, according to the selected level, beginning at $7.95 for 5 hours of email. GEnie is the consumer portion of General Electric's internal computer network. Further information is available at (800) 638-9636.

Prodigy Online

Prodigy is another popular online service. It hosts various chat rooms and bulletin boards of interest to people with disabilities. You can explore Prodigy for one free month, which includes 20 hours of online time. After that you will be billed $9.95 per month (includes 5 hours of online time). Prodigy is connected to the Internet only through Windows 3.1 or higher. Call (800) 776-3449 for more information.

Using the Internet

Commercial services, such as those described above, now provide an easy way to get onto the Internet. The advantages of this approach are ease in getting started as well as low cost, if you don't plan to spend much time on the Internet. Another advantage is that there is a substantial amount of disability-related content on the commercial services. Almost all now have an area for software, resources, sharing, and support.

If you are planning to spend a significant amount of time on the Internet, however, you may want to consider using an Internet Service Provider (ISP). These companies provide direct unlimited access to the Internet via local numbers for a monthly rate. This approach may be a bit daunting at the beginning, as you configure your system and find a web browser, but connecting directly to the net is a very cost-effective approach for serious Internet users.

288

Computer
Resources
for People
with
Disabilities

FidoNet and other local bulletin boards provide a third option: a no-cost, email-only route. You can't surf the net, but you can have an email address and communicate with people who are interested in similar topics through free, local bulletin board services. A local computer user group is the best place to ask for local bulletin board numbers that might offer disability-related postings.

What's on the Internet

The Internet is often described as a "network of networks." This means you can access information and resources on computers across the world as easily as the one on your desk by using your computer, modem, and telephone line. There are a variety of formats people typically use to get information. A couple of the most popular ways to use the Internet include:

World Wide Web
The World Wide Web (WWW) offers extensive information and resources in a format that is comfortable and intuitive for many people. Reviewing this information requires software known as a browser. Some popular prowsers are Netscape, Mosaic, and Lynx, among many. Browsers are graphics oriented, which creates potential barriers for users who rely on text-based material. Web sites can be developed with text options, and some organizations are offering alternate formats for their sites.

Each web site has an address known as its URL (Uniform Resource Locator). Typing in the URL allows you to visit the web site you have indicated. The following organizations and their URLs will help you get started on the Web. Happy surfing!

Alliance for Technology Access
http://marin.org/npo/ata/

The Disability Mall
http://disability.com

EASI (Equal Access to Software and Information)
http://www.isc.rit.edu/~easi/

Trace Research and Development Center
http://www.trace.wisc.edu/

Yahoo's Disability Resources
http://www.yahoo.com/yahoo/Society_and_Culture/Disabilities/

Job Accomodation Network
http://janweb.icdi.wvu.edu/

UCPA Assistive Technology Funding and Systems Change Project
http://www.assisttech.com/atfsc.html

RESNA
http://www.resna.org/resna/hometa1.html

Webable-Directory of Websites for People with Disabilities
http://webable.com/

Visit your favorite web sites frequently, as they are updated often and will provide valuable and current information.

In addition to World Wide Web sites, there are many other formats on the Internet that offer innumerable resources on virtually any topic of interest to you. Different formats include news groups, bulletin boards, gopher sites, list serves, and discussion lists. Your local library will no doubt have many books available that more thoroughly describe the different parts of the net. Some sample sites to visit are listed below. Remember, this is only a starter list. As with the web, the numbers of new resources are growing rapidly, bringing unbelievable amounts of information and connections with helpful, knowledgeable people.

Sample List Serves

EASI (Equal Access to Software and Information) deals with issues related to technology and people with disabilities. To join, send a message with a blank subject line to listserv@stuvm.stjohns.edu. In the body of the message type "subscribe easi firstname lastname." To post to the list, send a message to easi@sjuvm.stjohns.edu.

The BlindFam mailing list is for discussions of all aspects of family life as they are affected by the blindness of one or more family members. All family members are invited to join, and people are encouraged to send descriptions of themselves and their families. To subscribe to BlindFam, send an electronic mail message to listserv@sjuvm.stjohns.edu.

The Deaf Discussion List provides "Deaf Magazine" to subscribers. Send an electronic mail message to deaf-request@clark.net. Leave the subject line blank and type in the body of the message, "SUB DEAF firstname lastname."

Handicap Digest is an electronic journal for individuals interested in disability-related issues. An electronic journal is the computer network equivalent to a printed magazine. To subscribe to Handicap Digest,

290

Computer
Resources
for People
with
Disabilities

send an electronic mail message to: wtm@bunker.shel.isc-br.com and request a subscription to Handicap Digest.

LD-List (Learning Disability Discussion List) is an open, unmoderated, international forum that provides information for individuals interested in learning disabilities. Subscribers include people with learning disabilities, family members and friends, educators and administrators, researchers, and others wishing to know more about the subject. To subscribe to LD-List, send an electronic mail message to: ld-list-request@east.pima.edu. In the body of the message type only, "SUBSCRIBE."

Sample Newsgroups
alt.education.disabled includes information regarding the education of people with disabilities.
alt.comp.blind-users includes information about computer use for people with blindness.
alt.support.arthritis includes information of interest about arthritis.

Some Gopher Sites
St. Johns Electronic Rehabilitation Resource Center
gopher://sjuvm.stjohns.edu/11/disabled

Cornucopia of Disability Information at Buffalo
gopher://val-dor.cc.buffalo.edu/1

National Rehabilitation Information Center
gopher://val-dor.cc.buffalo.edu/11/.naric

DO IT (Disabilities Opportunities Internetworking Technology)
gopher://hawking.u.washington.edu

Technology Vendors

The following list indicates vendors and developers in the field today. This list is not exhaustive but represents many of the products currently available. Contact vendors directly for a full list of their products. Many of the vendors included on this list are members of the Alliance for Technology Access (indicated by an asterisk). The Alliance for Technology Access is a growing organization with new vendor members joining regularly. If you are interested in becoming a vendor member of the Alliance for Technology Access please contact them for information and an application.

Ability Research
P.O. Box 1721
Minnetonka MN 55345
email: ability@skypoint.com
website: http://www.skypoint.com/~ability/
- Electronic Pointing Devices
- Switches and Switch Software

(612) 939-0121
(612) 943-3809, fax

*AbleNet, Inc.
1081 Tenth Avenue SE
Minneapolis MN 55414
- Assistive Communication Products
- Environmental Controls
- Interface Devices
- Switches

(800) 322-0956
(612) 379-0956
(612) 379-9143, fax

*Academic Software, Inc.
331 West 2nd Street
Lexington KY 40507
email: asiwel@aol.com
- Interface Devices
- Switch Software

(800) VIA-ADLS (842-2357)
(606) 233-2332
(606) 231-0725, fax

ACS Technologies
1400 Lee Drive
Coraopolis PA 15108
- Assistive Communication Products
- Environmental Controls

(800) 227-2922
(412) 269-6656
(412) 269-6675, fax

ADAMLAB
33500 Van Born Road
Wayne MI 48184
email: kaminsk@wcresa.k12.mi.us
- Assistive Communication Products

(313) 467-1415
(313) 326-2610, fax

Adaptability
P.O. Box 575
Colchester CT 06475-0575
- Arm and Wrist Supports

(800) 266-8856
(800) 566-6678, fax

Adaptivation
224 SE 16th Street
Ames IA 50010
- Assistive Communication Products
- Switches and Switch Software

(800) 723-2783
(515) 233-9185, fax

292

Computer
Resources
for People
with
Disabilities

Adlib, Inc.
5142 Bolsa Avenue, Suite 106   (714) 895-9529
Huntington Beach CA 92649
• Pointing and Typing Aids

Advanced Gravis Computer Technology, Ltd.
101–3750 North Fraser Way   (604) 431-5020
Burnaby BC   (604) 431-5155, fax
Canada V5J 5E9
email: info@gravis.com
website: http://www.gravis.com
• Joysticks

Advanced Ideas Inc.
591 Redwood Highway, Suite 2325   (415) 388-2430
Mill Valley CA 94941   (415) 388-6575, fax
• Reading Comprehension Programs

Affinity Microsystems
934 Pearl Street, Suite H   (303) 442-4840
Boulder CO 80302   (303) 442-4999, fax
email: affinity@aol.com
tempo@affinity.com
• Abbreviation Expansion and Macro Programs

Aicom Corporation
2381 Zanker Road, Suite #160   (408) 577-0370
San Jose CA 95131   (408) 577-0373, fax
• Speech Synthesizers

Ai Squared
P.O. Box 669   (802) 362-3612
Manchester Center VT 05255-0669   (802) 362-1670, fax
email: zoomtext@aisquared.com
• Screen Enlargement Programs

Alliance for Technology Access
2175 East Francisco Blvd., Suite L   (415) 455-4575
San Rafael CA 94901   (415) 455-0654, fax
email: atafta@aol.com
website: http://marin.org/npo/ata/

American Printing House for the Blind, Inc.
P.O. Box 6085
Louisville KY 40206
email: info@aph.org
website: http://www.aph.org
- Notetakers
- Screen Readers
- Speech Synthesizers
- Talking Software

(502) 895-2405
(502) 899-2274, fax

*American Thermoform Corporation
2311 Travers Avenue
City of Commerce CA 90040
- Braille Embossers, Translators
- Refreshable Braille Displays

(800) 331-3676
(213) 723-9021
(213) 728-8877, fax

*Apple Computer, Inc.
Worldwide Disability Solutions
1 Infinite Loop MS 38-DS
Cupertino CA 95014
email: appledsg@applelink.apple.com
website: http://www.dsg.apple.com
- Access Utilities
- Menu Management Programs
- Screen Enlargement Programs
- Voice Recognition

(800) 600-7808
(408) 974-7911, TTY
(800) 462-4896, fax

*Arkenstone, Inc.
1390 Borregas Avenue
Sunnyvale CA 94089
email: info@arkenstone.org
website: http://www.arkenstone.org
- Electronic Reference Tools
- Reading Machines

(800) 444-4443
(408) 752-2200
(800) 833-2753, TTY
(408) 745-6739, fax

Artic Technologies
55 Park Street, Suite 2
Troy MI 48083
- Screen Enlargement Programs
- Screen Readers
- Speech Synthesizers

(810) 588-7370
(810) 588-2650, fax

294

Computer
Resources
for People
with
Disabilities

*Articulate Systems, Inc.
600 West Cummings Park, Suite 4500   (800) 443-7077
Woburn MA 01801   (617) 935-5656
email: sales@artsys.com   (617) 935-0490, fax
website: http://www.artsys.com
• Voice Recognition

AT&T Accessible Communication Products
14250 Clayton Road   (800) 233-1222, TTY
Ballwin MO 63011   (314) 891-7896, fax
• TTYs

A/V Concepts Corporation
30 Montauk Blvd.   (516) 567-7227
Oakdale NY 11769   (516) 567-8745, fax
• Educational Software

*Berkeley Systems, Inc.
2095 Rose Street   (510) 549-2300
Berkeley CA 94709   (510) 540-0709, TTY
website: http://www.berksys.com   (510) 540-5630, fax
• Screen Enlargement Programs
• Screen Readers

BEST
63 Forest Street   (617) 277-0179
Chestnut Hill MA 02167   (617) 277-1275, fax
• Interface Devices

Beyond Sight, Inc.
26 East Arapahoe Road   (303) 795-6455
Littleton CO 80122   (303) 795-6425, fax
• Braille Embossers and Translators
• CCTVs
• Screen Enlargement Programs
• Screen Readers
• Speech Synthesizers

Biolink Computer Research and Development, Ltd.
140 W. 15th Street, Suite 105   (604) 984-4099
North Vancouver BC   (604) 985-8493, fax
Canada V7M 1R6
email: 72604.367@compuserve.com
• Screen Readers

*Blazie Engineering, Inc.
105 E. Jarrettsville Road   (410) 893-9333
Forrest Hill MD 21050   (410) 836-5040, fax
email: info@blazie.com
website: http://www.blazie.com
- Braille Embossers, Translators
- Notetakers

Blissymbolics Communication International
1630 Lawrence Avenue West, Suite 104   (416) 242-9114
Toronto ON   (416) 244-6543, fax
Canada M6L 1C5
email: ortckse@oise.on.ca
- Writing Composition Programs

BrainTrain, Inc.
727 Twin Ridge Lane   (804) 320-0105
Richmond VA 23235   (804) 320-0242, fax
- Cognitive Training Software

*Brøderbund Software, Inc.
500 Redwood Blvd., Box 6121   (800) 521-6263, ordering
Novato CA 94948-6121   (415) 382-4400
website: www.broder.com   (415) 382-4582, fax
- Educational Software

*Brown & Company, Inc.
14 Midoaks Street   (914) 783-2713
Monroe NY 10950
- Interface Devices
- Switches

Bytes of Learning
150 Consumers Road, Suite 203   (800) 465-6428
Willowdale ON
Canada M2J 1P9
- Talking Word Processors

Cables to Go
1501 Webster Street   (800) 225-8646
Dayton OH 45404   (513) 496-2666, fax
- Monitor Additions

296

Computer
Resources
for People
with
Disabilities

Caere Corp.
100 Cooper Court   (800) 535-SCAN (535-7226)
Los Gatos CA 95030   (408) 354-8471, fax
• Optical Character Recognition Software

Carolyn's Products for Enhanced Living
1415 57th Avenue West   (800) 648-2266
Bradenton FL 34207   (941) 739-5555, fax
• CCTVs
• Keyboard Additions
• Visual Aids

Center for Applied Special Technology (CAST)
39 Cross Street   (508) 531-8555
Peabody MA 01960   (508) 531-0192, fax
email: cast.org
• Educational Software
• Reading Comprehension Programs
• Talking and Large Print Word Processors

CE Software, Inc.
1801 Industrial Circle   (800) 523-7638
West Des Moines IA 50265   (515) 224-1995
website: http://www.cesoft.com   (515) 221-1806, fax
• Abbreviation Expansion and Macro Programs

*Claris Corporation
5201 Patrick Henry Drive, C-56   (408) 987-7000
P.O. Box 58168   (408) 987-3002, fax
Santa Clara CA 95052-8168
• Home and Business Software

*Closing The Gap, Inc.
P.O. Box 68   (612) 248-3294
Henderson MN 56044   (612) 248-3810, fax
email: ctgap@aol.com
• Information Resources

Colorado Easter Seal Society, Inc.
Center for Adapted Technology   (303) 233-1666
5755 W. Alameda   (303) 233-1028, fax
Lakewood CO 80226
• Switch Software

Compusult Limited
P.O. Box 1000   (709) 745-4914
Mt. Pearl NF   (709) 745-7927, fax
Canada A1N 3CP
email: management@compusultnf.ca
• Speech Synthesizers

*Compu-Teach
16541 Redmond Way, Suite 137C   (206) 885-0517
Redmond WA 98052   (206) 883-9169, fax
email: cmpteach@wolfe.net
website: http://www./wolfe.net/~compteach
• Educational Software
• Reading Comprehension Programs

Computers to Help People, Inc.
825 E. Johnson Street   (608) 257-5917
Madison WI 53713
• Switch Software

Conover Company
P.O. Box 155   (800) 933-1933
Omro WI 54963   (414) 231-4809, fax
email: 102354.1136@compuserve. com
• Software: Work Skills

*Consultants for Communication Technology
508 Bellevue Terrace   (412) 761-6062
Pittsburgh PA 15202   (412) 761-7336, fax
• Environmental Controls
• Interface Devices
• Speech Synthesizers
• Switch Software

Continental Press, Inc.
520 East Bainbridge Street   (800) 233-0759
Elizabethtown PA 17022   (717) 367-1836
• Reading Comprehension Programs   (717) 367-5660, fax

Corporate Facilities, Inc.
919 North 5th Street   (215) 440-8840
Philadelphia PA 19123   (215) 440-8845, fax
• Furniture

298

Computer
Resources
for People
with
Disabilities

Costar Corp.
100 Field Point Road
Greenwich CT 06830-6406
website: http://www.costar.com
• Trackballs

(800) 426-7827
(203) 661-9700
(203) 661-1540, fax

*Creative Learning, Inc.
206 Sacramento Street, Suite 305
Nevada City CA 95959
• Reading Comprehension Programs
• Writing Composition Programs

(800) 842-5360
(916) 265-0584

Creative Switch Industries
P.O. Box 5256
Des Moines IA 50316
• Switches

(800) 257-4385
(515) 287-5748

Crestwood Company
6625 N. Sydney Place
Milwaukee WI 53209-3259
• Assistive Communication Products
• Pointing and Typing Aids

(414) 352-5678
(414) 352-5679, fax

Data Cal Corporation
531 East Elliot Road, #145
Chandler AZ 85225-1118
• Keyboard Additions

(800) 223-0123
(602) 545-1234
(602) 813-3100, fax

Davidson & Associates, Inc.
19840 Pioneer Avenue
Torrance CA 90503
website: http://david.com
• Educational Software
• Reading Comprehension Programs
• Talking and Large Print Word Processors
• Writing Composition Programs

(800) 545-7677
(310) 793-7600
(310) 793-0601, fax

Digital Equipment Corporation
P.O. Box 9510 m/s mk01-2/625
Merricack NH 03054
website: http://www.digital.com
• Speech Synthesizers

(800) 344-4825
(508) 467-5111
(800) 676-7517, fax

*Discis Knowledge Research, Inc.
90 Sheppard Avenue, 7th Floor   (800) 567-4321
Toronto ON
Canada M2N 3A1
email: discis@goodmedia.com
website: http://www.goodmedia.com/discis/
• Reading Comprehension Programs

*Don Johnston, Inc.
P.O. Box 639   (800) 999-4660
1000 N. Rand Road, Bldg. #115   (708) 526-2682
Wauconda IL 60084
• Alternate Keyboards
• Assistive Communication Products
• Interface Devices
• Keyboard Additions
• Reading Comprehension Programs
• Switches and Switch Software
• Talking and Large-Print Word Processors
• Word Prediction Programs
• Writing Composition Programs

Don Johnston Special Needs
c/o NW SEMERC   (44) 1925 241 642
18 Clarendon Court—Calver Road
Windwick Quay Warrington WA2 8QP
United Kingdom

Dragon Systems
320 Nevada Street   (800) 825-5897
Newton MA 02160   (617) 965-5200
email: info@dragon.sys.com   (617) 527-0372, fax
website: http://www.dragonsys.com
• Voice Recognition

*DU-IT Control Systems Group, Inc.
8765 TR 513 Township Road   (216) 567-2001
Shreve OH 44676   (216) 576-9217, fax
• Environmental Control Units
• Switches and Switch Software

TECHNOLOGY VENDORS | D

300

Computer
Resources
for People
with
Disabilities

*Dunamis, Inc.
3423 Fowler Boulevard
Lawrenceville GA 30244
email: dumanis.ben@aol.com
• Alternate Keyboards

(800) 828-2443
(404) 932-0485
(404) 932-0486, fax

Duxbury Systems, Inc.
435 King Street
P.O. Box 1504
Littleton MA 01460
email: duxbury@worldstd.com
• Braille Embossers, Translators

(508) 486-9766
(508) 486-9712, fax

EBM Corporation
2249 S. Grout Road
Gladwin, MI 48624
• Accessible Furniture

(800) 815-5719
(517) 426-7354, fax

*Echo Speech Corporation
6460 Via Real
Carpinteria CA 93013
• Speech Synthesizers

(800) DSP-ECHO (377-3246)
(805) 684-4593
(805) 684-6628, fax

*Edmark Corporation
6727 185th Avenue NE
P.O. Box 3218
Redmond WA 98073
website: http://www.edmark.com
• Educational Software
• Menu Management Programs
• Reading Comprehension Programs
• Switch Software
• Touch Screens

(800) 426-0856
(206) 556-8400
(206) 556-8402, TTY
(206) 556-8430, fax

Educational Activities, Inc.
P.O. Box 392
Freeport NY 11520
email: edact@panix.com
• Reading Comprehension Programs

(800) 645-3739
(516) 223-4666
(516) 623-9282, fax

*Educational Press/Learning Well
1720 H Belmont
Baltimore MD 21224
email: 73444, 2412@compuserve.com
• Educational Software

(800) 645-6564
(800) 413-7442, fax

*Education TURNKEY Systems, Inc.
256 North Washington Street   (703) 536-2310
Falls Church VA 22046
• Consulting Services

EduQuest
2929 North Central Avenue   (800) 426-4338
Phoenix AZ 85012   (800) 214-1436, fax
website: http://www.solutions.IBM.com/K12
• Educational Software
• Large-Print Word Processors

EKEG Electronics Company, Ltd.
P.O. Box 46199, Sta. D   (604) 857-0820
Vancouver BC   (604) 857-2726, fax
Canada V6J 5G5
email: richmush@direct.ca
• Alternate Keyboards

Enabling Technologies Company
3102 SE Jay Street   (800) 777-3687
Stuart FL 34997   (407) 283-4817
email: enabling@aol.com   (407) 220-2920, fax
• Braille Embossers, Translators

ErgoFlex Systems
XYBIX Ergonomic Systems   (800) 788-2810
145540 E. Freemont Avenue   (303) 766-8266, fax
Englewood CO 80112
email: ergosales@xy.com
website: http://www.csn.net/~barryc/
• Arm and Wrist Supports

Exceptional Computing, Inc.
450 NW 58th Street   (352) 331-8847
Gainesville FL 32607   (352) 331-4164, fax
email: ecit@aol.com
• Alternate Keyboards
• Switches and Switch Software

Extensions for Independence
555 Saturn Boulevard #B-368   (619) 423-1748
San Diego CA 92154
• Alternate Keyboards
• Pointing & Typing Aids

302

Computer
Resources
for People
with
Disabilities

Fellowes
1789 Norwood Avenue   (800) 945-4545
Itasca IL 60143   (708) 893-1600
• Trackballs

Fliptrack OneOnOne Computer Training
2055 Army Trail Road, Suite 100   (708) 628-0500
Addison IL 60101   (708) 628-0550
• Audio Training Tapes

Florida New Concepts
P.O. Box 261   (800) 456-7097
Port Richey FL 34673   (813) 842-3231
• Monitor Additions   (813) 845-7544, fax

Franklin Electronic Publishers, Inc.
One Franklin Plaza   (609) 386-2500
Burlington NJ 08016   (609) 387-7420, fax
email: customer_service@franklin.com
• Electronic Reference Tools

Fred Sammons, Inc.
P.O. Box 5071   (800) 323-5547
Bowlingbrook IL 60440-5071   (800) 325-1745, TTY
• Pointing and Typing Aids   (800) 547-4333, fax

Global Computer Supplies
2318 Del Amo Road   (800) 8-GLOBAL (845-6225)
Compton CA 90220   (310) 637-6191, fax
• Keyboard Additions

The Great Talking Box
2211 B Fortune Drive   (408) 456-0133
San Jose CA 95131   (408) 456-0134, fax
email: 102375,3351@compuserve.com
• Assistive Communication Products

Great Wave Software
5353 Scotts Valley Drive   (408) 438-1990
Scotts Valley CA 95066   (408) 438-7171, fax
email: greatwave@aol.com
• Reading Comprehension Programs

*Gus Communications
1006 Lonetree Court (360) 715-8580
Bellingham WA 98226 (360) 715-9633
email: gus@gusinc.com
website: http://www.gusinc.com
- Abbreviation Expansion and Macros
- Access Utilities
- Alternate Keyboards
- Assistive Communication Producers
- Environmental Controls
- Speech Sythesizers
- Switch Software
- Talking and Large-Print Word Processors
- Touch Screen
- Word Prediction Programs

GW Micro
725 Airport North Office Park (219) 489-3671
Fort Wayne IN 46825 (219) 489-2608, fax
email: support@gwmicro.com (219) 489-5281, BBS
- Braille Embossers, Translators
- Screen Enlargement Programs
- Screen Readers
- Speech Synthesizers

Hach Associates
P.O. Box 11754 (800) 624-7968
Winston Salem NC 27116 (919) 744-7280
- Alternate Keyboards (800) 410-7282, fax
- Interface Devices
- Switches
- Touch Screens

Handykey Corporation
141 Mount Sinai Avenue (800) 638-2352
Mt. Sinai NY 11766 (516) 474-4405
email: handykey@mcimail.com (516) 474-3760, fax
website: http://www.handykey.com
- Alternate Keyboards

HARC Mercantile Ltd.
P.O. Box 3055 (800) 445-9968
Kalamazoo MI 49003-3055 (616) 324-2387, fax
- TTYs

304

Computer
Resources
for People
with
Disabilities

Harding & Harris Behavioral Research, Inc.
344 West 920 North, Suite 2   (801) 224-2014
Orem UT 84057   (801) 224-6595, fax
email: 73672.437@compuserve.com
• Professional Products

Harris Communications, Inc.
6541 City West Parkway   (800) 825-6758
Eden Prairie MN 55344-3248   (800) 825-9187
email: harrisco@winternet.com   (612) 946-0924, fax
• TTYs

*Hartley Courseware, Inc.
3001 Coolidge Road, Suite 400   (800) 247-1380
East Lansing MI 48823   (619) 587-1835, voice/TTY
• Reading Comprehension Programs   (619) 622-7873, fax
• Software Features: Built-in Utilities
• Talking and Large Print Word Processors

Hear More Inc.
P.O. Box 3413   (516) 752-0738, voice/TTY
Farmingdale NY 11735   (516) 752-0689, fax
• TTYs

Hear You Are, Inc.
4 Muscontcong Avenue   (201) 347-7662 voice/TTY/fax
Stanhope NJ 07874
• TTYs and TTY Modems

Henter-Joyce, Inc.
2100 62nd Avenue North   (800) 336-5658
St. Petersburg FL 33702   (813) 528-8900
website: http://www.hj.com   (813) 528-8901, fax
• Screen Readers

Hexagon Products
P.O. Box 1295   (847) 692-3355
Park Ridge IL 60068
email: 76064.177@compuserve.com
website: http://www.ourworld.compuserve.com/homepages/hexagon
• Screen Enlargement Software
• Talking and Large-Print Word Processors

HITEC Group International
8160 Madison Street
Burr Ridge IL 60561
(800) 288-8303
(708) 654-9219, fax
• TTYs

Hooleon Corporation
411 South 6th Street
Cottonwood AZ 86326
(800) 937-1337
(520) 634-7515
• Keyboard Additions
(520) 634-4620, fax

Houghton Mifflin School Division
13400 Midway Road
Dallas TX 75244
(800) 733-2828
(214) 980-1100
• Reading Comprehension Programs
(214) 480-6814, fax

*Humanities Software
P. O. Box 950
408 Columbia Street
Hood River OR 97031
email: human@gorge.net
• Writing Composition Programs
(800) 245-6737
(541) 386-6737
(541) 386-1410, fax

HumanWare, Inc.
6245 King Road
Loomis CA 95650
email: info@humanware.com
website: http://www.humanware.com
(800) 722-3393
(916) 652-7253
(916) 652-7296, fax
• Braille Embossers, Translators
• CCTVs
• Notetakers
• Refreshable Braille Displays
• Screen Enlargement Programs
• Screen Readers
• Speech Synthesizers

Hunt Manufacturing; Media Mate Division
P.O. Box 5819
Statesville NC 28687-1836
(800) 879-4868, consumer line
(800) 283-1707, office
• Monitor Additions: Monitor Mounts
(704) 872-1766, fax

306

Computer
Resources
for People
with
Disabilities

*IBM Special Needs Systems
Building 904, Internal Zip 9448   (800) 426-4832
11400 Burnet Road   (800) 426-4833, TTY
Austin TX 78758   (512) 838-9367, fax
- Access Utilities
- Keyboard Additions: Keyguards
- Reading Comprehension Programs
- Screen Readers
- Talking and Large Print Word Processors
- TTYs
- Voice Recognition
- Writing Composition Programs

Imaginart
307 Arizona Street   (800) 828-1376
Bisbee AZ 85603   (520) 432-5741
- Communication Aids   (800) 737-1376, fax
- Keyboard Additions

Index Braille Printer Company
Box 155, S-954   +46 (0) 920-57135
23 Gammelstad   +46 (0) 920-57249, fax
Sweden
email: indexbrl@everyday.se
- Braille Embossers and Translators

Infogrip, Inc.
1141 E. Main Street   (800) 397-0921
Ventura CA 93001   (805) 652-0770
email: infogrip@infogrip.com   (805) 652-0880, fax
website: http://www.infogrip.com/infogrip
- Alternate Keyboards

*Information Services, Inc.
28 Green Street   (800) 462-9198
Newbury MA 01951
- Writing Composition Software

Information Strategies Incorporated
1200 E. Campbell, #108   (214) 234-0176
Richardson TX 75081   (214) 234-5936, fax
email: windows!mail1john@isio1.attmail.com
- Touch Screens

Infra-Link, Inc.
P.O. Box 1008
Portland OR 97207-1008
• Environmental Controls

(800) 395-3596
(503) 598-7531, fax

*Innocomp
26210 Emery Road, Suite 302
Warrensville Heights OH 44128
• Augmentative Communication
• Electronic Pointing Devices
• Switches

(800) 382-VOCA (382-8622)
(216) 464-3636
(216) 464-3638, fax

Innovation Management Group, Inc.
21550 Oxnard Street, Suite 300
Woodland Hills CA 91367
• Alternate Keyboards

(818) 346-3581
(818) 346-3973, fax

Innovative Designs
2464 El Camino, Suite 205
Santa Clara CA 95051
• Word Prediction Programs

(408) 985-9255
(408) 247-6624, fax

Innoventions
5921 S. Middlefield Road, Suite 102
Littleton CO 80123-2877
• Monitor Additions

(303) 797-6554
(303) 797-1320, fax

Inspiration Software
7412 SW Beaverton Hillsdale Highway, Suite 102
Portland OR 97225
website: http://www.inspiration.com
• Writing Composition Programs

(800) 877-4292
(503) 297-3004
(503) 297-4676, fax

Institute on Applied Technology
850 Boylston Street, Suite 106
Chestnut Hill MA 02167
• Large Print Word Processors
• Speech Synthesizer
• Switch Software

(617) 731-6466
(617) 731-5201, fax

Intelligent Peripheral Devices
20380 Town Center Lane, Suite 270
Cupertino CA 95014
email: info@alphasmart.com
• Notetakers

(408) 252-9400
(408) 252-9409, fax

308

Computer
Resources
for People
with
Disabilities

*IntelliTools
55 Leveroni Court, Suite 9
Novato CA 94949
email: intellitoo@aol.com
- Access Utilities
- Alternate Keyboards
- Keyboard Additions
- Switch Software
- Talking and Large-Print Word Processors

(800) 899-6687
(415) 382-5959
(415) 382-5950, fax

*In Touch Systems
11 Westview Road
Spring Valley NY 10977
- Alternate Keyboards

(800) 332-6244

Jostens Home Learning
9920 Pacific Heights Boulevard, Suite 500
San Diego CA 92121-4430
- Talking and Large-Print Word Processors

(619) 622-5096
(619) 622-7877, fax

*Judy Lynn Software
278 Dunhams Corner Road
East Brunswick NJ 08816
- Switch Software

(908) 390-8845

K-12 MicroMedia Publishing
16 McKee Drive
Mahwah NJ 07430
- Educational Software
- Reading Comprehension Programs

(800) 292-1997
(201) 825-8888

Kare Pillows, Inc./Ergo Kare
P.O. Box 2295
Boulder CO 80306
- Arm and Wrist Supports
- Ergonomic Products

(800) 927-5273
(303) 443-4243, fax

Kensington Microware
2855 Campus Drive
San Mateo CA 94403
- Monitor Additions: Anti-glare Filters
- Trackballs

(800) 535-4242

Keytec
1293 N. Plano Road
Richardson TX 75081
• Touch Screens

(214) 234-8617
(214) 234-8542, fax

Kidsview Software
P.O. Box 98
Warner NH 03278
• Enlarged Text Software
• Large-Print Word Processors

(800) 542-7501
(603) 927-4428

KidTECH/SoftTouch
4182 Pinewood Lake Drive
Bakersfield CA 93309
• Adaptivation
• Assistive Communication Products
• Switch Software

(805) 396-8676
(805) 396-8760, fax

Kinetic Designs, Inc.
14231 Anatevka Lane SE
Olalla WA 98359
• Access Utilities

(800) 244-8882

KLAI Enterprises
P.O. Box 43
Garden City MI 48136
• Arm and Wrist Supports

(313) 425-1165
(313) 425-9033, fax

Kurzweil Applied Intelligence
411 Waverley Oaks Road
Waltham MA 02154
• Voice Recognition

(800) 380-1234
(617) 893-7653, fax

KY Enterprises/Custom Computer Solutions
3039 E. 2nd Street
Long Beach CA 90803
• Environmental Controls
• Joysticks
• Switches

(310) 433-5244
(310) 433-3970, fax

310

Computer
Resources
for People
with
Disabilities

*Laureate Learning Systems, Inc.
110 East Spring Street   (800) 562-6801
Winooski VT 05404   (802) 655-4755
• Educational Software
• Reading Comprehension Programs
• Switch Software
• Writing Composition Programs

*Lawrence Productions
1800 South 35th Street   (800) 421-4157
Galesburg MI 49053   (616) 665-7075
• Educational Software   (616) 665-7060, fax
• Independent Living Software

LC Technologies, Inc.
9455 Silver King Court   (800) 393-4293
Fairfax VA 22031   (703) 385-7133
email: jlahoud@lctinc.com   (703) 385-7137, fax
• Environmental Controls

Learning Company
6493 Kaiser Drive   (800) 852-2255
Fremont CA 94555   (510) 792-2101
• Educational Software
• Reading Comprehension Programs
• Writing Composition Programs

Less Gauss, Inc.
187 East Market Street   (914) 876-5432
Rhinebeck NY 12572
• Arm and Wrist Supports
• Monitor Additions: Magnifiers

Lexia Learning System, Inc.
114 Lewis Street   (800) 435-3942
Lincoln MA 01773
• Reading Comprehension Programs

Logitech, Inc.
6505 Kaiser Drive   (510) 795-8500
Fremont CA 94555
• Trackballs

Looking Glass Learning Products, Inc.
3858 Hull (800) 545-5457
Skokie IL 60076
- Reading Comprehension Programs

***LS&S**
P.O. Box 673 (800) 468-4789
Northbrook IL 60065 (847) 498-9777
email: lssgrp@aol.com (847) 498-1482, fax
- CCTVs
- Visual Aids

Luminaud, Inc.
8688 Tyler Blvd. (216) 255-9082
Mentor OH 44060 (800) 255-3408, fax
- Assistive Communication Products (216) 255-2250, fax
- Switches and Switch Software

Maddak, Inc.
6 Industrial Road (800) 443-4926
Pequannock NJ 07440 (800) 541-3311, fax
- Pointing and Typing Aids

***Madenta Communications**
9411A–20th Avenue (800) 661-8406
Edmonton AB (403) 450-8926
Canada T6N 1E5 (800) 852-0815, fax
email: madenta@applelink.apple.com (403) 988-6182, fax
madenta@aol.com
madenta@ccinet.ab.ca
- Alternate Keyboards
- Environmental Controls
- Switch Software
- Word Prediction Programs

***MarbleSoft**
12301 Central Avenue NE (612) 755-1402
Blaine MN 55434 (612) 755-1402, fax
email: marblesoft@applelink.apple.com
- Early Childhood Software
- Reading Comprehension Programs
- Switch Software

312

Computer
Resources
for People
with
Disabilities

The Matias Corporation
178 Thistledown Boulevard
Rexdale ON
Canada M9V 1K1
email: ematias@dgp.toronto.edu
- Access Utilities

(416) 749-3129
(416) 740-4132, fax

*Mayer-Johnson Company
P.O. Box 1579
Solana Beach CA 92075
email: mayerj@aol.com
- Alternate Keyboards
- Assistive Communication Products
- Speech Synthesizers

(619) 550-0084
(619) 550-0449, fax

McIntyre Computer Systems Division
22809 Shagbark
Birmingham MI 48025
- Alternate Keyboards
- Joysticks
- Word Prediction Software

(810) 645-5090
(810) 645-6042, fax

MECC
6160 Summit Drive, N.
Brooklyn Center MN 55430
website: http://www.mecc.com/
- Educational Software
- Reading Comprehension Programs
- Writing Composition Programs

(800) 685-MECC (685-6322)
(612) 569-1551, fax

Med Labs Inc.
28 Vereda Cordillera
Goleta CA 93117
- Environmental Controls
- Switches

(800) 968-2486
(805) 968-2486, fax

*Microsoft Corporation
1 Microsoft Way
Redmond WA 98052
website: http://www.microsoft.com
- Access Utilities
- Menu Management Programs
- MS-DOS Version 6 Supplement
- Trackballs
- Voice Recognition
- Writing Composition Programs

(800) 426-9400, voice
(800) 892-5234, TTY

*Microsystems Software, Inc.
600 Worcester Road   (800) 828-2600
Framingham MA 01701   (508) 879-9000
email: hware@microsys.com   (508) 879-1069, fax
website: http://www.handiware.com   (508) 875-8009, BBS
- Access Utilities
- Assistive Communication Products
- Environmental Controls
- Screen Enlargement Programs
- Switch Software
- Word Prediction Programs

*MicroTalk
917 Clear Creek Drive   (903) 832-3471
Texarkana TX 75503   (903) 832-3517, fax
- Braille Translators   (903) 832-3722, BBS
- Screen Readers
- Speech Synthesizers

MicroTouch Systems, Inc.
300 Griffin Brook Park   (508) 659-9000
Methuen MA 01844   (508) 659-9100, fax
email: mts.mhs.compuserve.com
website: http://www.microtouch.com
- Touch Screens

*Millenium Software
3155 Fujita Street   (310) 530-0356
Torrance CA 90505
- Cognitive Training Software

Milliken Publishing Company
P.O. Box 21579   (800) 325-4136
1100 Research Blvd.   (314) 991-4220
St. Louis MO 63132   (800) 538-1319, fax
- Educational Software
- Reading Comprehension Programs

Mindplay
160 W. Fort Lowell Road   (800) 221-7911
Tucson AZ 85705   (520) 888-1800
email: mindplay@rtd.com   (520) 888-7904, fax
website: http://www.tucson.com\mindplay
- Educational Software
- Reading Comprehension Programs
- Writing Composition Programs

314

Computer
Resources
for People
with
Disabilities

Mindscape
88 Rowland Way
Novato CA 94945
• Educational Software

(800) 231-3088
(415) 897-8896, fax

Mobius Corp.
405 N. Henry Street
Alexandria VA 22314
email: bzdr14a@prodigy.com
website: http://www.america-tomorrow.com/mobius
• Early Childhood Software

(800) 426-2710
(703) 684-2919, fax

Mouse Systems, Corp.
47505 Seabridge Drive
Fremont CA 94538
email: support@mousesystems.com
FTP site: ftp.netcom.com Directory pub/mo/mouse
• Trackballs

(510) 656-1117
(510) 656-4409, fax

NanoPac, Inc.
4823 South Sheridan Road, Suite 302
Tulsa OK 74145-5717
email: info@nanopac.com
website: http://www.nanopac.com
• Switch Software
• Voice Recognition

(918) 665-0329
(918) 665-0361, fax

Nisus Software, Inc.
107 South Cedros Avenue
Solana Beach CA 92075
email: info@nisus-sost.com
website: http://www.nisus-sost.com
• Access Utilities

(800) 890-3030
(619) 481-7485, fax
(619) 481-6154, fax

North Coast Medical, Inc.
187 Stauffer Blvd.
San Jose CA 95125-1042
website: http://blvd.electronic.com
• Pointing and Typing Aids

(800) 821-9319
(408) 283-1950, fax

Now Software, Inc.
921 SW Washington Street, Suite 500
Portland OR 97205-2823
email: info@nowsoft.com
• Access Utilities

(503) 274-2800
(503) 274-0670, fax

Okay Vision-Aide Corporation
14811 Myford Road
Tustin CA 92680
• CCTVs

(800) 325-4488
(714) 669-1081, fax

***OMS Development**
610 B Forest Avenue
Wilmette IL 60091
email: ebohlman@netcom.com
• Screen Readers
• Word Prediction Programs

(847) 251-5787
(800) 831-0272
(847) 251-5793, fax

Optelec USA, Inc.
6 Lyberty Way
P.O. Box 729
Westford MA 01886
• CCTVs
• Screen Enlargement Programs

(800) 828-1056
(508) 692-6073, fax

Optimum Resources Inc.
5 Hilltech Lane
Hilton Head Island SC 29926
email: stickyb@stickybear.com
website: http://www.stickybear.com
• Educational Software
• Reading Comprehension Programs

(803) 689-8000
(803) 689-8008, fax

ORCCA Technology
218 McDowell Road
Lexington KY 40504
• Switches

(606) 268-1635
(606) 268-2595, fax

Origin Instruments Corporation
854 Greenview Drive
Grand Prarie TX 75050
email: sales@orin.com
website: http://www.orin.com
• Electronic Pointing Devices

(214) 606-8740
(214) 606-8741, fax

Parrot Software
6505 Pleasant Lake Court
West Bloomfield MI 48322
email: parrot@mcs.net
website: http://www.parrotsoft.com
• Cognitive Training Software

(800) 727-7681
(810) 237-7282
(810) 788-3224, fax

316

Computer
Resources
for People
with
Disabilities

*PEAL Software
8505 Gulana Avenue
Playa Del Rey CA 90293
• Language Acquisition Software
• Writing Composition Software

(310) 649-4546

Penny and Giles Computer Products Ltd.
163 Pleasant Street, Suite 4
Attleboro MA 02703
• Joysticks
• Trackballs

(508) 226-3008
(508) 226-5208, fax

Personal Data Systems, Inc.
100 West Rincon Avenue, #103
Campbell CA 95008
• Speech Synthesizers

(408) 866-1126
(408) 866-1128, fax

Phone TTY Inc.
202 Lexington Avenue
Hackensack NJ 07061
• TTYs and TTY Modems

(201) 489-7889
(201) 489-7890, TTY
(201) 489-7891, fax

Phonic Ear, Inc.
3880 Cypress Drive
Petaluma CA 94954
• Assistive Communication Products

(800) 227-0735
(707) 769-1110

Power Plus The Accessories People
4100 Caven Road
Austin TX 78744
email: pplus@io.com
website: www.io.com/-pplus
• Monitor Additions

(800) 878-5530
(512) 443-3518, fax

*Prentke Romich Company
1022 Heyl Road
Wooster OH 44691
• Alternate Keyboards
• Assistive Communication Products
• Electronic Pointing Devices
• Environmental Controls
• Joysticks
• Keyboard Additions
• Switches
• Word Prediction Programs

(800) 262-1984
(216) 262-1984
(216) 263-4829, fax

Presentation Electronics
4320 Anthony, Suite 1   (800) 888-9281
Rocklin CA 95677   (916) 652-9281
- Remote Control   (916) 652-9286, fax

Prime Performance Technologies, Inc.
13873 Park Center Road, Suite 315   (703) 318-0800
Herndon VA 22071-3232   (800) 227-5243, TTY
- TTYs and TTY Modems   (703) 318-0891, fax

Productivity Software International, Inc.
211 East 43rd Street, Suite 2201   (212) 818-1144
New York NY 10017   (212) 818-1197, fax
- Abbreviation Expansion and Macro Programs

Psychological Corporation
Communication Skill Builders
P.O. Box 839954   (602) 323-7500
San Antonio TX 78283-3954   (800) 232-1223, fax
- Writing Composition Programs

*Raised Dot Computing, Inc.
408 South Baldwin Street   (800) 347-9594
Madison WI 53703   (608) 257-9595
email:cnavy@delphi.com   (608) 257-4143, fax
website: http://www.well..com/user/dnavy
- Braille Editing Software
- Braille Embossers, Translators
- Screen Readers
- Speech Synthesizers

R.E.A.C.H., Inc.
1815 Ponce de Leon Avenue, NE   (404) 377-3836
Atlanta GA 30307   (404) 373-0058, fax
- Keyboard Additions

Reading Technologies
9269 Mission Gorge Road, Suite 108   (619) 685-7323
Santee CA 92071
- Braille Embossers and Translators
- Optical Character Recognition Software and Scanners
- Screen Enlargement Programs
- Screen Readers
- Speech Synthesizers

318

Computer
Resources
for People
with
Disabilities

Reasonable Solutions
1535 E. University Drive
Mesa AZ 85203
• Menu Management Programs

(800) 876-3475
(202) 668-9425, fax

*Rhamdec, Inc.
476 Ellis Street
Mountain View CA 94043-2240
• Computer Mounting Products

(800) 4-MYDESC (469-3372)
(415) 965-3251

*Richard Wanderman
P.O. Box 1075
Litchfield CT 06759
email: rwanderman@aol.com
website: http://www.tiac.net/users/poorrich
• Consulting Services
• Educational Software

(860) 567-4307

*R. J. Cooper and Associates
24843 Del Prado #283
Dana Point CA 92629
email: rj@rjcooper.com
website: http://www.rjcooper.com
• Alternate Keyboards
• Interface Devices
• Joysticks
• Switches, Switch Software

(800) RJ COOPER (752-6673)
(714) 240-4853
(714) 240-9875, fax

*Roger Wagner Publishing, Inc.
1050 Pioneer Way, Suite P
El Cajon CA 92020
email: rwagnerinc@aol.com
website: http://www.hyperstudio.com
• Authoring Software

(800) 421-6526
(619) 442-0522
(619) 442-0525, fax

SaundersErgo Source
4250 Norex Drive
Chaska MN 55318
• Arm and Wrist Supports

(800) 456-1289
(800) 375-1119, fax

Schamex Research
19201 Parthenia Street, Suite H
Northridge CA 91324
• Reading Machines

(818) 772-6644
(818) 993-2496, fax

Scholastic Software
555 Broadway
New York NY 10003
• Reading Comprehension Programs
• Writing Composition Programs

(800) 541-5513
(800) 724-6527, orders
(573) 635-5881, fax

Seeing Technologies Inc.
42 Executive Boulevard
Farmingdale NY 11735
• CCTVs
• Visual Aids

(800) 462-3738
(516) 752-0234, voice/TTY

*Sentient Systems Technology, Inc.
2100 Wharton Street, Suite 630
Pittsburgh PA 15203
email: sstsales@sentient-sys.com
• Assistive Communication Products

(800) 344-1778
(412) 381-4883
(412) 381-5241, fax

Shea Products
1721 W. Hamlin
Rochester Hills MI 48309
• Assistive Communication Products

(810) 852-4940
(810) 852-5298, fax

*Simtech Publications
134 East Street
Litchfield CT 06759
• Educational Software
• Switch Software

(203) 567-1173

Skills Bank Corporation
15 Governors Court
Baltimore MD 21244-2791
email: service@skillsbank.com
sales@skillsbank.com
website: http://www.skillsbank.com
• Reading Comprehension Programs
• Writing Composition Programs

(800) 451-5726
(410) 265-8855

SkiSoft Publishing Corporation
1644 Massachusetts Avenue, Suite 79
Lexington MA 02173
email: info@skisoft.com
website: http://www.skisoft.com
• Large-Print Word Processors

(800) 662-3622
(617) 861-0086, fax

320

Computer
Resources
for People
with
Disabilities

Society for Visual Education, Inc.
6677 N. Northwest Highway
Chicago IL 60631
• Electronic Reference Tools

(800) 829-1900
(312) 775-9550
(800) 624-1678, fax
(312) 775-5091, fax

Software Excitement
1106 E. Seymour, Suite 300
Muncie IN 47302
• Menu Management Programs

(800) 444-5457

Span-America Medical Systems, Inc.
P.O. Box 5231
Greenville SC 29606
• Keyboard Additions

(864) 288-8877
(864) 288-8692, fax

*Special Needs Project
3463 State Street, Suite 282
Santa Barbara CA 93105
• Books
• Electronic Reference Tools

(800) 333-6867
(805) 683-2341, fax

SSK Technology, Inc.
5619 Scotts Valley Drive, Suite 280
Scotts Valley CA 95066
email: writalk@aol.com
• TTYs

(800) 775-0759
(800) 775-1630 TTY
(408) 461-8909, fax

*Stone and Associates
7910 Ivanhoe Avenue, Suite 319
La Jolla CA 92037
• Educational Software
• Math Software
• Reading Comprehension Software
• Writing Composition Software

(800) 733-1263
(619) 693-6333
(619) 551-7899, fax

*Sunburst Communications
101 Castleton Street
Pleasantville NY 10570
email: sunburst4@aol.com
website: http://www.nyssunburst.com
- Alternate Keyboards
- Educational Software
- Large-Print Word Processors
- Math Software
- Reading Comprehension Programs
- Writing Composition Programs

(800) 321-7511
(914) 747-3310
(914) 747-4109, fax

Switch In Time
101 Clay Street
Cambridge MA 02140
email: adams@xensie.com
website: http://www.xensie.com/users/adams
- Switches and Switch Software

(617) 354-6577

Switch Kids
8507 Rupp Farm Drive
West Chester OH 45069
- Switches and Switch Software

(513) 860-5475
(513) 860-5475, fax

Symantec
10201 Torre Avenue
Cupertino CA 95014-1232
email: symantec@aol.com
- Menu Management Programs

(800) 441-7234
(541) 334-7400, fax

Sym Systems/The Great Talking Box Co.
2211 B Fortune Drive
San Jose CA 95131
email: 102375,3351@compuserve.com
- Assistive Communication Products

(408) 456-0133
(408) 456-0134, fax

Synergy
412 Plain Street
East Walpole MA 02081
- Switches and Switch Software

(508) 668-7424
(508) 668-4134, fax

322

Computer
Resources
for People
with
Disabilities

Syntha-Voice Computers, Inc.
800 Queenson Road, Suite 304   (800) 263-4540
Stony Creek ON   (905) 662-0568, fax
Canada L8G 1A7
email: help@synthavoice.on.ca
website: http://www.netaccess.on.ca
• Screen Enlargement Software
• Screen Readers

*TASH International, Inc.
Unit 1–91 Station Street   (800) 463-5685
Ajax ON   (905) 686-4129
Canada L1S 3H2   (905) 686-6895, fax
email: tashcan@aol.com
• Abbreviation Expansion and Macro Programs
• Alternate Keyboards
• Assistive Communication Products
• Environmental Controls
• Interface Devices
• Joysticks
• Keyboard Additions
• Switches and Switch Software

Taylor Associates Communications, Inc.
200-2 E. 2nd Street   (800) 732-3758
Huntington Station NY 11746   (516) 549-3000
• Reading Comprehension Programs   (516) 549-3156, fax

Teacher Support Software
1035 NW 57th Street   (800) 228-2871
Gainesville FL 32605   (904) 332-6404
• Reading Comprehension Programs   (904) 332-6779, fax
• Talking and Large-Print Word Processors
• Writing Composition Programs

Tech-Able
1140 Ellington Drive   (770) 922-6768
Conyers GA 30207   (770) 992-6769, fax
email: tekablega@aol.com
• Keyboard Additions (custom)
• Switches

Technology for Language and Learning
P.O. Box 327   (516) 625-4550
East Rockway, NY 11518-0327   (516) 621-3321, fax
• Switches and Switch Software

Teledyne Brown Engineering/Imperium Products Division

35805 Sparkman Drive   (800) 944-8002
Huntsville AL 35807   (205) 726-1743, fax
website: http://www.teledynebrownengineering
- Environmental Controls

*TeleSensory
455 N. Bernardo Avenue   (800) 227-8418
P.O. Box 7455   (415) 960-0920
Mountain View CA 94039-7455   (415) 335-1832, fax
website: http://www.telesensory.com
- Braille Embossers, Translators
- CCTVs
- Notetakers
- Reading Machines
- Refreshable Braille Displays
- Screen Enlargement Programs
- Screen Readers
- Speech Synthesizers
- TTYs

Texas School for the Deaf
Gerard Pollard   (512) 462-5463
1102 Smith Congress Avenue   (512) 562-5313, fax
P.O. Box 3538
Austin TX 78764
email: pollardg@tenet.edu
- Educational Software

TFI Engineering
529 Main Street   (617) 242-7007
Boston MA 02129   (617) 242-2007, fax
email: tfi@netcom.com
- Notetakers

Tom Snyder Productions
80 Coolidge Hill Road   (800) 342-0236
Watertown MA 02172-2817   (617) 926-6000
email: ask@teachtsp.com   (617) 926-6222, fax
- Educational Software
- Reading Comprehension Programs
- Writing Composition Programs

324

Computer
Resources
for People
with
Disabilities

Toucan Press (formerly Pelican Software)
Queue, Inc.
338 Commerce Drive
Fairfield CT 06430
email: queueinc@aol.com

(800) 232-2224
(203) 336-2481, fax

- Educational Software
- Writing Composition Programs

Toys for Special Children, Inc.
385 Warburton Avenue
Hastings on Hudson NY 10706

(800) 832-8697
(914) 478-0960
(914) 478-7030, fax

- Adapted Toys
- Environmental Controls
- Switches and Switch Software

Trace Research and Development Center
Room S-151, Waisman Center
1500 Highland Avenue
University of Wisconsin
Madison WI 53705
email: info@trace.wisc.edu

(608) 262-6966
(608) 263-5408, TTY
(608) 262-8848, fax

- Information Resources

Troll Touch
25510 Avenue Stanford, Suite 106
Valencia CA 91355
email: trolltouch@aol.com

(805) 295-0770
(805) 295-0771, fax

- Touch Screens

*UCLA Intervention Program for Young Handicapped Children
1000 Veteran Avenue, Room 23-10
Los Angeles CA 90095-1797

(310) 825-4821
(310) 206-7744, fax

- Alternate Keyboard Software
- Early Childhood Software
- Intellikeys Software
- Switches and Switch Software

Ultratec
450 Science Drive
Madison WI 53711

(800) 482-2424
(608) 238-5400
(608) 238-3008, fax

- Pay Phone Attachments
- Signaling Equipment
- TTYs

Visionware Software, Inc.
P.O. Box 1676   (800) 828-1056
Brookline MA 02146   (508) 392-0707
• Screen Enlargement Programs   (508) 692-6073, fax

Visuaide, Inc.
841 Jean-Paul Vincent Boulevard   (514) 463-1717, accepts collect calls
Longueuil PQ   (514) 463-0120, fax
Canada J4G 1R3
email: visuinfo@visuaide.gc.ca
• Switches and Switch Software

Visual Tech Connection
P.O. Box 898   (614) 899-9989
Westerville OH 43081
• Monitor Additions: Magnifiers

Volunteers for Medical Engineering
2301 Argonne Drive   (410) 243-7495
Baltimore MD 21218   (410) 467-3873, fax
• Computer Loan Closet for State of Maryland
• Environmental Controls
• Rehab Engineering Services

*Voice Communications
P.O. Box 29   (203) 775-3204
Wilton CT 06897
• Voice Recognition

*WesTest Engineering Corporation
1470 North Main Street   (801) 298-7100
Bountiful UT 84010   (801) 292-7379, fax
email: 75054.1230@compuserve.com
• Interface Devices

*William K. Bradford Publishing
16 Craig Road   (800) 421-2009
Acton MA 01720   (508) 263-6996
• Reading Comprehension Programs   (508) 263-9375, fax
• Writing Composition Programs

326

Computer
Resources
for People
with
Disabilities

*Words+, Inc.
40015 Sierra Highway, Bldg. B-145
Palmdale CA 93550
email: wwwordspls@aol.com
- Access Utilities
- Alternate Keyboards
- Assistive Communication Products
- Electronic Pointing Devices
- Environmental Controls
- Interface Devices
- Keyboard Additions
- Switches and Switch Software
- Word Prediction Programs

(800) 869-8521
(805) 266-8969, fax

*World Communications
245 Tonopah Drive
Fremont CA 94539
- Access Utilities
- Alternate Keyboards
- Assistive Communication Products
- Switches and Switch Software
- Word Prediction Programs

(800) 352-1979
(510) 656-0911
(510) 656-3005

X-10 (USA) Inc.
91 Ruckman Road
Closter NJ 07624
- Environmental Controls

(201) 784-9700
(201) 784-9464, fax

Xerox Imaging Systems, Inc.
9 Centennial Drive
Peabody MA 01960
- Optical Character Recognition Software
- Reading Machines

(800) 343-0311
(508) 977-2000
(508) 977-2148

Zygo Industries, Inc.
P.O. Box 1008
Portland OR 97207
- Alternate Keyboards
- Assistive Communication Products
- Environmental Controls
- Switches and Switch Software

(800) 234-6006
(503) 684-6006
(503) 684-6011, fax

Index

Names of commercial programs, services, and assistive hardware are indicated by ®.

A

AAC (augmentative or alternative communication) aid, 30, 50–51, 91, 179, 231–34
ABLEDATA®, 149
Abbreviation expansion software, 14, 46, 152, 169, 200–201
AccessDOS®, 171
Access Pack for Windows, 171
Access Utilities, 46, 152, 153, 169–72
Accessories, *see* Hardware
ADA (Americans with Disabilities Act), 28, 55, 58–59
  addresses, 265–67
  definition, 58
  employer requirement, 58, 92–93
  information sources, 59
  rights under, 92–93
  summary, 58
  technical assistance programs, 266–67
  technology resources, 265–66
Advisors, 22
Alliance for Technology Access (ATA), 4, 45, 65–66, 139
  addresses, 249–55
  description, 4
  on the Internet, 288
  services, 4–5, 97, 101, 139
Alternate labels, 172
America Online®, 286
Americans with Disabilities Act, *see* ADA
Apple Macintosh computer, 39–40
Apple Plain Talk®, 185
Application, definition, 37
Arm support, 46, 119, 198–99
Assistive communication products, 231–34, *also see* AAC
Assistive technology, 21, 44–52

  ability desired, 148, 151–57
  approach, 148, 151–57
  books, 281–85
  books by mail, 276
  classes, 69–70
  conferences, 101, 273–75
  defining needs, 65, 107–109
  definition, 59–60
  differences with conventional technology, 36
  difficulty, 148, 151–57
  input, 47–49, 53, 163–99
  information sources, 149, 249–90
  list, 46–47
  local resources, 64–72
  magazines, 66, 276–81
  mandated by ADA, 92–93
  newsletters, 276–81
  output, 49, 53–54, 213–30
  processing, 49, 53, 200–212
  purpose, 5
  in schools, 79
  selection charts, 151–57
  sharing knowledge about, 151–57
  similarities with conventional technology, 36–37
  tools, 148, 151–57
  training in use, 125–26
  trends, 141–43
  used equipment, 97
  vendors, 71, 290–326
  Assistive Technology Funding and Systems Change Project, 98
ATA, *see* Alliance for Technology Access
Auditory cues, 154, 155, 160
Augmentative or alternative communication, *see* AAC
Augmentative communication clinic, example, 51
Augmentative communication products, guide to, 234
Autism, 23
  example, 31, 78

328

Computer
Resources
for People
with
Disabilities

330

Computer
Resources
for People
with
Disabilities

332

Computer
Resources
for People
with
Disabilities

336

Computer
Resources
for People
with
Disabilities

SPIRIT OF CHANGE: Voices of Hope for a Better World
by Christopher Titmuss

Interviews with Joanna Macy, Fritjof Capra, Thich Nhat Hanh, and others who are at the forefront of the new environmental and spiritual consciousness that is sweeping through the global community. The interviews yield a positive vision of the role of the individual in the world today, in the voices of remarkable people who offer hope and inspiration for individuals seeking to change their lives and contribute to society.

256 pages ... paperback ... $9.95

FROM ACUPRESSURE TO ZEN: An Encyclopedia of Natural Therapies
by Barbara Nash

An accessible introduction to over 70 therapies, from ayurvedic medicine and Bach flower remedies to homeopathy, T'ai Chi, and Zen. Each entry includes information on the therapy's origin, how it helps, and how traditional doctors feel about it. It also lists more than 150 ailments and suggests natural therapies to treat them.

> **"A masterful compendium — presented with conviction and authority — with a clear eye to practical application." —** *NAPRA REVIEW*

288 pages ... 24 illus. ... paperback $15.95 ... hardcover $25.95

WRITING FROM WITHIN: A Guide to Creativity and Life Story Writing
by Bernard Selling

Any writer can create vivid stories and life narratives using the techniques taught in this book, which are from Selling's widely followed classes and workshops. This program enables everyone interested in writing to explore their lives, rediscover forgotten experiences, and find out hidden truths about themselves, their parents, and their family histories.

256 pages ... paperback $14.95 ... spiral $22.95 ... 3rd edition ... January 1997

IN YOUR OWN VOICE: Using Life Stories to Develop Writing Skills
by Bernard Selling

Based on the method outlined in the author's book WRITING FROM WITHIN, this curriculum guide shows educators how to teach students *of all ages* to write using their own life experiences. The techniques inspire even the youngest writers to enjoy—not fear—writing. The book emphasizes the importance of supportive, non-judgmental group feedback, and contains curriculum outlines.

192 pages ... 19 illus. ... paperback $14.95 ... spiral $22.95

THE PLEASURE PRESCRIPTION: To Love, to Work, to Play—Life in the Balance
by Paul Pearsall, Ph.D.

A leading exponent of the relationship between pleasure, stress, the immune system, and brain chemistry, Dr. Pearsall says that "Balanced pleasure is the natural way to physical and mental wellness, and the best remedy for the delight dyslexia that's killing the joy in Western culture." Drawing on the beliefs and practices of the Polynesian people, he offers an alternative based on enjoying life, connecting with others, and caring for the planet. It is a way to happiness and health that can bring us a new contentment and is founded in age-old wisdom and the latest science.

288 pages ... paperback $13.95 ... hardcover $23.95 ... August 1996

Prices subject to change without notice ... see over for order form

ORDER FORM

NAME

ADDRESS

CITY/STATE   ZIP/POSTCODE

PHONE   COUNTRY (outside U.S.)

TITLE	QTY	PRICE	TOTAL
Computer Resources . . . (paperback)		@ $ 17.95	
Computer Resources . . . (spiral bound)		@ $ 17.95	
Computer Resources . . . (hardcover)		@ $ 17.95	
Computer Resources . . . (ASCII disk)		@ $ 17.95	
List other titles and prices below:			
		@ $	
		@ $	
		@ $	
		@ $	
		@ $	
		@ $	
		@ $	

SHIPPING COSTS:
First book: $2.50 by book post ($4.50 by UPS or to ship outside the U.S.)
Each additional book: $1.00
For bulk orders call us at (510) 865-5282

TOTAL
Less discount @_____%
TOTAL COST OF BOOKS
Calif. residents add sales tax
Shipping & handling
TOTAL ENCLOSED
Please pay in U.S. funds only

☐ Check   ☐ Money Order   ☐ Visa   ☐ M/C   ☐ Discover

Card # _____ Exp date _____

Signature _____

Complete and mail to:

Hunter House Inc., Publishers
P.O. Box 2914, Alameda CA 94501-0914
Orders: 1-800-266-5592
Phone (510) 865-5282 Fax (510) 865-4295
☐ Check here to receive our FREE book catalog

CTS2 9/96